Leicester-Nottingham   Studies   in   Ancient   Society

Volume   1

PATRONAGE IN ANCIENT SOCIETY

PATRONAGE
IN
ANCIENT SOCIETY

Edited by
ANDREW WALLACE-HADRILL

R

ROUTLEDGE
London and New York

First published 1989 by Routledge
11 New Fetter Lane, London EC4P 4EE
29 West 35th Street, New York NY 10001

© 1989 Andrew Wallace-Hadrill
and individual contributors

Set in Times by Classics Department, University of Reading
Printed in Great Britain by T.J. Press (Padstow), Padstow, Cornwall.

British Library Cataloguing in Publication Data
Patronage in ancient society. - (Leicester-Nottingham studies in ancient
society; v.1).
1.   Ancient world. Patronage. Social aspects
I.   Wallace-Hadrill, Andrew, 1951-
II.   Series
306′.3

Library of Congress Cataloging in Publication Data

Also available

ISBN 0-415-00341-5

CONTENTS

Introduction

Ancient historians have, in recent years, become increasingly willing to cooperate with colleagues in other disciplines, including sociology, anthropology and social history. At times the attempt to build bridges can lead to frustration. Moses Finley, always one of the foremost proponents of interdisciplinary study, seems to have felt such frustration in the specific area of patronage study. Discussing the importance of patronage as a means of control of the masses in both Athens and Rome, he adds in a footnote an uncompromising aside:

> I make scarcely any reference to the recent outpouring of sociological and anthropological literature on patronage because I have found little of it helpful. The field of study is restricted to an odd combination of small societies in the colonial (or ex-colonial) world, backward agrarian regions in the Mediterranean basin, and machine politics in big American cities. The vast expanse of historical societies is ignored, so that e.g. A. Weingrod has produced a typology in which Roman *clientela* cannot be accommodated (though patron and client are of course words coined by the Romans) ...   (Finley 1983, 35 n.25)

Five years later, Finley would hardly have written in such terms. There has been considerable rapprochement between sociologists and historians. Sociologists have started to take markedly more interest in patronage in historical societies: notable here is the impressive study of Eisenstadt and Roniger (1984), with its case studies ranging from the Mediterranean to the Near and Far East and Latin America. In contrast to most of the earlier cross-cultural books and collections on patronage (e.g. Gellner and Waterbury 1977, Schmidt et al. 1977, Eisenstadt and Lemarchand 1981), Rome takes pride of place at the head of these case studies, and Roniger prepared the way with a study of clientelism in republican Rome (1983). At the same time, historians have shown more interest in that 'outpouring of sociological and anthropological literature', and have started to approach the phenomenon of patronage in the societies they study with new questions in mind, and in a way more likely to engage the interest of sociological colleagues. Most important here from the Roman side has been the work of Finley's own pupil, Richard Saller (1982), which approaches patronage under the early empire both from the basis of a sociological definition of patronage, and with the benefit of models derived from comparative reading (particularly the model of 'brokerage' to account for the relationship between members of the elite and their clients on the one hand and the emperor on the other). In France at the same time Norbert Rouland had examined patronage in Rome, first in an exhaustive study of literary passages (1979), but subsequently with an eye to its broader historical significance (1981). Historians of other periods too have caught an interest in a sociologically inspired approach: among several recent works one may single out Sharon Kettering's study of seventeenth-century France (1986) and Bourne's of Victorian England (1986).

It is against this rapidly changing background that the present volume has been composed. The members of the Ancient History Seminar jointly run by the Classics Departments of Leicester and Nottingham Universities wanted to select a theme for their meetings over a period of time which would encourage cross-fertilisation with their colleagues in other disciplines. Patronage seemed a particularly suitable theme: Finley's statement threw down the gauntlet, and Saller's book offered a good model of how it might be picked up. Various colleagues showed considerable interest in the proposal, above all in the Sociology Department at Leicester, where the work of several members was concerned with patronage. A series of seminars was therefore organised, during the period 1984/6. At each meeting there were at least two papers: sometimes both on a related aspect of patronage in the ancient world, sometimes one on the ancient world and the other by a sociologist, medievalist or modern historian.

As an experiment in interdisciplinary cooperation, the venture was exciting if somewhat lopsided, for inevitably the main focus was on the ancient world and the interests of ancient historians (several of whom attended sessions faithfully from across the country) dominated. But all were agreed that much of value had been learnt both from individual papers and from the process of cooperation, and that a collection of papers should be published based on the seminars.

This volume, then, is the direct product of the seminar. But it is designedly not a 'conference proceedings' type of publication which reproduces all papers in more or less the form delivered. Two measures have been taken to give it greater coherence. First, we decided to focus the volume more narrowly on the ancient world. It would indeed be valuable to present a collection of studies of patronage in historical societies from antiquity to the present, but that would require fewer papers on antiquity and more on subsequent periods than we could muster. A small scatter of post-antique papers would appear distracting and we therefore decided to omit them, though their role in the seminar in helping participants to approach antiquity from a comparative angle was vital. Instead, we turned to the sociologists, who had played an enthusiastic part in the seminar throughout, setting the scene in the opening session with a panorama of sociological approaches to patronage, and subsequently offering a perceptive commentary on the majority of the papers, to make one final major contribution by entering into dialogue with the papers of ancient historians as they finally appeared.

The second measure aimed at increasing coherence was to circulate all contributions among the most regular participants in the seminar. Attendance at the seminar had varied, inevitably, from session to session, so that few of the contributors had been present at all sessions, and some only at one. We wished the various papers of the volume, however diverse they might be in opinion, to be seen against a common background of debate. Contributions, therefore, having been recast in the light of discussion at the seminar and further thought, were read and commented upon by a small group of the most regular participants in the seminar. Each contributor then revised his paper to a greater or lesser extent in the light of these comments. The result is, we hope, not a conspiracy of viewpoint, but an awareness of shared concerns.

About certain issues there is among the contributors a broad measure of agreement. First is the essential matter of definition - essential because without it one can hardly know what a volume on 'patronage' is about. Most contributors would subscribe (and several do so explicitly) to the tripartite definition offered by Saller based on Boissevain: patronage is a social relationship which is essentially (i) reciprocal, involving exchanges of services over time between two parties, (ii) personal as opposed to e.g. commercial, and (iii) asymmetrical, i.e. between parties of different status. Most would accept a fourth element added by Garnsey and Woolf, namely that it is voluntary, not legally enforceable. Such a degree of consensus is remarkable, not least because it goes against a wariness ingrained in ancient historians of sociological definitions: it is a tribute to the influence of Saller's book. A traditional definition would lay more emphasis on the Roman vocabulary of *patronus/cliens*, and would wholly ignore the Greek world in view of its lack of corresponding vocabulary. But it would be futile to restrict discussion to passages where the signpost words occur: Saller has shown there to be a whole nuanced vocabulary associated with Roman patronage relations, often deliberately avoiding 'naming' the thing; following him, Rich has shown that even in investigating the metaphorical extension of patronage language to foreign relations, it is necessary to pursue associated concepts like *fides*. Nor does the adoption of a sociological definition lead to conflict with Roman definitions: Saller shows in this volume that elements of the 'Roman' definition which have been claimed to be in conflict with his own, like exclusivity (one patron per client) and non-elite status for the client (contradicting the idea that young senators were promoted through patronage) are not in fact borne out by the texts. Another worry may also be laid to rest, that we are obscuring the thought world of antiquity by imposing modern concepts. On the contrary (I have suggested below), one of our first tasks must be to study the Roman ideology of patronage which forms a vital part of the social reality we are analysing; but to define the phenomenon strictly in terms of Roman concepts is to invite confusion of ideal and reality. In this sense we need to take our stand outside the Roman value system in order to understand it.

But if the ancient historians in this volume are more or less agreed on one particular sociological definition, the major voice of dissent is paradoxically that of the sociologists (Johnson and Dandeker). Perhaps a subconscious motive of inviting the participation of sociologists was to win added authority for the ideas which we imagined we were borrowing from them; given that some of our own colleagues might have doubts about the legitimacy of our methods, it would be nice to have professional sociologists to reassure us that we were pointing in the right direction. If so, this is certainly not what they have done. Instead they offer something more exciting: a critique of our positions which questions several of our underlying assumptions and simultaneously questions some of the sociological thought on which we had based our own. The result is a significant advance in the sociology of patronage using the Roman world as its main case study, though also looking for comparison at British naval promotions in the eighteenth century.

The essence of their argument is that our attempts to define patronage have focused too narrowly on relations between individuals instead of the system. What matters is not to establish whether individual clientelistic relations subsist in a society, but whether it is characterised by the presence of an interconnected network of patronal exchanges. This cuts to the heart of one of our major definitional problems. Approached from a systemic rather than relational viewpoint, the question of whether individual relationships between members of the ruling elite should be characterised as patronage or merely friendship loses its relevance. We may indeed hesitate to describe Pliny and some young senatorial protégé as patron and client, in deference to Roman sensibilities; but if the favours and services they exchange form part (as we may scarcely doubt) of a wider network which operates by the mediation of resources through personal links of exchange lasting over a period of time between men of unequal status, then their 'friendship' is part of a system of patronage. This is a step forward in definition which probably few of the contributors would want to quarrel with, and which would lead to a considerable amount of rethinking.

A second important observation made by Johnson and Dandeker is that ancient historians tend to assume that patronage lies outside the operations of 'the state' and is in some sense in conflict with it. We see an 'official' system of laws and offices and courts and powers, and an 'unofficial' system of personal links and patronage. Yet, their argument runs, if the state depends on patronage for its operation, then patronage itself is a vital part of the relationships of power which constitute the state. Here we still possibly live under the shadow of Mommsen. Patronage forms no part of Mommsen's conception of the *Staatsrecht*; for him the state is a network of legal and constitutional rights and limitations, and it is notable that the aspect of patronage which attracted his interest was the archaic period, when, so he believed, it formed part of the legal framework. It is not clear that the Romans themselves, who ascribed the introduction of this traditional institution to the founder of their state, Romulus, would have conceived patronage as lying 'outside' the *res publica*. Forming part of the *mos maiorum*, it could hardly be thought of by them as conflicting with legal institutions; indeed, they would probably have found it hard to envisage the state running at all, let alone smoothly, without the operation of patronage, on which courts, elections, and much of the senate's running of the empire depended. Here too we may find that we agree, and that the sociologists, far from giving us a seal of approval, have led us to reassess our positions.

If this volume contains unresolved tensions of this sort, that does nothing to diminish its value. For the whole aim of the seminar and of the volume was not to establish new orthodoxies, but to raise problems and stimulate debate. Many of the authors underline the difficulties of evidence and interpretation that surround various aspects of patronage. Early Roman *clientela*, which modern historians have long tried to reconstruct as the 'true' archetype of Roman patronage, emerges from Drummond's rigorous survey as an area of acute uncertainty that can only be caught by moving back tentatively from the better known later period, with some help from comparative data. The importance of *clientela* as a model for structuring Rome's external relations with her allies, the subject of Badian's classic study (1958), is a matter, Rich shows, of still unresolved dispute: whether the victorious Rome could in any real sense act as patron of her subjects to whom there was no choice, and whether the Romans even claimed that she did, is far from clear, though Rich gives qualified support to the idea that the language and ideology of loyalty and dependence applied to the allies is linked to that of patronage. Whether or not Rome itself was regarded as a patron, the patronage by individual Romans of the communities Rome ruled was a vital instrument of imperialism. But Braund underlines the difficulties in assessing an imperialism shot through with patronage: at one level it oiled the wheels of government; at another it led to what we would have no doubt in characterising as corruption, destroying the credibility of Roman control from within.

Patronage of the poor, and especially the rural poor, emerges as another major area of difficulty. The relationship between peasant and big landowner may be seen as the archetypical patron-client relationship, both in many anthropological studies (like Pitt-Rivers' *People of the Sierra*), and even in the classical sources. Yet though there can be little doubt of the importance of rural patronage throughout the Roman Mediterranean, its study proves surprisingly elusive. As Garnsey and Woolf reveal, the sources disdain to discuss it until in the fourth century it becomes a focus of conflict, challenging the power basis of the urban elite. But oblique approaches can also be fruitful. Taking the rough terrain of Isauria in Asia Minor, notorious for its brigandage, as a case study, Hopwood examines the problems of maintaining order in a society with deep divides between town and country, rich and poor, and points to patronage as the key to social control. Building on the studies of bandits of Hobsbawm and others, he suggests that Isaurian brigandage may also be understood within the patterns of patronage, since it might be the great landowners themselves who harboured and gave support to bandit groups for their own protection, and to operate as a protection racket for others. A similar hypothesis lies behind Drinkwater's study of the controversial brigands of late Roman Gaul, the Bagaudae. Van Dam (1985) has argued that the Bagaudae should be seen as the product of old patronage patterns in a period of uncertain central control. The big landowner/patrons, who in times of strong central government act in support of the state and law and order, in times of disintegration of central control take the law into their own hands, local strong men exercising armed violence, and are seen by central government as so many petty usurpers or brigands. Drinkwater offers an alternative scenario: rural patronage as the guarantee of order in times of peace, brigandage as disorder produced under stress by the disintegration of patronal ties. Whichever way we see it, these scholars have in common the sense that rural patronage was crucial for the maintenance of social order in provinces of the empire as widely separated as Gaul and Cilicia.

Even the political patronage of the late republic has now become controversial, and it is paradoxical that the period which has always provided the clearest evidence of patronage at work is also one in which a whole constellation of factors were at work which tended to undercut traditional patterns of patron-client relations. But despite all controversies and difficulties of evidence and interpretation, there remains an underlying consensus among the contributors: that if we want to understand the structure of social relationships in antiquity, patronage study is an essential tool of analysis. None of the contributors would want to claim exclusive importance for patronage. On the contrary, it is better understood as one of a number of alternative and competing systems that coexist: both Millett and Garnsey and Woolf bring out the way patronage competes with kinship and neighbourhood solidarity on the one hand, and state support on the other. Equally, patronage and bureaucracy should not be seen as mutually exclusive: I suggest below that under the imperial system they supplement and support each other. This is why, as Johnson and Dandeker stress, it is inadequate simply to look for the presence of patron-client relations: these may well be virtually universal in human societies, and what we need to look at is the strategic function of such relations within a particular social system as a whole. In classical Athens, this was successfully reduced to a minimum; in Rome, from its origins to late antiquity, most of the contributors see it playing a strategic role in maintaining the social order. Whether this should be characterised as exploitative is debatable: we may plead that individual relationships were voluntary, but there is nothing voluntary about a social system which succeeds in perpetuating inequalities. What is equally important to remember is that patronage in antiquity was only one of the available forms of inequality. That of master and slave, universal in the societies under discussion, was far harsher, less flexible and nuanced, and was legally enforceable. Patrons and clients were (mostly) fellow citizens, equal in theory before the law, and it is therefore a crucial feature of this particular structure of human inequality that it had to be compatible with the ideology of citizenship. Patronage, slavery and citizenship form a tight nexus in classical culture, and the fate of all three may be seen as closely linked as the Christian culture of the middle ages supervenes.

*   *   *

If this volume aims at coherence, that does not imply that it has any pretensions to completeness. Though some attempt was made to cover what we saw as the most important aspects of the subject in the seminar, various pressures prevented several participants in the seminar from contributing to the volume, so that there are major gaps even within the original design. Some of the larger omissions call for comment. First, though the title seems to offer a study of the whole of Greco-Roman antiquity, only one paper concerns classical Greece. However, as Millett explains in that paper, this is the result of the state of the historiography of the subject: while Roman historians have long been concerned with patronage, for obvious reasons, it has not been regarded as an issue by Greek historians. That is indicative of a sharp contrast between Greek and Roman societies; but there is still much to be learnt, as Millett shows, from investigating the reasons for this contrast and exploring the alternative structures to patron/client relations in Greek societies. The further we move from classical democratic Athens, the less likely it is that relationships of personal dependence can be discounted. More remains to be said on this front: the operation of patronage in Sparta has been discussed illuminatingly by Hodkinson (1983) and recently by Cartledge (1987, 139ff.), while Gabriel Herman's study of ritualised friendship in Greece (1987) underlines the importance and continuity of personal relationships in aristocratic circles, even if such *philia* is not marked by the asymmetry typical of Roman society.

A second, perhaps more glaring omission, is the whole issue of literary patronage. This is deliberate. Literary and artistic patronage have attracted considerable discussion in recent years, and are the subject of a fairly recent volume of essays (Gold 1982). Recent studies have tended to stress that the poet/patron relationship can only be understood in the context of client/patron relationships in society (so White 1978). Indeed, it is particularly striking how it is those poets who have most to say about literary patronage - Horace, Martial, Juvenal - who are also our most forthcoming informants about early imperial *clientela*. Not that this makes them reliable informants: as Cloud argues in the case of Juvenal, the representation of contemporary social realities may prove an elaborate literary construct which the historian trusts at his peril. Even the degree of attention the satirists lavish upon patronage may be the product of their own obsession with literary patrons. Nevertheless, in making this link, and generalising the poet's plight as ill-supported client into the abuse of clients at large, as does Juvenal, or by moving, as does Horace, from his own relationship with Maecenas to the archetypical patron/client pair of Philippus and Mena (*Epistles* 1.7), the poets themselves underline the need to see their situation in terms of a broader social context. Just as ancient historians tend incautiously to treat a literary text as unproblematic, and read it naively as a 'social document', so literary critics treat social institutions as unproblematic, and write as if patronage were something fixed and fully understood. It is to be hoped that this volume will indeed attract the attention of literary critics concerned with the patronage of poets, despite its failure to meet the question head on, and that they will draw a lesson from the difficulties which historians find in reconciling Roman ideology and practice. One lesson at least must emerge clearly: that patronage was not a sharply defined relationship with a predictable set of services exchanged between men of a given social distance. Rather, we are dealing with a varied, ill-defined and unpredictable set of exchanges unified by reference to values deeply embedded in Roman ideology. It may emerge that the anxiety of the poets to integrate their own activity within this Roman value system and legitimate the ambiguous figure of the poet is more revealing than the connections with specific social practices.

A final, major omission, in this case of accident not design, is in the area of late antiquity. Two papers at least are in large part concerned with the period - Garnsey and Woolf on rural patronage and Drinkwater on the Gallic 'Bagaudae'. But much remains to be said about the special conditions of late antiquity, notable for its combination of strong elements of continuity from classical antiquity with profound transformations. Thus we meet on the one hand the pagan aristocracy of Rome exercising a perfectly familiar traditional patronage, to Ammianus' disgust (14.6.12ff.), and on the other the striking role of holy men and bishops in usurping the functions of pagan patrons (Brown 1971, Van Dam 1985). In particular we meet tensions and conflicts surrounding various aspects of patronage on a scale not seen before. Patronage is now frequently presented to us as 'corruption'. So the role of patronage in appointment to public office becomes problematic in a new way: *venale suffragium* or the sale of support for office becomes a perennial problem against which emperors legislate in vain, not indeed because patronage is in itself seen as objectionable, but because it is believed to be abused (de Ste. Croix 1954, Goffart 1970, Barnes 1974, de Ste. Croix 1981, 364ff., Veyne 1981 etc.). Ties between individual governors and the court are blamed for catastrophic provincial misgovernment, as in Tripolitana (Ammianus 28.6). Even the social power-base of a potentate is a source of abuse, as in the vivid portrayal by Ammianus (27.11) of Petronius Probus as driven to office 'by the lawless behaviour of his countless dependants, whose excessive greed could never be satisfied in an innocent way'. In fact there is nothing new in the abuse of patronage, as Braund's study of function and dysfunction shows: Cicero had seen quite clearly how obligations of patronage could drive a governor to corruption. What is new is the way in which the sources constantly revert to the problematic aspects, and it is characteristic that our most explicit picture of rural patronage in antiquity comes from Libanius' tirade against its abuse. The explanation may lie, as Garnsey and Woolf hint, in the new clash of rival systems of authority, city elites, imperial government, and of course the churches. Where systems of authority themselves conflict, the social basis on which the authority rests appears as corrupt. The whole question still lies open, as does the transformation and transmission of traditional Roman social patterns after the collapse of central government in the West.

*　　　*　　　*

This volume is a cooperative venture, and thanks are owed to the many who have contributed in various ways to its making: to the Departments of Classics at Leicester and Nottingham which hosted and financed the original seminar series, and to the many colleagues, including those from other disciplines, whose papers and comments, even when they do not form part of this collection, were an essential part of its background: in particular among ancient historians to Tim Cornell (London), John Davies (Liverpool), John Matthews (Oxford), Nicholas Purcell (Oxford), Dominic Rathbone (London), and among colleagues in other disciplines Aubrey Newman (Leicester, History), Clive Ashworth and John Scott (Leicester, Sociology), Jane Everson (Leicester, Italian), and Ian Wood (Leeds, Medieval History). A small group of members of the seminar made valuable comments on first drafts of many of the papers, especially Tim Cornell, John Davies, and John Rich, though naturally neither they nor the editor bear responsibility for the views of individual authors. The plan of turning the seminar series into book form has been made possible by the enthusiasm and understanding of Richard Stoneman of Croom Helm (now absorbed within Routledge). Rhoda Lee took on the labour of eliminating the worst inconsistencies from the bibliography. Typesetting, including indexing, has been done within the Department of Classics at Reading with advice from the Department of Typography and Graphic Communication; to accomplish this the Department Secretary, Mrs Sybil Lowery, assisted by Miss Samantha Woodford, has gone beyond the skill and patience normally demanded of a typist in mastering a new and trying technology. Imperfections doubtless remain, but the editor can shelter behind no further apology, and expresses warmest gratitude to all who have made this enterprise an enjoyable one.

Andrew Wallace-Hadrill

Bibliography

Badian, E. (1958), *Foreign Clientelae (264 - 70 B.C.)*. Oxford.
Barnes, T.D. (1974), 'A law of Julian', *Classical Philology* 64, 288-91.
Bourne, J.M. (1986), *Patronage and Society in Nineteenth Century England*. London.
Brown, P. (1971), 'The rise and function of the holy man in late antiquity', *Journal of Roman Studies* 61, 80-101.
Cartledge, P. (1987), *Agesilaos and the Crisis of Sparta*. London.
Eisenstadt, S.N. and Lemarchand, R. eds. (1981), *Political Clientelism: Patronage and Development*. London.
Eisenstadt, S.N. and Roniger, L. (1984), *Patrons, Clients and Friends. Interpersonal relations and the structure of trust in society*. Cambridge.
Finley, M.I. (1983), *Politics in the Ancient World*. Cambridge.
Gellner, E. and Waterbury, J. eds. (1977), *Patrons and Clients in Mediterranean Societies*. London.
Goffart, W. (1970), 'Did Julian combat venal *suffragium*? A note on CTh 2.29.1', *Classical Philology* 65, 145-51.
Gold, B.K. ed. (1982), *Literary and Artistic Patronage in Ancient Rome*. Austin, Texas.
Herman, G. (1987), *Ritualised Friendship and the Greek City*. Cambridge.
Hodkinson, S.J. (1983), 'Social order and the conflict of values in Classical Sparta', *Chiron* 13, 239-81.
Kettering, S. (1986), *Patrons, Brokers, and Clients in Seventeenth-Century France*. Oxford.
Pitt-Rivers, J. (1954), *The People of the Sierra*. New York.
Roniger, L. (1983), 'Modern patron-client relations and historical clientelism: some clues from ancient republican Rome', *Archives Européennes de Sociologie* 24, 63-95.
Rouland, N. (1979), *Pouvoir politique et dépendance personnelle dans l'antiquité romaine. Genèse et rôle des rapports de clientèle* (Coll. Latomus no. 166). Brussels.
Rouland, N. (1981), *Rome, démocratie impossible? Les acteurs du pouvoir dans la cité romaine*. Paris.
Ste. Croix, G.E.M. de (1954), 'Suffragium: from vote to patronage', *British Journal of Sociology* 5, 33-48.

Ste. Croix, G.E.M. de (1981), *The Class Struggle in the Ancient Greek World.* London.

Saller, R.P. (1982), *Personal Patronage under the Early Empire.* Cambridge.

Schmidt, S.N., Guasti, L., Landé, C.H. and Scott, J.C. (eds.) (1977), *Friends, Followers and Factions. A reader in political clientelism.* Berkeley, London.

Van Dam, R. (1985), *Leadership and Community in Late Antique Gaul.* California.

Veyne, P. (1981), 'Clientèle et corruption au service de l'État: la vénalité des offices dans le Bas-Empire romain', *Annales E.S.C.* 36:3, 339-60.

White, P. (1978), '*Amicitia* and the profession of poetry in early imperial Rome', *Journal of Roman Studies* 68, 74-92.

Chapter 1
Patronage and its avoidance in classical Athens

Paul Millett

A bibliography on the subject of patronage in the ancient Greek world would be brief almost to the point of non-existence. Outside the specialist areas of literary and artistic patronage (see, for example, Webster 1972, Roberts 1983, 148-208), I am not aware of a single book or article having as its main or even subsidiary theme the relationship between patron and client in classical Greece. A glance at the indexes of the usual socio-economic histories of Greece has failed to produce a single entry for either 'patron' or 'client'.[1]

In shunning ancient Greek patronage as a subject repaying study, historians have done no more than follow the lead that the ancient sources themselves seem to suggest. The traditional point of departure for ancient historians engaged in institutional analysis has been terminology, and the Greek material is almost entirely devoid of a terminology of patronage (Herman 1987, 38). The word 'almost' is deliberately included here, as there are hints of a terminology appropriate to patronage to which I will return below; but there is nothing at all comparable to the *cliens/patronus* vocabulary familiar

---

[1] If such studies exist, they have failed to enter the mainstream of secondary literature. Faced with the assumption that patron-client relationships did not, as a rule, exist in ancient Greece (see, for example, Strasburger 1976, 111-16), the few historians who introduce the concept of patronage do so defensively (Whitehead 1986, 309). For attack as the best form of defence, see Finley (1983), 39-47: the only attempt known to me to apply a patron-client model to the Greek world. In what follows, my debt to this and others of Finley's writings will be obvious.

from the earlier Roman world. That need not, of course, be final, and the absence of an explicit, stable terminology does not necessarily mean that patron-client relationships are not taking place. The point is well brought out by Saller (1982, 8-11), in his study of patronage under the early principate. He shows how the usual patron/client vocabulary was not the only way of signalling the personal patronage that was a key institution of the early empire (see, briefly, Garnsey and Saller 1987, 148-59). The elements that Saller sees as indicative of a patron/client type of relationship are three in number, and in what follows I take them as the basis of my own working definition. They are (i) an exchange of goods and/or services that is reciprocal; (ii) the relationship must be a personal one, and of some duration; (iii) the relationship must be asymmetrical, inasmuch as the two parties are of unequal status, offering each other different sorts of goods and services. To these three elements I would tentatively add a fourth: namely, that the relationship was conducted along lines largely determined by the party of superior status. It is this that opens up the way for the exploitation that is so common in patron-client relations.[1]

It seems incredible - almost inconceivable - that relationships like this never occurred in the ancient Greek world. In fact, they did occur, and some of the more obvious examples are given below. But these instances are so peripheral and so few in number that they do not appear to exert any pronounced influence on the ordering of society; not in the same, central way as patron/client relations in the Roman world, amply documented by other papers in this volume. At first sight, this seems surprising. Like many other Mediterranean societies, past and present, ancient Greece was a relatively poor, pre-industrial, agrarian society, with a few rich people and very many poor people. Patronage is one of the methods by which the rich seek to control the poor, and the poor try to protect themselves in a potentially hostile environment (Gellner 1977, Davis 1977, 132-50). In this respect, *modern* Greece is no exception: it is sufficient to

---

[1] Saller's tripartite definition is based on modern anthropological and sociological studies; my fourth element was suggested by a reading of Wrightson (1982), 57. The exploitative tendency inherent in patron-client relations is not always represented in modern discussions, which lay too much emphasis on the symbiotic aspects of the relationship (Theobald 1983, 141-2).

point to the classic study of a modern Greek mountain community by Campbell (1964), called 'Honour, Family and *Patronage*'. Why, then, should it have been any different for *ancient* Greece?

It will have called for no very close attention to realise that in spite of the promise of my title, with its reference to classical Athens, the discussion so far has been conducted in terms of ancient Greece as a whole. That is deliberate, and the terms have not - and will not - be used indiscriminately. Lurking behind this distinction there is a bias in the ancient sources which, however obvious, needs to be made explicit. The great bulk of the surviving evidence about virtually every aspect of Greek social history - including patronage - comes from Athens. It is probably fair to say that, with the partial exception of Sparta, the only Greek state for which we can attempt anything like a comprehensive account of economy and society is Athens (Finley 1985, 61-6); and Athens was not a typical *polis*. The ways in which Athens differed from other Greek states are many and various, but one which seems especially relevant here is the status of Athens as the most developed and stable of ancient democracies. With only two, brief oligarchic interludes in 411 and 404, the basic structures of the democracy remained stable for almost one-and-a-half centuries (462-322). When Aristotle in his *Politics*, which probably dates from the 320s, wants to list the characteristics of a developed democracy, it is almost certainly Athens that he takes as his model (1317b18-18a2).[1]

It is an easy step to connect the strength and longevity of the Athenian democracy with the apparent absence of information about patronage. It seems a plausible hypothesis that the democratic ideology, with its emphasis on political equality, was hostile to the idea of personal patronage, which depended on the exploitation of inequalities in wealth and status. So Aristotle prefaces his analysis of *stasis* or political conflict with the observation that:

> Democracy arose from the idea that those who are equal (*isous*) in any respect are equal absolutely. All are alike free (*eleutheroi*), therefore they claim that they are all equal absolutely.
> (*Politics* 1301a 29-31)

[1] For Aristotle's references to, and views on, 'extreme democracy', see Ste. Croix (1981), 76. Such changes as occurred within the structure of the fourth-century democracy are discussed by Rhodes (1980).

More generally, there is the stress on the notion of equality in the common synonyms for *demokratia*: *isonomia* ('equality before the law') and *isegoria* ('equality of the right to speak'). For details of references, both ancient and modern, see de Ste. Croix (1981), 285.

There can be nothing novel about this hypothesis relating democracy to absence of personal patronage, which must have occurred - if only subconsciously - to the great majority of ancient historians. But the argument cannot be allowed to rest there. In spite of effective measures to bring about a degree of political equality in Athens, the distribution of property and status was manifestly *not* equal (Davies 1981, 15-37). Moreover, even widespread hostility to the idea of patronage does not automatically bring about its abolition. In what follows, I will try to argue that deliberate and, in large measure, effective steps were taken to minimize the scope for patronage in classical Athens. Also, where patronage, or something very like it, still occurred, efforts were made to conceal or disguise it. Alternatively, dependent relationships typical of patrons and clients are either criticized or ridiculed as something shameful to be avoided. It is this hostile material that constitutes one of our major, though indirect, sources of information about patronage in democratic Athens.

Patronage before democracy

The corollary of the argument offered above, linking absence of patronage to presence of democracy, is that outside Athens, where democratic institutions were less secure or non-existent, there was a lot more patronage about, with little or no effort to disguise it. But this is where the 'Athenocentricity' of our sources becomes an obvious handicap, because there is no typical oligarchic state that can be used as a control. The best that can be managed is Sparta: certainly an oligarchy (Xenophon *Hellenica* 2.3.34), but hardly a typical representative of non-democratic *poleis* (see Cartledge 1980). Nevertheless, even amongst the Spartan elite, with their heavy emphasis on uniformity, a case can be made out for patronage as an integral part of the system (Hodkinson 1983). Apart from Sparta, the usable evidence from other non-democratic states that has come to my attention is meagre. By itself, it cannot be used to recreate the structure of patron-client relations as they might have existed outside Athens. Against this, there do survive several potentially relevant items of information from pre-democratic Athens; that is, Athens before the development of the mature democracy, around the middle of the fifth century. By combining these two strands, it is possible to build up a sequence of pictures, tracing the possible development of patronage in and around Attica, down to the so-called 'Democratic Revolution' of 462.

The sequence actually starts outside Attica, in the neighbouring region of Boeotia in the early archaic period; to be more precise, in Hesiod's village of Ascra, c.700. I have argued elsewhere that in the *Works and Days* Hesiod gives a valuable account of social relations within a small peasant community, typical of countless others in archaic and classical Greece. As such, it has a general significance, and the relationships between peasant households as described in the *Works and Days* are an appropriate starting point for a study of the development of patronage.[1]

If the *Works and Days* has a single theme, it is how to maintain, or even increase, the prosperity of the peasant *oikos* or household (e.g. vv.493-5). This is to be achieved through a judicious blend of piety, good management and hard work (vv.465-78). A major element in all this is the need to strive after self-sufficiency; but it is also envisaged that temporary imbalances between households will be corrected by reciprocal exchanges (vv.342-51): A gives to B on the assumption that, at some future date, A will himself need something back from B. The situation is ideally one of overall equilibrium, with the exchanges taking place between near equals. It conforms closely to the mechanism identified in modern peasant societies by Foster, as described in a classic paper called 'The dyadic contract' (1967). Like Foster's Mexican peasants, Hesiod is adamant that the successful member of the community will do everything in his power to avoid being on the receiving end of any exchange (as in vv.364-7, 407-9, 453-7), even going to the lengths of keeping in stock a prefabricated plough, should the one in regular use break (vv.432-4). If it is necessary to borrow grain, the lender must be paid back with the

---

[1] The analysis that follows is given in fuller form in Millett (1984), 93-103. The picture of peasant reciprocity derived from Hesiod has close affinities with the account of patronage of the poor in the Roman world given by Garnsey and Woolf in this volume.

archaic equivalent of interest. Says Hesiod:

> Take fair measure from your neighbour and pay him back fairly
> with the same measure, or better, if you can; so that if you are in
> need afterwards, you may find him sure. (vv.349-51)

In other words, far from remaining under an obligation to a
neighbour, the tables are turned, so that the obligation is imposed
upon him.

At various points in the poem (esp. vv.352-63), Hesiod stresses
the desirability of giving rather than receiving. If a man continues to
take without giving back, the relationship ceases to be reciprocal,
between near equals, and turns into one of dependence. Hesiod's
objections to dependent relationships are based, not on any proto-
democratic ideology, but rather on practical fears about the future.
Neighbours are not so willing to help out a person who does nothing
but take. 'Two or three times', says Hesiod, you may persuade your
neighbours to give you food, 'but if you trouble them further, it will
not avail you, and all your talk will be in vain, and your word-play
unprofitable' (vv.401-4). It is to avoid this end - or even worse - that
Hesiod counsels his combination of hard work, careful management,
and a proper attitude towards the gods: 'In order', he says, 'that you
may buy another man's holding, and not another man yours' (v.341).
Again, this notion that one man's gain must necessarily involve
another's loss is apparently a characteristic of modern peasant
societies (Foster 1965).

What Hesiod apparently envisages may be expressed schematically
as the conversion of a reciprocal relationship between equals - a
horizontal relationship - into a vertical relationship between superior
and inferior partners; and that is one of the criteria of patronage. Two
points need clarification. Hesiod himself has no ethical objection to
this vertical relationship, so long as he is at the upper end. Also, the
world of Hesiod is not to be seen as in any kind of crisis, or even on
the verge of a crisis, resulting from excessive dependence of the poor
on the rich. For the first signs of that, we have to wait for a century
or more, and transfer our attention to Attica in the time of Solon
(c.600).[1]

---

[1] The account of the Solonic crisis given in the text is necessarily brief; for
detail, see Finley (1965), 156; Andrewes ((1982) 377-81. The idea of

The detail of the Solonic crisis is highly controversial, and certainty is impossible. But insofar as any consensus has emerged, it seems to be agreed that in the period leading down to Solon's archonship of 596, the poorer peasantry of Attica were being reduced to a position of extreme dependence on the rich. As the author of the Aristotelian *Constitution of the Athenians* wrote in the later fourth century (2.2): 'The poor together with their children and wives were enslaved (*edouleuon*) to the rich.' Although that is probably a loose exaggeration, it gives some impression of the severity of the crisis (Finley 1965, 156-7). Immediately after are given the terms used to describe those in positions of dependence: 'They were called *pelatai* and *hektemoroi*'. The precise meaning of *hektemoros* is obscure. The word is usually said to represent a type of sharecropper, tied to the land and compelled to hand over one sixth of all produce as rent (see Rhodes 1981 *ad loc.*). Whereas *hektemoros* occurs only in the context of the Solonic crisis, *pelates* crops up elsewhere, and in ways which have a direct bearing on the question of patronage. The literal meaning of the word (from the common verb *pelazo*) is 'one who approaches another' (e.g. Sophocles *Philoctetes* v.1164), and, by extension, 'a neighbour' (Aeschylus *Persae* v.49). But it seems also to have the sense of 'one who approaches another *for protection*' - like a client. The word occurs only once with this sense in a classical context (Plato *Euthyphro* 4C, discussed below). It is, however, significant that *pelates* reappears three centuries later in the writings of Dionysius of Halicanassus as the Greek equivalent of the Latin *cliens* (2.9.2; cf. Plutarch *Romulus* 13; and generally, Hahn 1983).

Here is possible evidence for widespread dependence in early sixth-century Attica that was severe enough to distort the structuring of Athenian society. By a process not entirely clear to us, the depressed peasants were able to resist the pressure of increasing exploitation, and, by the legislation of Solon, it was made illegal for a citizen to use his own person as security (*Constitution of the Athenians* 6.1). For evidence that this successful resistance on the part of the peasantry was not limited to Attica, we may turn aside to the neighbouring state of Megara at approximately the same time as

increasing dependence on the part of the Attic peasantry is retained in the recent re-interpretation of the evidence by Gallant (1982). In support of the traditional date for Solon's archonship of 594/3: Wallace (1983).

Solon's archonship.[1] Plutarch, in his *Greek Questions* 18, poses the problem: 'What is return-interest (*palintokia*)?', and then offers the following solution:

> When the Megarians had expelled Theagenes their tyrant, for a short time they were well-disciplined in their government. But later, when the demagogues had poured a heady draught of freedom for them, as Plato says, they were utterly corrupted. Among the shocking acts of misconduct towards the wealthy, the poor would enter their homes and insist on being entertained and banqueted sumptuously. But if they did not receive what they demanded, they would treat all the household with violence and insult. Finally, they enacted a decree whereby they received back from the lenders the interest they happened to have given. They referred to the affair as 'return-interest'.

Plutarch's source for this passage is probably the lost *Constitution of the Megarians* attributed to Aristotle. Apart from the debtors' revolt - a partial and contemporary parallel for the Solonic *seisachtheia* - there is the striking feature of the wealthy being compelled to offer hospitality to the poor. Referring back to the definition of patronage with which this study opened, the Megarian episode looks like a deliberate inversion of the usual patron/client relationship, with the poor replacing the rich as the exploitative partner.

What subsequently happened in Megara we do not know; about Attica after Solon, we are rather better informed. It has often been remarked that in spite of his abolition of the legal status of dependence, Solon is not known to have addressed the deeper problems underlying the poor peasants' dependence on the wealthy. This may help to explain the eventual success of Pisistratus in establishing a popular tyranny in Athens some fifty years later (c. 550).[2] Pisistratus was remembered as having given practical help to

---

[1]   A precise date for the Megarian debt-crisis is unattainable. Asheri (1969), 14-16 argues for the years after 570, while Legon (1981) favours a date shortly before 600. In an otherwise perceptive treatment of the *palintokia*, Figueira (1985), 149-6 clouds the issue by identifying the introduction of coinage as the critical factor in precipitating the crisis. He accordingly favours a late date for the *palintokia* of 544/1, a generation after the earliest minting of silver coins in Greece.

[2]   For the background to Pisistratus' tyranny, see Pleket (1969), 40-7. The

peasants who were in difficulties:

> He made advances of money (*proedaneize chremata*) to those who
> were without resources, in order to support their work, so that
> they should continue to maintain themselves by farming.
>
> *(Constitution of the Athenians* 16)

The effect of this would presumably be to reduce peasants' dependence on local, wealthy landowners, and transfer their allegiance to the tyrant, thereby centralising patronage and buttressing the tyranny. It is a reasonable assumption that the loan fund was supported by the levy on agricultural produce described in a later section (16).[1] It is also reasonable to assume that both loans and levy were abolished in the aristocratic reaction that followed on the overthrow of the tyranny in c. 510.

As for what replaced this attempt to centralise patronage, we have some indication in the career of Cimon, the Athenian aristocrat *par excellence* who dominated the political scene in the second quarter of the fifth century. The relevant passage comes from the *Philippica* of Theopompus, a fourth-century historian, whose works survive only in fragmentary form:

> Cimon the Athenian stationed no guard over the produce in his
> fields or gardens, so that any citizen who wished might go in and
> harvest and help himself, if he needed anything on the estate.
> Furthermore, he threw his house open to all, so that he regularly
> supplied an inexpensive meal to many men, and the poor
> Athenians approached him and dined. And he tended to those who

theory of Ellis and Stanton (1968), 99-110, that Solon deliberately set about engineering an economic boom in industry and trade to compensate for a depression in agriculture, depends on an anachronistic reading of the evidence.

[1] In this way, the peasant loans could have a redistributive function, as the tax in kind would fall most heavily on the larger landowners. The anecdote that follows in the text of the *Constitution of the Athenians* (16.6), about Pisistratus' grant of exemption to a struggling hill farmer as the origin of the term 'tax-free land' (*chorion ateles*), implies that the poorest peasants were free from the levy. In support of the argument that *prodaneizein* refers to loans which were interest-free, see Wyse (1982), with additional comments by Korver (1934), 136-43 and Migeotte (1980). For arguments in favour of popular support for Pisistratus, see Chambers (1984).

day by day asked something of him. And they say that he always
took around with him two or three youths who had some small
change, and ordered them to make a contribution whenever
someone approached and asked him. And they say that he helped
out with burial expenses. Many times also, he did this: whenever
he saw one of the citizens ill-clothed, he would order one of the
youths who accompanied him to change clothes with him. From
all these things, he won his reputation and was first of the
citizens. (Theopompus, fr. 89, 135 = Athenaeus 12, 532f-533c)

The substance of this passage is repeated by Plutarch in his *Life of
Cimon* (10. 1-2), and part of it also occurs in the Aristotelian
Constitution of the Athenians (27. 3), where Cimon is made to limit
his largesse to fellow-demesmen.[1] Whatever the scale of his handouts,
Cimon's behaviour has regularly been identified as patronage on a par
with the politicians of republican Rome (Davies 1981, 97; Finley
1983, 39-40; Whitehead 1986, 309). Cimon's wealth was as
extensive as his aristocratic connections - 'worthy of a tyrant', says
the *Constitution of the Athenians* (27. 3; see Davies 1971, no. 8429,
esp. XVI). His reputation for generosity mixed in with military
successes against the Persians proved a winning combination. By
way of confirming Theopompus' assessment that Cimon was 'first of
the citizens' was his election as commander or *strategos* every year
from 477 to 461: a record with which even Pericles could not
compete (Hignett 1952, 191 n.4).

It may be presumed that Cimon was unique only in the scale of
his patronage and the level of success he achieved. This would
explain how memories of his methods came to be preserved in
anecdotal form. In the absence of appropriate evidence, he has to stand
proxy for other, lesser aristocrats, deploying their wealth along

---

[1] In a detailed discussion, Whitehead (1986), 306-8 argues in favour of
limited generosity to fellow-demesmen. Even if Cimon was not in a position
to help out the whole citizen body, he would still enjoy a *polis*-wide
reputation for doing the decent thing. It is possible that the common source
from which Theopompus and the *Constitution of the Athenians* derived their
information of Cimon as patron was a work by Critias - the leading oligarch
of late-fifth-century Athens (Wade-Gery 1938). Although only fragments of
his writings survive, one of them reads (fr.8): 'I would wish for the wealth of
the Scopadae, the magnanimity of Cimon, the victories of Arcesilaus of
Sparta' - a splendidly oligarchic recipe for power.

similar lines. The whole period from 479 to 462 has been summed up as 'The Indian summer of the Athenian aristocracy' - the definition is Hignett's (1952, 192). But, somehow, everything went wrong, and in 461 Cimon was ostracized. This is not the place to speculate why it was that things went so badly wrong for Cimon and his aristocratic supporters; it is sufficient to note that the year or so before the exile of Cimon is dominated by what is conventionally called 'The Democratic Revolution of 462'. Precisely what happened to politics and the *politeia* in 462 is problematical to say the least; but the effect seems to have been to develop and extend democratic institutions, and foster what was loosely referred to above as the 'democratic ideology'. It is with this political shift that private patronage on a grand scale disappears from the record, a development that is surely not coincidental. What replaced private, personal patronage, I will suggest in the final section below.[1]

Democratic Athens

For the 140 years from the Revolution of 462 down to the destruction of the democracy in 322, we have a series of hints and glimpses of patronage in Athens. Although the material is scattered and fragmentary, most of it shares the idea that patron-client relationships, inasmuch as they are generated by inequality and are a constraint on an individual's freedom, are inappropriate to democracy. That said, my analysis opens with an exceptional text that supports by reverse logic the general rule about the incompatability of patronage and democracy. This is a long passage in defence of patronage from the *Areopagiticus* of Isocrates, a political pamphlet from the middle of the fourth century. In spite of the stability of the fourth-century democracy, there were those in Athens who would have preferred an oligarchic *politeia*. But such was the strength of the prevailing democratic ideology that they were forced to conceal or

[1] For a short but sensitive assessment of the events of 462 and their impact, see Davies (1978), 63-75; full citation of sources in Hignett (1952), 193-213. The democratic shift of 462 may represent a delayed response to the popular, anti-aristocratic reforms of Clisthenes, half a century earlier (c.508/7). On the possible implication of Clisthenes' measures for aristocratic patronage, see Finley (1983), 42-9.

disguise their views. One such crypto-oligarch was Isocrates, and in the *Areopagiticus* he appeals for a reconstruction of the democratic constitution along more 'traditional' lines. His technique is reminiscent of the oligarchs of 404, appealing not to oligarchic principles, but to the 'democracy handed down to us by our forefathers' (§15). The only way, he says, that the Athenians can achieve again their former greatness is by 'restoring that earlier democracy which was instituted by Solon ... and which was re-established by Clisthenes' (§16). This requires the abolition of selection for public office by lot, and also of pay for public office (§21-7): cornerstone and capstone of the developed democracy.

This is the covertly oligarchic context of Isocrates' praise of patronage, harking back to the 'Good Old Days' in a long but illuminating passage:

...in their private lives as well, they [the Athenians] showed that degree of consideration for each other which is due from men who are right-minded and partners in a common fatherland. The less well-off among the citizens were so far from envying those of greater means that they were as much concerned about the great estates as their own. They considered that the prosperity of the rich was a guarantee of their own well-being. Those who possessed wealth, on the other hand, did not look down on those in humbler circumstances. Instead, they regarded poverty among citizens as their own disgrace, and came to the rescue of the sufferings of the poor. To some they handed out farmland at a moderate rent (*epi metriais misthosesi*), they sent out some to engage in trade, and to others they supplied what was needed to start up in occupations (*eis tas allas ergasias aphormen parechontes*). They had no fear that they might suffer either of two things: they they might lose the lot, or, after a great deal of trouble, recover only a small part of what they had layed out (*ton proethenton*). On the contrary, they felt as confident about what they had given out (*dedomenon*) as about that which they had stored at home. ... if the rich were to stop lending (*proiemenoi*), they would be deprived of only a small revenue (*mikron prosodon*), whereas if the poor should lack the help of their supporters (*ton eparkounton*) they would be reduced to desperate straits. And because of this confidence, no one tried to conceal their wealth, or hesitated to lend it out (*symballein*). Instead they were happier to see men borrowing than paying back. In this way, they experienced a double satisfaction which should appeal to all those with any sense, of helping their fellow citizens; and at the same time, they made active use of their property. This was the result of their treating each other fairly. The ownership of property was secured to those to whom it justly belonged, and the enjoyment of property was shared by all the citizens who needed it. (*Areopagiticus* 32-5)

Heartwarming stuff, but hardly the stuff of history. Historians have tried to locate this Golden Age anywhere between the time of Solon and Isocrates' own youth during the Peloponnesian War.[1] But what it really amounts to is an apologia for the idea of patronage, seen through an oligarchic haze. With considerable rhetorical skill, Isocrates paints a picture of admiration, assistance and mutual respect, whereas one suspects that what he had in mind was a great deal of forelock-tugging. The Hesiodic warning that receiving without giving back can result in dependence is presented as a paradox: the wealthy preferred to see the poor taking rather than making repayments.[2]

---

[1]   The passage has been used by Erxleben (1974), 471-3 and Bravo (1974), 151-3, (1977), 4-5; in each case as the key to different theories about the organization of maritime trade. Both place too much reliance on the commitment of Isocrates to historical veracity. The Orators are notoriously cavalier in dealing with specific events in the past (Pearson 1941, Nouhaud 1982, esp. 359-61, Perlman 1961). With generalized references as in the *Areopagiticus*, there is more scope for romancing and even downright lies. As a further warning, there is a disturbingly close parallel in the *Archidamus* of Isocrates, written in c.365, a decade or so before the *Areopagiticus*. Here, Isocrates contrasts the fortunate condition of the Peloponnese under Spartan rule with its present state of wretchedness. Apparently, the notion of the rich helping the poor, and receiving respect in return, was a *topos* in Isocrates' stock description of a successful society that no longer existed.

[2]   Right through the passage, the terminology is cleverly manipulated to diminish the exploitative overtones of the rich lending to the poor at interest: *parechontes, proethenton, dedemenon, proiemenoi* and *symballein* are normally associated with credit transactions *not* involving payment of interest (Korver 1934, 89-95). Tribute must be paid to Isocrates' ability to mislead readers across the ages. The *Areopagiticus* passage is cited by Fuks in a collection of material intended to show as a theme in Greek history the motif of the rich helping the poor by the voluntary sharing of property (1979/80, 177-9). It is possible that other passages in the collection conceal patronal control of the poor under the guise of humanitarian concern (e.g. Strabo 14.2.5 on Rhodes).

Elsewhere in the pamphlet, Isocrates explains how this near-utopia originally came about under the guardianship of the state by the aristocratic council of the Areopagus (§§37-55). An important part of his formula for the regeneration of the Athenian spirit is therefore the restoration of the powers of the Areopagus. According to popular tradition (*Constitution of the Athenians* 23. 1-2, 25), responsibility for whittling down the authority of the Areopagus lay with the Revolution of 462 and the men behind it; so the spirit of Isocrates' proposals may fairly be called neo-Cimonian.

In his attack on the fourth-century democracy, justifying the need for change, Isocrates argues that key democratic concepts have been debased (§20). *Demokratia*itself has, he says, become 'insolence' (*akolasia*), and *isonomia* (equality before the law) has turned into 'slanderous behaviour' (*parrhesia*). We have already encountered *isonomia*as promoting the idea of overall equality inimical to patronage, and in the following section, Isocrates is at pains to distinguish between two types of equality: 'that which makes the same award to all alike, and that which gives to each man his due'; needless to say, only the latter secures Isocrates' approval. In his catalogue of debasement, Isocrates cites a further attribute of democracy in 'freedom' (*eleutheria*), which he claims has degenerated into 'lawlessness' (*paranomia*). *Eleutheria* is perhaps best understood as 'freedom to do as you like', and is seen by both sides as the chief characteristic of democracy (de Ste. Croix 1981, 600 nn. 4 & 7). Widespread commitment to the possession of 'freedom to do as one chooses' constitutes a formidable stumbling-block to the progress of personal patronage, with its insistence on obligation and dependence. In his *Rhetoric* (1367a28), Aristotle defines the condition of a 'free man' (*eleutheros*) as 'not living in dependence on another man (*pros allon*)'. The full implication of this is brought out elsewhere by Aristotle, in his *Politics* (1337b19-21): if you do something 'because of other people' (*di' allous*), you are in danger of behaving in a servile way (*doulikon*). That this is not just Aristotle theorising can be illustrated by a familiar anecdote from Xenophon's *Memorabilia* (2.8; de Ste. Croix 1981, 181). Xenophon describes how Socrates fell in with his old friend Eutherus, who had lost all his property in the Peloponnesian War, and was now getting his living by manual labour. Socrates warns him that he will soon be too old to work in this way, and advises him to get a job as a farm bailiff or overseer. Eutherus' answer is revealing (§4): 'I would', he said, 'find slavery (*douleian*) hard to endure.' When Socrates remonstrates with him, he amplifies his objection (§5): 'Generally speaking, Socrates', he said, 'I don't take kindly to being held accountable to anyone.' From the context it is clear that the novelty of the dialogue lies in Socrates' advice and not in Eutherus' response.

Eutherus had originally been a man of property (§1), and would therefore be more sensitive to the humiliation of being at another person's beck and call. But a less well known passage from the opposite end of society suggests how close dependence on others could be assimilated to slavery. This is the sole surviving scene from Menander's comic play, *The Hero*, of which the setting is the country deme of Ptelea in Attica. Getas asks his fellow-slave Davus about two further 'slaves', a brother and sister called Gorgias and Plangon. Davus explains how their father, Tibeius, had once been a slave in their master's household. Having gained his freedom, he worked as a shepherd. Then a famine occurred, and in order to feed his two children, he borrowed two minas from his former master. Despite the loan, he died soon after, and Gorgias borrowed some more cash from Tibeius to bury his father. Davus continues (vv.34-6): 'After performing the rites, he came here to us, bringing his sister with him. And here he stays until the debt is worked off (*to chreos apergazomenos*).'

This scene is remarkable in suggesting that, in spite of the legislation of Solon (above), debt bondage continued to exist in Attica. The solution favoured by de Ste. Croix (1981) is to point to the date of the production of the play, after the destruction of the democracy in 322, when (163): 'forms of debt bondage could well have crept in and even received at least tacit legal recognition.' This is a possibility but the answer may be simpler. The abolition of debt bondage by law, and its actual disappearance, are two different things. Although debt bondage has to all intents and purposes been outlawed in the modern world, it continues to flourish under other names and through the use of legal fictions (Ennew 1981: a report of the still-active Anti-Slavery Society). If people are superficially willing - perhaps through starvation - to assign their own or their family's labour to another person, there is little that the law can do about it. I suspect that in the Menander fragment, Gorgias and Plangon are to be thought of as voluntarily discharging a 'debt of honour' on behalf of their dead father. As such, their service would fall outside the scope of Solon's law. This would explain the circumlocutory way in which

Davus describes Plangon's status (v.20). When asked outright whether the girl is a slave (*doule*), he replies: 'Yes - sort of - in a kind of way'. It should also be borne in mind that Gorgias and Plangon were portrayed as the children of a freedman and not of citizen status. They therefore had less *eleutheria* to be compromised.[1]

Although it will be argued below that the fictional case of Gorgias and his sister mirrors what occasionally happened in the real Athenian world, their debt-dependence represents an extreme form of patronage which was rare in classical Athens. In assessing types of patronage that were more common, it may prove helpful to think in terms of a 'spectrum of dependence'. At one end will be full and perpetual dependence, as close to chattel slavery as makes no practical difference; at the other end is a much milder form of dependence on other people for favours, perhaps on a casual basis. There is an impression that the form of patronage most commonly encountered in Athenian sources comes from the milder end of the spectrum. It is a species of dependence that gives rise to the character type of the *kolax* or 'flatterer', and his more specialist associate, the *parasitos* or 'parasite'. To clarify all the possible shades of meaning of these two terms over time itself would require a lengthy monograph. The summary that follows is adequate only for the purpose in hand.

The *locus classicus* for flatterers and parasites must be a rambling section of Athenaeus' *Deipnosophists* (6. 234c-261f), in which the learned diners reel off passage after passage in which the two types appear. From the range of references given, it is clear that they are stock characters in Comedy, with plays actually called 'The Flatterers'

---

[1] Similar circumstances may lie behind the appearance of a *pelates* in a dialogue of Plato (*Euthyphro* 44B-E) - the only appearance of the word in a classical context. Euthyphro is shown as prosecuting his father for murder. The victim was a *pelates* of Euthyphro, and the incident took place on Naxos, where he was labouring (*etheteuen*) on the family's property. Although the whole scenario is imaginary and the circumstantial detail cannot be pressed too far, a couple of points call for comment. If the *pelates* had placed himself under the protection of Euthyphro, that would explain his obligation to act against the murderer. Also, the status of the *pelates* remains a mystery. If he were a Naxian, his dependant status would be explicable: de Ste. Croix (1981), 163 is surely correct in his suggestion that debt bondage and other forms of dependence were always widespread outside Athens; to the references given (Lysias 12.98; Isoc. 14.48; Aristoph. *Plutus* vv.147-8) add *SIG* [3] 46, with Bogaert (1968), 271-2.

by Eupolis in the fifth century, 'The Flatterer' by Menander in the fourth, and 'The Parasite' by Alexis, Antiphanes and Diphilus (all from the fourth century). The terms may be provisionally defined as referring to people who perform trivial services for their social and material superiors in return for favours. Of the two words, *parasitos* tends to be the more specific, and has the dubious distinction of having experienced a decline in respectability. The original *parasitoi* were temple officials whose services to the gods were recompensed by free meals (*sitos*). From the mid-fourth century, the term acquires a subsidiary sense which eventually becomes dominant: a *parasitos* is a person who makes himself agreeable at dinner-parties in return for a decent meal (Arnott 1959). So far as precision is possible, a parasite received his reward as a result of a general ability to entertain and amuse, whereas a *kolax* attached himself to a single eminent person. But the two terms are to some extent interchangable (Athenaeus 236e), and *kolax* may do service for both of them.

The passages cited by Athenaeus give a fair impression of the duties that the *kolax* performed in return for his reward. Eupolis makes his chorus of flatterers say:

... And when I catch sight of a man who is rich and thick, I at once get my hooks into him. If this moneybags happens to say anything, I praise him vehemently and express my amazement, pretending to find delight in his words.

(Eupolis, 236f = Kock I fr. 301)

But the fullest and most closely observed description of a kolax comes in the sketch by Theophrastus that is one of his *Characters*.[1] He begins by defining flattery (*kolakeia*) as (2. 1): '... an attitude or relationship which is degrading in itself, but profitable to the one who flatters.' The opening sentences give the flavour of the study:

---

[1] To be sure, the *Characters* are meant to amuse rather than provide realistic portraits of Athenian society; but as a general rule, comic effects in the individual characters do not depend on fantasy, after the fashion of the Old Comedy. Instead, much of the humour seems to lie in the piling-up of elements which, taken individually, are true to life; but which, when strung together, add a touch of the absurd. Theophrastus apparently wrote a serious study of flattery (*peri kolakeias*, Athenaeus 10. 425e), which has not survived.

The flatterer is the sort of person who will say to the man he is walking with: 'Do you notice how people look at you? You are the only man in Athens they study in that way.' Or he might say: 'You were being complimented yesterday in the colonnade. There was a group of thirty or more sitting talking and the question cropped up, who was our best citizen? Starting from that, we all came back finally to your name.' While he is going on like this, he picks a stray thread off the other's coat; or if a bit of chaff has blown into his hair, he takes it out and says with a laugh: 'Well look at that! Because I haven't seen you for two days, you've got a beard full of grey hairs; though if anyone's hair keeps its colour in spite of years, yours does'. (Theophrastus*Characters* 2. 2-3)

Theophrastus goes on to describe how the flatterer keeps silence while the great man speaks, says 'hear hear' in all the right places, clears the way for him, and runs his errands.

The emphasis in Theophrastus' sketch is understandably on the services performed by the flatterer. For the other side of the coin (literally) we turn to Aristotle, who says:

Of those who try to give pleasure, he who does this with no ulterior motive aims at being pleasant and is anxious to please (*areskos*); but he who does so in order that some advantage may fall to him in respect of money (*chremata*), or anything else that money procures, is a *kolax*.. (*Nichomachaean Ethics* 1127a 7)

A sequence of passages cited by Athenaeus (254c) makes exaggerated claims about the dangers that flatterers pose to rich men, draining them utterly dry.

This relation between the *kolax*and his rich 'victim' has many of the hallmarks of a client-patron arrangement. Attitudes towards the role of the kolax are almost invariably negative, ranging from the amused contempt of Theophrastus to the downright condemnation of Aristotle in the *Nichomachaean Ethics* (1124b30-5a2). In the context of his description of *megalopsychia* ('greatness of soul'), he argues that a man possessing this quality: 'must be unable to make his life revolve around another, unless it be a friend (*philon*); for that is slavish (*doulikon*), and for this reason all flatterers are hirelings (*thetikoi*) and those lacking in self-respect are flatterers.' In Aristotle's view, hired labour is on an ethical level with slavery - see de Ste.

Croix (1981), 182-5. The basis of all this disapproval is plain: the *kolax* is forced to compromise his *eleutheria* by adapting his behaviour to gratify his potential benefactor, on whose favours he is dependent. Aristotle does, however, allow the modification of behaviour where the motive is to help a friend (*philos*), and this points towards one of the obvious ways in which patronage could be disguised to make it more acceptable. A case in point occurs in Xenophon's *Memorabilia* (2. 9), where Socrates advises his friend Crito, who was being plagued by sycophants or blackmailers. They were threatening him with a court case on the assumption that he would pay up rather than take the trouble and risk of going to court. Socrates suggested that Crito might fight fire with fire, and find his own sycophant who would put pressure on the blackmailers. The person eventually chosen was one Archedemus, who is described in the following terms (§4):

> ... they discovered Archedemus - a person of considerable rhetorical ability, but poor (*peneta*), because he is not the sort of man to make money by any means; he was a man of good character, and skilled at getting money out of sycophants. So whenever Crito was getting in crops or grain (*sitos!*) or wine or wool, or any other useful farm product, he used to give a share to Archedemus. And whenever he gave a dinner, he invited him, and showed him every consideration of this kind.

The whole scheme was a great success, with Archedemus finding out unpleasant things about the people blackmailing Crito, and blackmailing them in return. The story has a tailpiece which is instructive (§8). When the enemies of Archedemus taunt him with the accusation that he is behaving like a *kolax*, Archedemus responds that he is really a 'friend' (*philos*) of Crito. This anticipates a common device of Roman patronage: preserving appearances by disguising clients as *amici*.[1]

If there is a common Athenian equivalent for 'client' it must be *kolax*. And yet, so far as I am aware, *kolax* is never used in conjunction with a word that might conceivably be rendered as 'patron'. Such a word is *prostates*, used by later authors as an

---

[1] Saller (1982), 11-15. For another euphemism, transforming *kolakeia* into *areskeia* ('willingness to oblige'), see Athenaeus 6. 255a.

equivalent for the Latin *patronus* (Plutarch *Romulus* 13). According to Liddell and Scott, *prostates* has a wide range of meanings: 'one who stands before', 'leader, chief (especially of a democracy)', 'ruler', 'presiding officer', 'one who stands before and protects, guardian, champion', 'patron who took charge of the interests of *metoikoi* (metics)'. This sequence of meanings gives a strong hint why it was that no Athenian citizen is ever described as having a personal *prostates*. Having leaders is inevitable, even in a democracy, and having protectors also seems unexceptionable, until it is appreciated what kind of people were being protected. The inferior status of the metic population of Athens has been well-documented by Whitehead (1977 and 1986a). One of the key institutions that marked off the metics from the citizen body was the legal obligation imposed upon each metic to have a citizen *prostates*. The punishment for failing to have a *prostates* was reputedly enslavement (Harrison 1968, 189-93). For some metics, the gulf between freedom and slavery was not wide; a proportion of the metic population were freed slaves. Freedmen automatically took as *prostates* their former master. When Tibeius, as conceived by Menander, turned to his former master for loans to buy food in time of famine, he was exploiting the idea of *prostates* as patron and protector. In the surviving sources, this kind of action is exceptional, and the major function of the *prostates* seems to have been mediation between non-citizen and *polis* institutions (Whitehead 1977, 89-92). Here, then, the picture was one of formalised superiority and inferiority, helping to explain why what was obligatory for a metic should be considered inappropriate for a citizen.[1] In only one text known to me does the *prostateia* (patronage) of citizens by another citizen seem to be envisaged. Some comments on this passage may serve as a conclusion to this section on the extent and nature of patron-client relations in classical Athens. In Xenophon's *Oeconomicus* 2, Socrates confronts Critobulus (son of

---

[1] Plutarch in his *Life of Alcibades* (5) has an anecdote about a metic who deliberately courted dependence on a powerful patron. The metic sold all his property, and presented the proceeds (100 staters) to Alcibiades. He was thereupon commanded, under pain of getting a beating, to attend the auction of the right to collect public revenues, where he was to outbid all the other tax-farmers. This he did, offering a whole talent more than the usual bidders. They were thrown into confusion, and demanded that the metic name his citizen guarantor. At this point Alcibiades stepped in, claimed the metic as his friend, and offered himself as guarantor. He allowed the metic to withdraw

Crito), whose property he estimates to be worth ten talents (§3), with the paradox that he is in reality extremely poor. When Critobulus demands an explanation, Socrates replies that wealth brings with it disproportionately heavy obligations. He points out (§§5-6) that he has a duty to offer lavish sacrifices 'lest you be on bad terms with gods and men', he has to entertain many strangers (*xenoi*) in grand style, and invite citizens to dinner, 'otherwise you will be without supporters *(symmachoi)*'. Socrates then details added burdens: 'For I see that the *polis* is already laying heavy expenses on you for the keeping of horses, paying for a chorus, or holding a gymnasiarchy, or *prostateia*.' The sense of *prostateia* is uncertain here. Austin and Vidal-Naquet (1977), in their version of the passage, translate it as (320) 'undertaking some important function' adding a note to the effect that: 'The Greek word *prostateia* has here a very general meaning.' As the term appears in a list of burdens imposed by the state, that may well be right; but a few lines later, the verb from *prostates (prostateuein)* occurs in a context making it clear that *personal* patronage is intended (§§7-9). Socrates envisages the not-unlikely situation in which Critobulus, having spent all his money, becomes hard-up: 'Your friends (*philoi*), even though they have ampler means for supporting their condition than you have for supporting yours, nevertheless look to you as if to receive benefits from you.' Critobulus is forced to acknowledge the strength of Socrates' arguments about poverty and wealth, and asks him for advice: 'It is now time for you to act the *prostates (prostateuein)* towards me, and prevent me from becoming pitiable in reality.' Socrates cannot resist the temptation to crow a little over his refutation of Critobulus, who had earlier laughed at the idea that Socrates, though poor, was in reality the better-off. He says: '... you now desire me to be your *prostates (prostateuein)*, and take care that you do not become utterly and undeniably poor (*penes*).' I interpret all this in the following way. Running through this dialogue, there is an antithesis between wealth and poverty: Critobulus, having lost his wealth, will become poorer than his *philoi* (polite for clients?), but

bid only on condition that the other tax-farmers bought him off with a talent by way of compensation. Plutarch contrasts Alcibiades' treatment of the deferential metic with the contempt he regularly showed to citizen admirers. Only a story, but it shows both the advantages and disadvantages for a metic of having a powerful patron.

they will still expect him to help them out. Critobulus then picks out the theme of patronage and applies it both paradoxically and metaphorically by asking Socrates, a poor man, to act as his patron and prevent him becoming poor.

Provided that this is a correct reading of the passage, Socrates sees Critobulus as a patron of poorer people, with no implication that they be thought of as non-citizens. There need be nothing remarkable about this. Critobulus was, like his father, a wealthy man, and even in democratic Athens, wealth on a grand scale attracted its fair share of hangers-on. Such was the fate of Nicias, a major public figure of the late fifth century, and rich through his exploitation of the silver mines (Davies 1971, no. 10808). According to Plutarch in his *Life of Nicias* (§4), he was always surrounded by spongers, 'who not only pressed him for money, but got it out of him.' What we have in the case of Critobulus looks like a patron-*kolax* relationship seen from the position of the patron. Socrates is too polite to suggest that Critobulus is a prey to flatterers; or perhaps Xenophon's Socrates approved of the principle of patronage. In picking out the denunciations of the comic playwrights and the moralists, we are in danger of forgetting that wealthy men might actually enjoy being lionized. If they did not, there would have been no scope for *kolakes*. In addition, there is the hint of a practical side to Critobulus' patronage in the lavish dinners that he lays on for citizens. Without these dinners, says Socrates, you will be without *symmachoi*, which Austin and Vidal-Naquet (1977) take as referring to supporters in politics (320): a faded replica of Cimonian political patronage.[1]

What calls for comment here is not the survival of personal patronage in classical Athens, but its vestigial and peripheral existence. What should have emerged from the sequence of texts cited above is the conclusion that patronage in Athens was a minor social phenomenon, with minimal political and economic implications. If Critobulus was no Cimon, neither was Archedemus a pre-Solonic *pelates*. We are expressly told that he was *penes* (§4); that is, poor enough to have to work for a living, but certainly not destitute (Finley 1985a, 40-1). There is nothing to suggest that *kolakes* were either a large group in society, or that they were forced into a dependent relationship through economic hardship such as faced

[1] Alternative methods of winning political support are listed by Rhodes (1986).

Gorgias and his sister, or the plebs in the Roman Republic. They are criticised on moral grounds as people who have chosen an easy, if degrading, way of making a living. Under certain circumstances, the position of *kolax* was almost a profession.[1] But disapproval cannot by itself account for the relative absence of personal patronage from classical Athens. In other Mediterranean societies, the protection of a patron provides people living at or close to the margin of subsistence with 'crisis insurance'. Given a sufficiently high level of economic pressure on the Athenian demos, any amount of ideological objections would have been overridden. In the final section, I return to the question posed towards the beginning of the paper: why it was that poor Athenian citizens were exceptional in having no need of wealthy patrons.

Alternatives to patronage

The survival of the Athenian system of democracy depended on the participation of the *demos*, which in turn relied on preserving their independence of the wealthy. Political equality was actively promoted (Finley 1983, 70-96); I would argue that deliberate steps were also taken to underwrite the economic independence of the poor. These measures did not involve the pursuit of economic equality. As noted above, the distribution of property in Athens was grossly unequal, even among the citizen body. The solution to the problem of economic independence seems to lie, not with the distribution of property, but rather with the redistribution of income. If Athens was unique in the intensity of the democracy and (possibly) in the low level of personal patronage, it also differed sharply from other *poleis* in the size and frequency of transfers of cash to poor citizens: what is

---

[1] Athenaeus (6. 284d-252f) names some of the characters who held what amounted to full-time posts as the *kolakes* of 'great men', including Philip and Alexander (see Herman 1980/1). With this may be contrasted the refusal of the Athenian statesman Phocion to accept a gift from Alexander of one hundred talents, lest his reputation for independent action be compromised (Plutarch *Phocion* 18; cf. 30). According to passages cited by Athenaeus (6. 252f-254c), the whole population of post-democratic Athens was transformed into flatterers, as citizens vied with one another in toadying to the Macedonian ruler, Demetrius Poliorcetes.

conventionally referred to as 'public pay'.[1]

The idea that public pay might act as a practical antidote to personal patronage is not new. It is precisely, though briefly, formulated by Finley, who takes as his key text Pericles' introduction of pay for jurors, as explained by the Aristotelian *Constitution of the Athenians* (27.3; Finley 1983, 39-40). The author interprets this innovation as a political device to counter the calculated generosity of Cimon. After detailing the extent of Cimon's personal wealth and the way in which he deployed it, the text continues:

> The property of Pericles was insufficient for this kind of expenditure. He was therefore advised by Daminides of Oe ... that since he was less well supplied with private property, he should give the common people (*hoi polloi*) their own property; and so he devised payment for the jurors.
>
> (*Constitution of the Athenians* 4)

Ignoring the way in which the conflict is brought down to a personal level, Finley detects here an alternative form of 'crisis insurance'. With the introduction of public pay, a poor citizen who experienced difficulties and fell below the level of subsistence could turn, not to a wealthy landowner, but to the state.

It will be appreciated how this link with public pay compliments the survey given above of patronage before the revolution of 462. State pay appears as a democratic substitute for the peasant loans of Pisistratus, reflecting the changed condition of the Athenian *politeia*. It also helps to explain why conservative theorists like Plato and Isocrates disapproved so vehemently of state pay: not only did it enable the *demos* to participate in politics, it also weakened the hold that the wealthy might reasonably expect to have over *hoi polloi* (Markle 1985, 271-2). Abolition of pay was therefore high on the agenda of the oligarchs in their short-lived revolutions of 411 and 404 (Gabrielsen 1981, 13-56). In spite of the apparent logic of the argument, it has to be conceded that Finley's hypothesis linking public pay with the suppression of patronage has not found universal favour. The main objections seem to be the trivial size of the sums

[1] What matters here is not the principle of public pay, but its overall scale: see Finley (1978), 310 n. 53, with the comments by de Ste. Croix (1975) and (1981), 602 n. 24.

involved and the impossibility of guaranteeing that payments went to the citizens most in need. The remainder of this paper is concerned with meeting these objections.

The phrase 'public pay' is misleadingly narrow in the range of payment it implies. Transfers of cash available to poorer citizens included disbursements for holding public office, serving as jurors, attending the assembly and rowing in the fleet; to which may be added the occasional handouts known as *theorika*. To give a detailed, documented account of all these types of expenditure calls for a treatment beyond the scope of this paper. The material presented here is therefore impressionistic in nature, with references to the secondary literature as appropriate.

It cannot be a coincidence that the introduction and extension of transfer payments was broadly contemporary with the Athenians' acquisition of their empire (Finley 1978, 122-3). The Aristotelian *Constitution of the Athenians* (24. 1-2) represents more than twenty thousand citizens as being supported by a combination of imperial tribute and internal revenues (cf. Aristophanes'*Wasps* vv. 707-11). If that figure is an obvious exaggeration, it at least expresses the idea that public pay, deriving from the empire, was something substantial, and significant as a source of income for individuals. Altogether more credible is the figure that follows in the text (§3) of seven hundred officials maintained in Athens, vigorously defended by Hansen (1980) as appropriate for both fifth and fourth centuries. Adding the five hundred citizens serving on the *boule* or council gives a total of 1200 persons receiving state pay, to say nothing of unknown numbers outside Attica, at least down to 404. That all these officials received anything up to a drachma a day is argued for the fifth century by Hansen (1979) and for the fourth by Gabrielsen (1981). As for jury and assembly pay, it has consistently been doubted whether daily payments were large enough to compensate even poor citizens for time spent away from work (Jones 1957, 50). A recent, exhaustive study by Markle (1985), carefully comparing costs and expenses, concludes that even the lowest rate of pay (three obols a day) would have been enough to attract the less well-off. In any case, the implied assumption of the availability of full-time employment for every citizen is demonstrably false. The same can be said for rowing in the fleet. Although payment seems to have declined from a peak of one drachma per day in the Peloponnesian War (Jordan 1972, 111-16) to as little as two obols in the fourth century (Demosthenes 4. 28), service in the fleet still made up a significant slice of some citizens' incomes. In the pseudo-Demosthenic speech *Against Polycles* (50), the speaker twice refers to the crewmen depending on prompt receipt of their wages to pay household expenses (§§11-12). Concerning the theoric fund, no firm conclusion is possible. Estimates of the annual expenditure from the fund going direct into citizens' pockets range from six talents (Jones 1957, 33-5) to ninety talents (Buchanan 1962, 83-8 with the review by de Ste. Croix 1964). That the theoric payments had *some* significance for poor citizens may be inferred from the saying attributed to Demades, a late-fourth-century politician, that the theoric payments were the 'glue of the democracy' (Plutarch, *Platonic Questions* 1011B).

Any attempt to combine the above information to arrive at an average, aggregate figure for all these transfer payments is doomed to failure: too many estimates and unknowns are involved. By way of a substitute, I offer a passage from Aristotle's *Politics* which is solidly based on the assumption that state pay could be intended as a remedy against poverty. Aristotle often refers to public pay as being the hall-mark of a developed democracy (e.g. 1293a2-7, 1294a 40-1, 1298b 18), and it is plausibly assumed that the state he has in mind is Athens. In a longer passage, Aristotle explains the weakness in the system as he understands it:

> And inasmuch as the ultimate forms of democracy tend to have large populations and it is difficult for their citizens to sit in the assembly without pay ... Where, therefore, there happen to be no revenues (*prosodoi*), few meetings of the assembly must be held, and the law courts must consist of many members, but sit only on a few days ... Where there are revenues, men must not do what popular politicians (*hoi demagogoi*) do now, for they distribute the surplus, and as soon as the people get the money, they want more of the same; for this kind of help for the poor (*tois aporois*) is the proverbial jar with a hole in it. Instead, the truly democratic politician must consider how the bulk of the people (*to plethos*) may be saved from excessive poverty (*lian aporon*), for this is what causes democracy to be corrupt. (*Politics* 1320a17-b4)

As an alternative to state subsidies, with their continuing burden, Aristotle advocates that a central fund be set up, from which lump sums could be doled out to those in need. Ideally, these sums should be large enough to purchase a small plot of land (*eis gediou ktesin*). Failing that, they should be sufficient to set people up in trade or agricultural work (*pros aphormen emporias georgias*). The reference back to Pisistratus is irresistible.[1]

One problem remains: the objection that however large the sums available to the poor might be in aggregate, they will be thinly spread over the whole citizen body, without any guarantee of going where most needed to avoid destitution and dependence. On the face of it, this is a plausible argument. The man who cannot work and is in need through illness is not likely to take a place on a jury or in the assembly - still less on a rowing bench. I would counter this objection by drawing attention to a secondary redistributive mechanism, serving to focus funds where they were most desperately needed.

Athenian social relations are shot through with systems of reciprocal obligations which are most obvious between relatives, neighbours and friends. The three categories overlap, and may be subsumed under the single term *philoi*, for which 'friends' is an inadequate translation (Whitehead 1986, 231-2). These obligations extend from the borrowing of household goods (Theophrastus, *Characters* 10. 13) to the lending or giving of large sums of money (Demosthenes 53, 4-13); to explore them in any detail would require a separate study. By way of illustration of the concept, I turn to the paradigmatic institution of *eranos* credit. The mechanism of an *eranos* loan was relatively straightforward: a person who was in financial difficulties would go the rounds of his *philoi*, collecting from them small contributions, until he had raised the sum required. The obligation to give under these circumstances was matched by an equally pressing obligation to repay the contribution as soon as possible. To accuse a man of defaulting on his *eranos* repayments

[1] As is the contrast with Isocrates (above), who wants handouts to come directly from individuals, without being mediated through the state. What Aristotle objects to in the passage cited is not so much the failure of state handouts to prevent the poor from falling into destitution, as the perpetual burden they impose on *polis* finances, and, indirectly, on wealthy citizens. His preferred solution harks back to the preoccupation displayed elsewhere with peasants as the best type of citizen for a democracy, inasmuch as they are too busy to involve themselves in politics (1292b 25-9, 1318b 9-16, 1319a 26-32). The same could be said of those involved in overseas trade (*emporia*).

was to place him beyond the bounds of moral decency (Lysias fr. 38). This type of interest-free credit was commonplace in classical Athens. Even a short text like Theophrastus' *Characters* contains five references to *eranos* loans (1. 5, 15. 7, 17. 9, 22. 9, 23. 6). When the 'Hostile Man' gives an *eranos* contribution to a friend, he snarls: 'More money thrown away!'; if the 'Mean Man' sees someone in the distance whom he knows to be raising an *eranos* loan, he will hurry off down a sidestreet, and go home by a roundabout way. Particularly revealing is the connection of the 'Boastful Man' with *eranos* credit:

> In the food shortage, he gave handouts of more than five talents to
> needy citizens - he doesn't know how to refuse. He then tells the
> men sitting next to him, who are strangers, to set out some
> counters; and by reckoning in sums of a thousand drachmas and
> in round minas, and by plausibly attributing a name to each of
> them, he makes it ten talents. He says that these are the monies
> he has contributed in *eranos* loans. (*Characters* 23.5-6)

This is, of course, a gross caricature, but even the most outrageous of caricatures must retain a recognisable link with reality.

Theophrastus has his boaster link his fantastically large *eranos* loans with a food shortage, and it was a famine that Menander made the background to dependence in the *Hero*, where Gorgias and Plangon were placed in a position akin to debt bondage. This seems to suggest an alternative to dependence, in the shape of mutual support between citizens through *eranos* loans and other forms of reciprocal obligation between *philoi*. Citizens would necessarily tend to borrow from people who were on the same social level as themselves. Although the bulk of our evidence is concerned with citizens towards the upper end of society, there are hints that even slaves might raise *eranos* contributions (Demosthenes 59, 30-1). In the passage from Xenophon cited above, Socrates explains to Critobulus how, in spite of his being a poor man, he enjoys financial security:

> As for myself, even if I were in want, I am sure that you are aware
> that there are persons who would assist me, to the extent that even
> if each contributed only a little, they would drown my modest
> means in a flood. (*Oeconomicus* 2. 8)

Although the word *eranos* does not appear here, this is evidently the arrangement that Socrates has in mind.[1]

The expressions of obligation between *philoi* outlined above are complimented and extended as effective antidotes to patronage by the additional resource of state pay. If transfer payments, however substantial, redistributed wealth among poorer citizens indiscriminately, *eranos* and associated mechanisms served to divert income where it was most needed. Although the scale of operations is appreciably larger and the network of relationships more complex, my study of patronage and its avoidance ends more or less where it began in the world of Hesiod: with the maintenance of an equilibrium through reciprocal exchanges between people of similar status.

Bibliography

Andrewes, A. (1982), 'The growth of the Athenian state', *Cambridge Ancient History*, second edition, vol.3, pt.3, 360-91.

Arnott, G. (1959), 'Three problems in Alexis: the Parasite's name, the *Poenulus*, and the humourless scholars', *Bulletin of the Institute of Classical Studies* 6, 78-9.

Asheri, D. (1969), 'Leggi greche sul problema dei debiti', *Studi Classici e Orientali* 18, 5-122.

Austin, M.M. and Vidal-Naquet, P. (1977), *Economic and Social History of Ancient Greece: an Introduction*. London.

Bogaert, R. (1968), *Banques et banquiers dans les cités grecques*. Leiden.

Bravo, B. (1974), 'Une lettre sur plomb de Berezan: colonisation et modes de contact dans le Pont', *Dialogues d'histoire ancienne* 1, 111-87.

---

[1] Irrelevant here is whether the Socrates of 'real life' was rich or poor. In the dialogue with Critobulus, he is deliberately cast by Xenophon in the role of a poor man (*penes*), estimating the value of his property at only five minas (§5). For an account (possibly fictional) of Socrates' friends clubbing together to help him out, see Plato, *Apology* 38B.

Bravo, B. (1977), 'Remarques sur les assises sociales, les formes
  d'organisation et la terminologie du commerce maritime grec a
  l'époque archaïque', *Dialogues d'histoire ancienne* 3, 1-59.
Buchanan, J.J. (1962), *Theorika. A Study of Monetary Distributions
  to the Athenian Citizenry during the Fifth and Fourth Centuries
  B.C.* New York.
CAH ^{3} = *Cambridge Ancient History* (new edition). Cambridge,
  1970-.
Campbell, J.K. (1964), *Honour, Family and Patronage*. Oxford.
Cartledge, P.A. (1980), 'The peculiar position of Sparta in the
  development of the Greek city-state', *Proceedings of the Royal
  Irish Academy* 80 (C). 91-108.
Cartledge, P. and Harvey, F.D. eds. (1985), *CRUX. Essays presented
  to G.E.M. de Ste. Croix on his 75th Birthday* (*History of
  Political Thought* vol. 6 Issue 1/2). Sidmouth.
Chambers, M.H. (1984), 'The formation of the tyranny of
  Pisistratus', in J. Harmatta (ed.), *Proceedings of the VIIth
  Congress of the International Federation of the Societies of
  Classical Studies* vol. 1, 69-72, Budapest.
Davies, J.K. (1971), *Athenian Propertied Families 600-300 B.C.*
  Oxford.
Davies, J.K. (1978), *Democracy and Classical Greece*. London.
Davies, J.K. (1981), *Wealth and the Power of Wealth in Classical
  Athens*. New York.
Davis, J. (1977), *People of the Mediterranean*. London.
Ellis, J.R. and Stanton, G.R. (1968), 'Factional conflict and Solon's
  reforms', *Phoenix* 22, 95-110.
Ennew, J. (1981), *Debt Bondage - a Survey* (Anti-Slavery Society,
  Human Rights Series Report no.4). London.
Erxleben, E. (1974), 'Die Rolle der Bevölkerungsklassen in
  Aussenhandel Athens im 4. Jahrhundert v.u.Z.', in Welskopf
  (1974), 1, 460-520.
Figueira, T.J. (1985), 'The Theognidea and Megarian society', in
  Figueira and Nagy (1985), 112-58.
Figueira, T.J. and Nagy, G. (1985), *Theognis of Megara, Poetry and
  the Polis*. Baltimore.

Finley, M.I. (1965), 'La servitude pour dettes', *Revue historique de droit français et étranger* 43, 159-84; translated as (and cited from) 'Debt bondage and the problem of slavery', in Finley (1981), 150-66.

Finley, M.I. (1978), 'The fifth-century Athenian empire: a balance sheet', in Garnsey and Whittaker (1978), 103-26.

Finley, M.I. (1981), *Economy and Society in Ancient Greece*, B.D. Shaw and R.P. Saller (eds.). London.

Finley, M.I. (1983), *Politics in the Ancient World*. Cambridge.

Finley, M.I. (1985), *Ancient History, Evidence and Models*. London.

Finley, M.I. (1985a), *The Ancient Economy* (2nd ed.). London.

Foster, G.M. (1965), 'Peasant society and the image of the limited good', *American Anthropologist* 67, 293-315; reprinted in (and cited from) Potter, Diaz and Foster (1967), 300-23.

Foster, G.M. (1967), 'The dyadic contract: a model for the social structure of a Mexican peasant village', in Potter, Diaz and Foster (1967), 213-20.

Fuks, A. (1979/80), 'The sharing of property by the rich with the poor in Greek theory and practice', *Scripta Classica Israelica* 5, 46-63; reprinted in (and cited from) Fuks (1984), 172-89.

Fuks, A. (1984), *Social Conflict in Ancient Greece*. Jerusalem and Leiden.

Gabrielsen, V. (1981), *Remuneration of State Officials in Fourth Century B.C. Athens* (Odense University Classical Studies vol. 11). Odense.

Gallant, T.W. (1982), 'Agricultural systems, land tenure, and the reforms of Solon', *Annual of the British School in Athens* 77, 11-24.

Garnsey, P. and Saller, R.P. (1987), *The Roman Empire, Economy, Society and Culture*. London.

Garnsey, P. and Whittaker, C.R. eds. (1978), *Imperialism in the Ancient World*. Cambridge.

Gellner, E. (1977), 'Patrons and clients', in Gellner and Waterbury (1977), 2-6.

Gellner, E. and Waterbury, J. (1977), *Patrons and Clients in Mediterranean Societies*. London.

Hahn, I. (1983), 'Pelatai und Klienten', *Concilium Eirene* 17, 59-64.

Hansen, M.H. (1979), 'Misthos for magistrates in classical Athens', *Symbolae Osloenses* 56, 5-22.

Hansen, M.H. (1980), 'Seven hundred *archai* in classical Athens', *Greek, Roman and Byzantine Studies* 21, 153-73.

Harrison, A.R.W. (1968), *The Law of Athens* vol. 1. Oxford.

Herman, G. (1980/1), 'The "friends" of the early hellenistic rulers: servants or officials?',*Talanta* 12/13, 103-49.

Herman, G. (1987), *Ritualised Friendship and the Greek City*. Cambridge.

Hignett, C. (1952), *A History of the Athenian Constitution*. Oxford.

Hodkinson, S. (1983), 'Social order and the conflict of values in classical Sparta', *Chiron* 13, 239-81.

Jones, A.H.M. (1957), *Athenian Democracy*. Oxford.

Jordan, B. (1972), *The Athenian Navy in the Classical Period* (University of California Publications: Classical Studies vol. 13). Berkeley.

Korver, J. (1934), *De terminologie van het crediet-wezen in het Grieksch*. Amsterdam (reprinted New York, 1979).

Legon, R.P. (1981), *Megara: the Political History of a Greek City State to 336 B.C.* Ithaca.

Markle, M.M. (1985), 'Jury pay and assembly pay at Athens', in Cartledge and Harvey (1985), 265-97.

Migeotte, L. (1980), 'Note sur l'emploie de *prodaneizein*', *Phoenix* 34, 219-26.

Millett, P.C. (1984), 'Hesiod and his world', *Proceedings of the Cambridge Philological Society* 210, 84-115.

Nouhaud, M. (1982), *L'utilisation de l'histoire par les orateurs attiques*. Paris.

Pearson, L. (1941), 'Historical allusion in the Attic Orators', *Classical Philology* 36, 209-29.

Perlman, S. (1961), 'The historical example, its use and importance as political propaganda in the Attic Orators', *Scripta Hierosolymitana* 7, 150-66.

Pleket, H. (1969), 'The archaic tyrannis', *Talanta* 1, 19-61.

Potter, J.M., Diaz, M.N. and Foster, G.M. eds. (1967), *Peasant Society: a Reader*. Boston.

Rhodes, P.J. (1980), 'Athenian democracy after 403 B.C.', *Classical Journal* 75, 305-23.

Rhodes, P.J. (1981), *A Commentary on the Aristotelian 'Athenaion Politeia'*. Oxford.

Rhodes, P.J. (1986), 'Political activity in classical Athens', *Journal of Hellenic Studies* 106, 132-44.

Roberts, J.W. (1983), *City of Sokrates: an Introduction to Classical Athens*. London.

Saller, R.P. (1982), *Personal Patronage under the Early Empire*. Cambridge.

Ste. Croix, G.E.M. de (1964), review of Buchanan (1962) in *Classical Review* 14, 190-2.

Ste. Croix, G.E.M. de (1975), 'Political pay outside Athens', *Classical Quarterly* 25, 48-52.

Ste. Croix, G.E.M. de (1981), *The Class Struggle in the Ancient Greek World, from the Archaic Age to the Arab Conquests*. London.

Strasburger, H. (1976), *Zum antiken Gesellschaftsideal*. (Abhandlungen der Heidelberger Akademie der Wissenschaften, Philosophische-historische Klasse 4).

Theobald, R. (1983), 'The decline of patron-client relations in developed societies', *Archives européennes de sociologie* 24, 136-47.

Wade-Gery, H.T. (1938), 'Two notes on Theopompus, Philippika, X', *American Journal of Philology* 59, 129-34; reprinted in (and cited from) *Essays in Greek History* (Oxford, 1958), 233-8.

Wallace, R.W. (1983), 'The date of Solon's reforms', *American Journal of Ancient History* 8, 81-95.

Webster, T.B.L. (1972), *Potter and Patron in Ancient Athens*. London.

Welskopf, E.C. ed. (1974), *Hellenische Poleis* 3 vols. Berlin.

Whitehead, D. (1977), *The Ideology of the Athenian Metic*. Cambridge.

Whitehead, D. (1986), *The Demes of Attica 508-7 - ca. 250 B.C. A Political and Social Study*. Princeton.

Whitehead, D. (1986a), 'The ideology of the Athenian metic: some pendants and a reappraisal', *Proceedings of the Cambridge Philological Society* 212, 145-58.

Wrightson, K. (1982), *English Society 1580-1680*. London.

Wyse, W. (1892), 'Prodaneizein', *Classical Review* 6, 254-7.

Chapter 2
Patronage and friendship in early Imperial Rome: drawing the distinction

Richard Saller

In my study of patronage (1982) three features of a patronal relationship were stressed as characteristic: 'First, it involves the *reciprocal* exchange of goods and services. Secondly, to distinguish it from a commercial transaction in the marketplace, the relationship must be a personal one of some duration. Thirdly, it must be asymmetrical, in the sense that the two parties are of unequal status and offer different kinds of goods and services in the exchange - a quality which sets patronage off from friendship between equals.'[1]

The most common criticism of reviewers has centred on this definition: 'A definition so broad goes well beyond what the Romans technically understood by *patrocinium*. Indeed, the author sometimes sees patronage relationships where not only Romans, but also their modern interpreters would be surprised to find them. For instance, the younger Pliny and Corellius Rufus were men of comparably high rank and station ... To classify this relationship as one of "dependence", between "unequals", is rather to strain the meaning of

NOTES

[1] Saller (1982), 1. In this essay I am not concerned with the complex issues raised by literary patronage, except to show that some of the confident assertions about the semantic ranges of *amicus* and *cliens* are not well grounded. Versions of this paper were presented to seminars at the University of Leicester and Stanford University; I am grateful to the participants for their suggestions.

both words.'[1] Or, in the words of another critic, as for the 'relationships of senior and junior senators and of senators and equestrians, ... most of this is a far cry from what a Roman would recognise as touching *patronatus* and *clientela*. The status of a *cliens* evaporated, as Gaius Marius remarked, when a man secured curule rank. Yet the author regularly applies the terminology of clients and patrons to the whole range of senatorial society, where it is technically inadmissible. ... in the technical Roman sense ... a man can have only a single *patronus*.'[2]

The repeated references by respected scholars to the 'technical' definition of *patronatus* raised the possibility that my study omitted a significant feature of the institution. For while the historian should not be satisfied simply with describing the Romans' world in their own terms, an important first step in any analysis is to understand their categories through their linguistic usage, law and patterns of behaviour. If there was a formal sense of patronage in imperial society, it would certainly warrant close attention. In this paper I want to ask whether anything in imperial law, linguistic usage or social behaviour suggests a 'technical' definition in the minds of Romans. Could a patronage relationship exist only between men of substantially different rank? Could a *cliens* have only one *patronus*?

The belief in a 'technical sense' may arise from the recognition of the patron-client relationship in early Roman law and the regulation of the ex-master/libertus relationship in classical law. The well-known condemnation in the Twelve Tables of patrons defrauding their clients immediately comes to mind.[3] When Herennius invoked his patronage duty in his refusal to testify against Marius in the late second century BC, the *patronus-cliens* relationship still had some legal content, but the argument over the exact terms of the rules suggests confusion arising from disuse of an archaic rule.[4]

In classical law, as represented by the *Digest*, patronage in its general sense (as opposed to the *patronus-libertus* relationship) is

[1] D'Arms (1986), 95.

[2] Sherwin-White (1983), 272f.

[3] 'Patronus, si clienti fraudem fecerit, sacer esto', cited by Servius, *Aen.* 6.109; see Rouland (1979), 157-64.

[4] Plutarch, *Marius* 5.4; on this episode see Deniaux (1973). Deniaux rightly comments that in the second century BC clientage did not necessarily imply a lowly condition for the client (p.186).

conspicuous by its absence. The word 'cliens' appears only five times in the whole of the *Digest* and never in a context to suggest a specific legal content comparable to that found in early law.[1] In four of the passages, the *cliens* is one type of hanger-on who might be in a Roman's household or entourage. Consequently, there can be no *furti actio* against a *cliens*, *libertus* or *mercennarius*, because this action cannot be brought against members of the household (*Dig.* 47.2.90 [Paul]). On the positive side, a man granted *usus* of a house cannot rent it, but he can have his slaves, freedmen, *hospites* and *clientes* live in with him (*Dig.* 7.8.3 [Paul], and, similarly, 33.9.3.6 [Ulpian]). In these four passages *cliens* is found in series with other kinds of dependants and friends, without any suggestion of a formally defined category or special legal obligations.

The fifth passage deserves to be quoted because of its implications about the essential elements of patronage in the Roman mind. In the title on *postliminium* (49.15) the jurists had to define *hostis* in order to identify prisoners of war who could recover their full legal status and rights upon return across the frontier. Who qualified as a foreign enemy, as opposed to an internal rebel or bandit, was not always obvious, since not all areas of the empire were annexed and directly ruled by Rome.[2] According to Proculus, it was beyond doubt that there could be no *postliminium* from peoples who were in the category of *foederati et liberi*.

A free people is one that is subject to the *potestas* of no other people: likewise, a people is allied, whether it has come into friendship by an equal treaty, or has been united by a treaty to the effect that that people courteously maintain the *maiestas* of the other people (i.e. the Romans). Further, we add this point, that it is understood that the second people (the Romans) is superior, not that it is understood that the first is not free: indeed, just as we understand our *clientes* to be free, even though they are not equal to us in *auctoritas*, *dignitas* or *vires*, so also it is to be understood that those peoples are free who are obligated courteously to maintain our *maiestas*. (49.15.7.1)

---

[1] I have focused on *cliens* rather than *patronus*, because the latter had more common meanings than that associated with *cliens*.

[2] On the distinction between *bellum iustum* and other types of violence, Shaw (1984).

The jurist feels it necessary to go to some lengths here to explain how it is that a *populus* can be *liber* and yet not have the independence to be a potential *hostis*. The explanation lies in the notion of *clientela*: their inferiority in *auctoritas*, *dignitas* and *vires* placed them in a condition of dependence like *clientes*, who are nevertheless free. To the best of my knowledge, this is as close as the Romans come in the extant classical literature to a statement of the determinants of the patron-client relationship. It is patently one based not on legal definition or treaty terms, but on the realities of superior power and status, summed up in the terms *auctoritas*, *dignitas* and *vires*.[1] This understanding is not very different from the anthropologists' definition emphasizing asymmetry of resources and unequal social position.

If the law did not formally define patronage, do the patterns of usage of *patronus* and *cliens* suggest that these terms were informally reserved for a *humble* Roman's exclusive relationship with *one and only one* patron? *Cliens* certainly carried connotations of social inferiority, and, as a result, aristocratic authors most often used it with reference to humble men. As one reviewer pointed out, Cicerowrote that some Romans 'think it as bitter as death to have accepted a patron or to be called clients' (*Off*. 2.69).[2] Seneca shows that this attitude continued into the Empire (*De Ben*. 2.23; *De Brev. Vitae* 19.3). Nevertheless, imperial authors did refer to senators as *clientes* and exploited the connotations of inferiority and subservience by applying the label to outcasts such as the senatorial followers of Sejanus (Tac. *Ann*. 4.2, 4.34; Seneca, *Cons. ad Marciam* 6.22.4; cf. Tac. *Hist*. 3.66).

More important, the vocabulary of *patronus* and *cliens* can be found in Cicero's works and imperial inscriptions, applied without pejorative connotations to relationships within the leisured class. The Caecinae, for instance, were late republican local notables and 'almost certainly equestrian'.[3] In a letter of December 46 BC young Aulus Caecina described himself as a *cliens* of Cicero, an inherited bond

[1] See the discussion of Badian (1958), ch.1, rightly avoiding a legalistic approach to *clientela*.

[2] D'Arms (1986), 95.

[3] Nicolet (1974), 813.

going back to his father's relationship with the orator (*Ad fam.* 6.7.4). In another letter a month later Cicero also labelled the Caecinae *clientes*, but of the Servilii (*Ad fam.* 13.66).[1] In Cicero's prosecution of Verres (2.1.28) another local aristocrat, a Sicilian named Dio, was said to have *amici, hospites, patroni* (note the plurals) who had helped him pay off the avaricious governor. These examples contradict both 'technical' rules - that *clientes* were humble and that they could have only one *patronus*. The second rule is contradicted in other letters of Cicero. Atticus is said to have a *cliens*, who is also Cicero's *libertus* - a situation that implies two *patroni*. When Cicero counted the people of Sicily in his *clientela*, he was obviously not their sole patron. Similarly, after Trebatius requested that Cicero take the people of Ulubrae on as his *clientes* during Trebatius' service with Caesar, there is no reason to believe that these people ceased to be *clientes* of Trebatius. Of course, the Sicilians and people of Ulubrae were groups rather than individuals, but it is probable that Cicero's protection would have been extended to individuals within the group.

One passage in Cicero's corpus lends some support to the notion that the patron-client bond was ideally an exclusive one for the client. M'. Curius, the banker of Patras, wrote to Cicero in 45 BC, requesting a recommendation on his behalf to Sulpicius Rufus' successor as governor of Achaea. He playfully pledged Cicero to secrecy: 'But, my great *amicus*, do not show this letter to Atticus; allow him to continue to believe mistakenly that I am a good man and am not accustomed to whitewash two fences out of the same pail. Therefore, my *patronus*, farewell ...' (*Ad fam.* 7.29). The ideal of unique loyalty of a *cliens* to one *patronus* is understood in this passage, but the ideal could be jokingly manipulated in a way that shows that no 'technical' rule was at stake. Curius slips easily back and forth between the language of *amicitia* and *patronatus*, and shows why it was useful to have more than one supporter, however labelled, to call on in various circumstances.

Finally, it is worth noting that Cicero often mentions *clientes* in a series including other associates and dependants. At one point Atticus was asked to be sure to forward some books to Cicero by any means - *per amicos, clientes, hospites, libertos denique ac servos tuos* (by

---

[1] This case is noted in D'Arms' review (p.95).

your friends, clients, guest-friends, even your freedmen and slaves)
(*Ad Att.* 1.20). Similarly, Cicero promised to help Crassus' people -
amici, hospites, clientes - during Crassus' expedition against the
Parthians (*Ad fam.* 5.8.5).[1] The ambiguity of each category in these
catch-all series may frustrate the historians wishing to know into
what classification any given individual fell, but they were functional
for the Romans insofar as they absolved them of the need to make
potentially invidious distinctions.

An examination of imperial epigraphy demonstrates even more
clearly than Cicero's works that the 'technical' criteria suggested for
Roman patronage are modern attributions. An explanation for the
greater prominence of the words *patronus* and *cliens* in inscriptions
than in imperial literature was suggested in my book: the elite who
wrote the literature were not inclined for reasons of courtesy to refer
to their dependants and protégés as *clientes*, but the subordinates who
erected the honorary inscriptions could enhance the reputation of their
supporters by the use of such terms.[2]

My list of patronal inscriptions from North Africa offers a number
of dedications bearing on the issues raised in this paper.[3] Friendly
governors were not infrequently honoured by leading local aristocrats
as their personal *patroni*. For instance, M. Sedius Rufus, an advocate,
flamen perpetuus and *duumvir* dedicated an inscription to Q. Anicius
Faustus, his *patronus*, in the Numidian capital of Lambaesis (*AE*
1911, 99). Or again, the propraetorian legate C. Iulius Lepidus
Tertullus was acclaimed by M. Aemilius Felix, a magistrate of Diana
Veteranorum, as his *patronus optimus* (*AE* 1934, 26). Another pair
of local notables of Diana Veteranorum, the Aquili brothers, also
used the language of *patronus* in their inscription honouring the
governor, M. Valerius Maximianus (*CIL* 8.4600). Finally, special
attention should be paid to the dedication to the senior equestrian
governor of Numidia, L. Titinius Clodianus, a *rarissimus patronus*,
erected by C. Vibius Maximus, *eques Romanus, fisci advocatus* and
candidatus eius (*AE* 1917-18, 85). Clearly, the help given by a
senior equestrian official to his junior at the outset of his career could

---

[1]   See also *Ad Q. fr.* 1.2.16; *Verr.* 2.4.89 and 140; *Caec.* 66; *Cluent.* 94;
Rosc. Am. 106.

[2]   Saller (1982), 10f.

[3]   *Ibid.*, 195-9.

be described in the language of *patronatus*.

Less exalted officials than governors were similarly honoured. In Segermes a *flamen perpetuus* L. Sempronius Maximus described a procurator of the imperial estates in the region of Hadrumetum as his *patronus* (*CIL* 8.11174). Even *clarissimi pueri* received public acclaim as *patroni*, in one case by a leading man of Timgad (*CIL* 8.2400) and in another by an *eques Romanus* (*ILAlg.* 1.7). The last example once again falsifies the suggestion that the vocabulary of *patronatus* was not thought appropriate for relationships within the imperial aristocracy.

Several inscriptions are of particular interest for the question of multiple patrons. One enterprising Numidian advocate, L. Valerius Optatianus (*eques Romanus*), proclaimed himself *cliens* of the imperial legate T. Iulius Tertullus Antiochus, and then some fifteen years later (ca. AD 210) honoured another governor, M. Aurelius Cominius Cassianus as his *patronus* (*CIL* 8.2393; *AE* 1917-18, 73). He may also have dedicated inscriptions to the intervening governors, which have now disappeared. It is not difficult to think why an advocate would wish to advertise his special relationship with the province's principal dispenser of justice. The pair of dedications does not prove that Optatianus simultaneously had more than one *patronus*, but they do undermine the notion that *patronatus* was thought of exclusively as a permanent, even heritable, bond between a great man and his humble dependants. The proposition that patronage in its 'technical sense' required the client's undivided loyalty is more obviously falsified by *CIL* 8.11175, a dedication by Victor, *libertus Augustorum*, to C. Postumius Saturninus Flavianus, *procurator regionis Hadrimetinae*. Though as an imperial freedman Victor must have had emperors as his legal *patroni*, he described himself as *cliens* of Flavianus.

Two criticisms related to the problem of the definition of patronage have been directed at my list of inscriptions from North Africa. First, it has been suggested that the criterion for inclusion - some language signalling exchange between men of unequal social status - was not sufficiently narrow and discriminating; some *amici* were included.[1] Secondly, the list of fifty-three inscriptions is not very long by comparison with the tens of thousands of inscriptions

---

[1] Sherwin-White (1983), 272f.

found in North Africa.[1] The first objection can be answered by a comparison of *CIL* 8.25382 with the dedication by C. Vibius Maximus, the grateful *fisci advocatus* referred to above. In the former P. Sicinius Pescennius Hilarianus honoured his *amicus incomparabilis* L. Calpurnius Fidus Aemilianus. The latter was a senator and the former his *candidatus*. The use of the word *amicus* here rather than *patronus* as in the earlier case surely does not imply that the two relationships were so different that the one should be included in a study of patronage and the other excluded. The shortness of the list is to be explained by the low survival rate of inscriptions and the brevity of those that have survived. Many more short honorary dedications may be manifestations of a patronage relationship, but simply do not provide enough information to warrant inclusion on the list. There is no doubt in my mind that the list grossly under-represents the phenomenon of patronage in North Africa. It was offered for its illustrative value.

Before leaving this survey of the epigraphic evidence for the definition of patronage, I want to point out that the most detailed patronage inscription found in the western empire, the Thorigny Marble (*CIL* 13.3162), supports the positions advanced above. This grand inscription was put up in Gallia Lugdunensis in the third century and honoured one of the province's leading local notables, T. Sennius Sollemnis, a wealthy member of the provincial council. Sollemnis won the favour of more than one governor for his part in helping to suppress charges of maladministration that were being considered in the provincial council. Tiberius Claudius Paulinus, the senatorial governor of Lugdunensis who escaped prosecution, displayed his appreciation for Sollemnis' support with luxurious gifts and a position as assessor on his staff during his later governorship in Britain. In the same inscription Sollemnis described himself as *amicus et cliens* of Paulinus and as *cliens* of the subsequent governor, Aedinius Iulianus, later praetorian prefect. The fact that Sollemnis could be at once *cliens* and *amicus* of the same man belies any thought that *amicitia* and *patronatus* were quite separate categories in the Roman mind. If Sollemnis could advertise himself as *cliens* of both Paulinus and Iulianus, clearly multiple *patroni* (it hardly need be repeated) did not violate the Romans' sense of *patronatus*.

---

[1] D'Arms (1986), 97.

Patently, the Romans applied the language of patronage to a range of relationships, with both humble dependants and their junior aristocratic colleagues labelled *clientes*: usage was more fluid than usually supposed, and the connotations of *amicus*, *cliens* and *patronus* were subtly and variously manipulated in different circumstances. It must be admitted, however, that the typical word for a junior aristocratic associate and others further down the social ladder was *amicus*. More important than the language is what the patterns of behaviour and social conventions reveal about the Roman understanding of these relationships.[1]

To discuss bonds between senior aristocrats and their aspiring juniors in terms of 'friendship' seems to me misleading, because of the egalitarian overtones that word has in modern English. Though willing to extend the courtesy of the label *amicus* to some of their inferiors, the status-conscious Romans did not allow the courtesy to obscure the relative social standings of the two parties. On the contrary, *amici* were subdivided into categories: *superiores*, *pares* and *inferiores* (and then lower down the hierarchy, humble *clientes*).[2] Each category called for an appropriate mode of behaviour, of which the Romans were acutely aware (Pliny, *Ep.* 7.3.2, 2.6.2; Seneca, *Ep.* 94.14). The central question of this paper is whether *amici inferiores* can appropriately be analysed under the heading of patronage. Resemblances between the behaviour of aristocratic *amici inferiores* and *clientes* suggest that such an analysis would be a reasonable way of proceeding.

The social hierarchy of Rome was re-enacted and reinforced daily through the characteristically Roman institution of the *salutatio*. Every day lesser men showed up at the houses of the great. The *salutatio* provided a visible marker of status in two ways: the standing of the callers was indicated by the order in which they were received by the patron, and the patron's status was displayed by the number and importance of his callers. The verses of Martial (*Epig.* 10.70;74;82) suggest that the early morning scramble to the house of the patron was an imposition that put the caller in his place. Seneca claimed that the formal classification of callers could be traced back to

---

[1] Wiseman (1982) in a discussion of literary patronage very sensibly focuses on 'who does what, and when, and where' (p.28). A similarly pragmatic view is expressed by E. Badian in his review of this collection in (1985), 348f.

[2] White (1978), 80ff.

the second century BC when the custom was initiated by Gaius Gracchus and Livius Drusus (*De Ben.* 6.33.3ff.).

The ambitious attempts of new men aspiring to make their way in the imperial aristocracy were associated with the need to cultivate the favour of the great by attending *salutationes*. Plutarch advised a young municipal notable to be satisfied with a local *cursus* rather than pursuing 'the procuratorships and governorships of provinces from which much money may be gained and in pursuit of which most public men grow old haunting the doors of other men's houses and leaving their own affairs neglected' (*Mor.* 814D). In going to salutations, then, the young senator or equestrian hopeful of an appointment had to subordinate his interests and behave like a *cliens*.[1]

More generally, the ambitious new man depended for his success on his ability to attract and hold the favour of a *suffragator* who would speak on his behalf before the senate or emperor.[2] The supporter was customarily cultivated and shown respect: *colere et observare* was the characteristic Latin expression. This attitude of deference to the more powerful was again associated with *clientes* - so much so that the etymology of *cliens* was traced back to *colere*. Servius in his commentary on the *Aeneid*, for example, claims that 'if *clientes* are *quasi-colentes* and *patroni* are *quasi-patres*, then to wrong a *cliens* is as bad as to wrong a son' (on *Aeneid* 6.609).[3] Thus, in certain important matters of social ritual and attitudes, the *amicus inferior* or junior colleague fell into a category with ordinary *clientes*.

It would perhaps be profitable to turn attention finally to the particular relationships that have provoked the critics, those of Gavius Clarus and Fronto, and of the younger Pliny and Corellius Rufus. First, however, a brief comment about the example of Herennius and Marius, cited above, may be in order. It has been used

[1] Even consulars like Pliny were occasionally called upon to go from house to house canvassing on behalf of their protégés up for election, but this is different from the situation described by Plutarch, insofar as a consular's canvassing was very infrequent and was matched by other consulars calling at his door for the same purpose. A consular's canvassing did not imply dependence because his role was interchangeable with the man on whom he was calling, in contrast to the ambitious local notable seeking office in Rome.

[2] de Ste. Croix (1954).

[3] Similarly, Isid., *Orig.* 10.53 and Remigius 97. For modern thoughts about the etymology, see Rouland (1979), 19-22.

to argue that in the Roman view there could be no patronage relationships between 'senior and junior senators'. On the contrary, the fact that Marius ceased to be a *cliens* only upon reaching a curule magistracy demonstrates that new men entering the senate continued to be considered *clientes* until they had advanced well into their *cursus*. The less successful, on the rule as stated, might never break the patronage bond.

The imperial examples are, of course, more relevant and deserve close attention. Fronto in AD 163 wrote a recommendation to his former student, the emperor Lucius Verus, on behalf of his close personal associate, the senator Gavius Clarus. He described their relationship in the following terms:

> From an early age Gavius Clarus has attended me in a friendly
> fashion not only with those *officia* by which a senator lesser in
> age and station properly cultivates (*colit*) a senator senior in rank
> and years, earning his goodwill; but gradually our *amicitia*
> developed to the point that he is not distressed or ashamed to pay
> me the sort of deference which *clientes* and faithful, hardworking
> freedmen yield - and not through arrogance on my part or flattery
> on his. But our mutual regard and true love have taken away from
> both of us all concern in restraining our *officia*. (*Ad Verum* 2.7)

This passage is rich in its implications about social rank and personal relationships. On the one hand, Fronto draws a clear distinction between Gavius Clarus and ordinary *clientes* and *liberti*. On the other, Clarus' attainment of a curule office, the praetorship, did not entitle him to friendship on an equal footing with Fronto, because their *auctoritas*, *dignitas* and *vires* were still far from equal. As a junior senator Clarus was expected to cultivate (*colit*) his senior, whose help and connections he still relied on to maintain his position. Fronto says that if he had been wealthier, he would have provided Clarus with financial support in time of need, but he can at least use his powerful influence with the imperial court to help Clarus secure an inheritance. According to Fronto, their personal relationship became so close that Clarus performed duties that would normally have been expected of a *cliens*. In sum, though Clarus was not labelled a *cliens*, his relationship as a junior senator with his senior was marked by inequality, shows of deference, and even a limited dependence.

The subordination of young senators to their seniors was institutionalized through the practice of *suffragium*.[1] The younger Pliny enjoyed a very successful career in part through the *suffragium* of Verginius Rufus and Corellius Rufus. As one of my critics himself wrote of the relationship:

> Pliny's first steps in the public career would *depend* on the sort of assistance from powerful friends that he himself later gave to ambitious young equestrians, such as Erucius Clarus and Junius Avitus (my italics).[2]

Pliny's own description of his relationship with Corellius Rufus (*Ep.* 4.17) indicates that in return for support Pliny (like Gavius Clarus) showed deference to his *suffragator* and followed his advice. Like Gavius Clarus, Pliny was not labelled a *cliens*; nevertheless, his relationship with Corellius Rufus was obviously not one of friendship between equals insofar as their roles were not reversible. To treat their relationship as one of 'inequality' and 'dependence' should occasion far less 'surprise' than the contrary claim stressing similarity of rank. To minimize the inequality by describing the junior friends as men 'of the same or much the same status who were destined to be their (seniors') successors in eminence'[3] misrepresents the nature of the bond by underestimating the Roman sensitivity to social differentiation and by treating the success of new men as if it were automatic. Of course, it was not; Sherwin-White was correct to write that Pliny's success 'depended' on the influence of Corellius Rufus and a few others.

This paper has sought to establish the following points. In the imperial age, the *patronus-cliens* relationship had no 'technical sense' and no formal standing in law. Nothing precluded a Roman from having more than one *patronus*. Linguistic usage reveals that the words *patronus* and *cliens* were applied to a wide range of bonds between men of unequal status, including junior and senior aristocrats. This is not surprising, since Proculus' basic condition for

[1] It is curious that de Ste. Croix (1954), in his article on *suffragium*, described the support of *suffragatores* as 'patronage' without drawing criticism for unduly stretching the concept.

[2] Sherwin-White (1966), 71.

[3] Brunt (1982).

clientage was the superiority of one party in *auctoritas, dignitas* and *vires*. This condition was an accepted part of the relationship between junior and senior equestrians and senators.

The broad semantic fields of *amicitia* and *clientela*, and the considerable overlap between them, should not be allowed to obscure the fine gradations of Roman personal relationships. The Romans recognized the difference between a junior senator and a humble client, however they might be labelled. To express the gradation in English one might translate *amici superiores inferioresque* directly and write of 'superior and inferior friends', as distinct from clients, but that solution to the problem of translating Roman categories seems inordinately awkward in English. Furthermore, it separates *amici* from *clientes* more clearly than the Romans themselves did. The solution adopted in my book was to use the labels 'patron' and 'protégé' for relationships between senior and junior aristocrats.[1] 'Protégé, a man under the care and protection of an influential person (as a sponsor, instructor, or patron) usually for the furthering of his career',[2] seems to describe the situation of Gavius Clarus or the young Pliny particularly well. In addition, the fact that both clients and protégés have patrons as their counterparts captures some of the ambiguity and overlap in Latin of *amicitia* and *clientela*.

Bibliography

Badian, E. (1982), Review of Saller (1982), *Classical Philology* 80, 348f.

Badian, E. (1958), *Foreign Clientelae* (264-70 BC). Oxford.

Brunt, P.A. (1982), Review of Saller (1982), *Times Literary Supplement*, 1276.

Deniaux, E. (1973), 'Un probleme de clientele: Marius et Herennii', *Philologus* 117, 1976-96.

D'Arms, J.H. (1986), Review of Saller (1982), *Classical Philology* 81, 95-98.

---

[1]   Upon rereading, I believe that I was careful to avoid calling senators *clientes* except where the Latin text justified it.

[2]   *Webster's Third New International Dictionary*.

Gold, B.K. (ed.) (1982), *Literary and Artistic Patronage in Ancient Rome*. Austin, Texas.

Nicolet, Cl. (1974), *L'ordre équestre à l'époque républicaine (312-43 av J.-C.)*. Paris.

Rouland, N. (1979), *Pouvoir politique et dépendance personnelle dans l'antiquité romaine, Genèse et rôle des rapports de Clientèle* (Collection Latomus no. 166). Brussels.

Ste. Croix, G.E.M. de (1954), '*Suffragium*: from vote to patronage', *British Journal of Sociology* 5, 33-48.

Saller, R.P. (1982), *Personal Patronage under the Early Empire*. Cambridge.

Shaw, B.D. (1984), 'Bandits in the Roman Empire' *Past and Present* 105, 3-52.

Sherwin-White, A.N. (1966), *The Letters of Pliny: A Historical and Social Commentary*. Oxford.

Sherwin-White, A.N. (1983), Review of Saller (1982),*Classical Review* n.s. 33, 271-273.

White, P. (1978), '*Amicitia* and the profession of poetry in early imperial Rome', *Journal of Roman Studies* 68, 74-92.

Wiseman, T.P. (1982), '*Pete nobiles amicos*: Poets and patrons in late Republican Rome', in B.K. Gold (ed.), *Literary and Artistic Patronage in Ancient Rome*, 28-49. Austin, Texas.

Chapter 3
Patronage in Roman society: from republic to empire

Andrew Wallace-Hadrill

The Roman self-image

To stand at the door of an upper-class Roman house of the late republic or early empire is already to glimpse something of the centrality of patronage in Roman society. From the threshold a vista opens out, elaborately and symmetrically framed: between the walls of the entrance passage (*fauces*), the sightline passes over the rectangular light-well of the impluvium, its central axis marked by an ornamental marble table, and through the great square opening of the tablinum; and resting briefly there, passes on through a smaller opening in the back wall to the balanced columns of the peristyle garden beyond, with a central fountain perhaps playing amid plants and graceful statuary; and then still on beyond to mountain peaks rising in the blue distance (Bek 1980). The vista is striking; yet it lacks a central focus, like an elaborate frame without a picture, unless we repopulate it in our imagination. At the focal point, in the centre of the tablinum, belongs the master of the house, seen as Cicero pictures the great noble of an earlier generation: 'both walking about in the forum and sitting at home on his throne, he was approached, not just about questions of law, but about marrying a daughter, buying a farm, cultivating the land, in fact about any point of social obligation or business' (*De oratore* 3.133).

The physical structure of the house, as the architect Vitruvius reminds us, must be seen in the context of the social structure of activities to which it forms the setting (Wiseman 1982, Wallace-Hadrill 1988). The way the Roman house invites the viewer from the front door, unparalleled in the Greek world, flows from the patronal rituals so often described in the Roman sources: the opening of the doors at dawn to the crowd of callers, the accessibility of the dominus to the public, his clients and his friends. Patronage was at all periods for which we have information central to the way the Roman upper class wished to present itself to the world. Passages widely separated in date illustrate the continuity.

Plautus' *Menaechmi*, dating from the years immediately after the Second Punic War, presents the hero returning tired and frustrated from a morning's business in the forum (571ff.) Menaechmus has been engaged in representing a client in a lawsuit, though he regards the client as a rogue and the suit as a nuisance. But, like other members of his class, he is trapped; 'What a stupid, irritating practice we have, and one the best people follow most! Everyone wants lots of clients. They don't bother to ask whether they're good men or bad; the last thing that counts is the reliability (*fides*) of the client, and how dependable he is (*clueat*, punning on *cliens*). If he's poor and no rogue, he's held good for nothing; if he's a rich rogue, he's treated as a solid client.' Which, Menaechmus elaborates, only gets the patron into deep waters, since the rich rogues drag them irresponsibly into indefensible suits.

Though the play is based on a Greek original, this passage is evidently one of those Plautine additions designed to give local Roman colour. Here, in one of the earliest pieces of Roman literature, patronage is seen as a characteristic activity of the upper class, and one which in practice falls short of the ideal. The client should be marked by dependability, one for whom the patron can pledge his faith (*fides*); but anxiety to maximise following and profits lead to neglect of moral considerations.

We are to find the same thought recurring later in Cicero (*de Officiis* 2.69-71). There are obvious financial and political advantages that derive from the patronage of the wealthy and influential in preference to the poor but worthy man, and few in practice hesitate to lend their support to the wealthy. Yet, Cicero urges, there is a strong argument for taking the opposite line, for the patronage of the poor appears disinterested and wins widespread and lasting support, whereas the rich dislike being held under obligation and hate 'like death' to be treated as clients whether in deed or name (a much but only partially quoted passage).

Six centuries after Plautus, a Gallic aristocrat, Paulinus of Pella, voiced his bitter regret at the passing of a way of life shattered by the Visigothic invasions of the early fifth century, 'when my house was happy and prosperous ... and when the display of my rank was very important, magnified and bolstered by deferential crowds of clients' (quoted in Van Dam 1985, 151). His regrets mirror the standard image of a fall from power such as was evoked by an Augustan rhetorician: 'I have seen hallways deserted by their ambitious crowd of clients put up for sale by a master under forfeit' (Seneca, *Controversiae* 2.1.1).

Numerous passages throughout the intervening period (collected e.g. by Friedländer 1922) tell the same story: that the Roman noble felt himself almost naked without an entourage of dependants, which he expanded to the best of his ability, and who acted as the visible symbol of his social standing. Patronage was central to the Roman cultural experience, in a way in which it was foreign to the Greek cultural experience. It represented a vital part of conscious Roman ideology, of their own image of how their world both was and ought to be. It does not follow (and there are many grounds for questioning) that practice squared with ideal; that patronage 'worked', for the benefit of either party; that it represented the only power-base for the upper class; or that the type of relationships characterised (and legitimised) as patronal remained constant over the centuries (cf. Rouland 1979). What however does demand some explanation is why on the cultural and ideological level patronage remained so central.

Ideal and reality

One of the difficulties in dealing with patronage is to determine at what level the analysis is to be conducted. Is it a pattern of relationships that exists objectively in certain societies whether or not the participants themselves acknowledge or approve it, or is it a way in which the actors perceive and formulate the relationships in which they are engaged? That is to say, are we talking about a structure or an ideology? We need only formulate this question (which I owe to Silverman 1977) to see that the answer is both. We cannot simply study one or the other. Thus Finley rightly anticipates and dismisses the objection that we cannot talk about 'clients' at Athens simply because the Greek language has nothing comparable to *clientela*. If there is an objective exchange of goods and services whereby political support is given in exchange for material benefits, one can properly speak of patronage even if the Greeks didn't have a word for it (Finley 1983, 41). On the other hand, there is something in Millar's protest:

> It can even be claimed that we are entitled to apply to ancient societies the now established common-language (or sociological) use of terms like 'clientage' and 'patronage' without regard to the presence, or precise use, of equivalent terms in the society in question. But to say that is to say that curiosity about exact nuances of ancient social and political relationships is superfluous. (Millar 1984, 17)

Certainly, to declare the ideology and language of the society studied irrelevant is to miss a vital dimension; on the other hand to identify the ideology with the social reality is to invite confusion - exemplified in the argument which seeks to estimate the actual importance of Roman patronage on the basis of frequency of the use of the words *patronus* and *cliens* (see Saller above). We need to study both structure and ideology and the relationship between the two. The importance of the *patronus-cliens* relationship in Roman ideology does not in itself prove that 'patronage' in the modern sense was important in their social structure; but it does constitute an invitation to us to explore the structural significance of patronal relationships.

The gulf between ideology and social reality, and the complexity of the relationship between the two, emerges from the one passage we have that purports to offer an explicit analysis of the patron-client bond. As a Greek writing, at least partly, for a non-Roman audience, Dionysius of Halicarnassus, when describing how Romulus as founder of Rome also 'founded' patronage, spells out what the mutual obligations of patron and client were (*Roman Antiquities* 2.9-11, see Appendix for text). One of the most striking features of this description is its lack of overlap with contemporary realities of the late first century BC. Romulus' patrons are identical with the patricians, his clients with the plebeians; by the late republic this had long since ceased to be the case. Romulus' patron-client bond is enshrined in the law: the parties might not take legal action or vote against each other, on pain of being declared accursed; yet historical Roman patronage is a moral and not a legal relationship, and the one famous instance of invoking the principle is a quaint anachronism - the rising Marius is far from flattered when a Herennius refuses to testify against him on the grounds that the Marii were hereditary clients of his family (Plutarch *Marius* 5). Finally, the relationship is clearly seen as exclusive and binding: each client has 'his' patron to whom he is obliged, and the patron will pass on his hereditary clients to his heir. Historically, we are more struck by the fluidity and multiplicity of patronal bonds: the client could sustain many links simultaneously, and pick and choose to suit the moment, like Cicero's clients (in court) the Roscii, who 'had many patrons and hospites inherited from their ancestors, whom they ceased to cultivate and pay observance to, and betook themselves to the *fides* and *clientela* of Chrysogonus (the upstart ex-slave of the dictator Sulla)' (*Pro Roscio Amerino* 106).

Of course, the misfit between the 'Romulan' patronage of Dionysius and contemporary reality is partly chronological. This picture of the 'original' pattern is meant to represent something lost and gone; it has formed the basis of reconstructions of the 'original' patronage of early Rome from Mommsen on (see Drummond's discussion below). But it also has a strong idealistic dimension. Any Roman description of ancestral ways, the *mos maiorum*, particularly when associated with the authoritative figure of Romulus, tends to represent an ideal, one indeed from which the present generation has fallen off, but which nevertheless it ought to imitate. Dionysius brings this out in his open praise for Romulus' system. The division between the master class of patricians, who act as priests, magistrates, judges and patrons, and the working class of plebeians, who are farmers, craftsmen and clients, is one, in Dionysius' view, well designed to avoid social conflict (sedition). Patronage means that ruling class and ruled are held together by mutual bonds of affection: 'It is remarkable how intensely both parties competed with each other in their demonstrations of goodwill, each anxious not to be outdone in generosity by the other: clients resolved to perform every service they could for their patrons, whilst patrons were anxious to inconvenience their clients as little as possible and accepted no gifts of money.' The abuse by the ruling class of the ruled that was disastrous in Greek cities was thus, according to the historian, avoided.

There is enough contact in this picture with contemporary realities (notably in the listing of the mutual services of patron and client) to invite the reader to draw links with contemporary patterns of behaviour: at the same time it is remote enough to be recognisable as an ideal and a reproach to contemporary practice. We have, in fact, myth serving a characteristic function: to legitimate current practice. The fact that they had fallen away from their ancestors made it easier for Romans to apply the myth to circumstances quite unlike those attributed to Romulus. The Roman could no longer live as if he was a subject of Romulus; even so, the more closely his social relationships resembled the lost ideal, the better and more legitimate they were. The old division of patrician and plebeian, with which Dionysius links patronage, had long since ceased to have importance; but it was easy to see in contemporary social divisions an analogue. The Roman of Augustus' day who exercised 'patronage' even dimly resembling the Romulan model could be seen as acting in the interest of the state, for by his actions he reconstructed the ideal society of the past.

Patronage in politics

In most recent discussion, the practical importance of Roman clientage has been located in the workings of internal politics. Yet what Fustel de Coulanges (1890) offered was an insight into the structure of Roman society. 'Patronage', according to Fustel, 'explains how in the context of laws of equality, the great families always kept their power ... Clientele was not in the laws ... but it reigned in society.' Patronage was central to the structure of Roman society as feudalism was to medieval: it constituted the dominant social relationship between ruler and ruled. Matthias Gelzer (1912) expanded and deepened this insight, documenting the way in which the republican nobility maintained their dominance through the channels of personal links of dependance and obligation:

> The entire Roman people, both the ruling circle and the mass of
> voters whom they ruled, was, as a society, permeated by
> multifarious relationships based on *fides* and personal connections,
> the principal forms of which were *patrocinium* in the courts and
> over communities, together with political friendship and financial
> obligation. These relationships determined the distribution of
> political power. To maintain their rights citizens and subjects
> alike were constrained to seek the protection of powerful men ...
>
> (1969, 139)

Gelzer's slim essay was a seminal contribution to social history. Yet his successors were more interested in writing political than social history. His analysis of personal bonds, in boiled down and dogmatised form, became the basis of a new type of political history in which 'Who knew whom?' became the only significant question. Patronage was no longer a relationship to explore, but one to take for granted as the basis for the pattern of links between individual members of the elite (e.g. Scullard 1951, 12ff.). Much of this work has been naive and mechanistic; and it has provoked a reaction which questions whether clientage can explain much about the working of Roman politics (Brunt 1988[1]; Millar 1984 and 1986; Rouland 1979 and 1981). As a result, we are beginning to learn something of the limitations of patronage; to see it as one factor coexisting with others in the structure of politics. Some of the salient points may be briefly summarised.

First, if patronage is seen as a system primarily political in its orientation, in which the payoff for the patron's support and protection is the vote, we may doubt that it affected even the majority of the population by the late republic. Poor citizens scattered throughout Italy were too far from the political centre in Rome to be worth courting for their vote; while the 250,000 or so urban poor of the capital were simply too numerous to enter into significant personal relations with the few hundred members of the political elite. Their votes were, for the little that they were worth, more effectively courted by 'bread and circuses'. The massive expansion of the population of the capital rendered traditional social relationships impotent; old structures of deference broke down to the point at which military force became necessary to 'police' the behaviour of the mob (Nippel 1984). Nor is it easy to account for the debt crises, urban and rural, of the last century BC, encapsulated in the Catiline episode, and the recurrent stories of dispossession, if the majority of the poor enjoyed active protection from their patrons (Brunt 1979). 'Debt' in a patronal society should form part of the nexus of mutual obligations of patron and client: a debt crisis implies a crisis of patronage.

---

[1] Although this fundamental paper appeared too late to be taken into consideration, I am grateful to Professor Brunt for discussing his arguments with me in advance of publication.

Secondly, it is at best part of the political process on which vertical relationships could have effect. The elections are one thing (and even here patronage is one among several factors); legislation is another, and it would be hard indeed to build up an argument that the popular assembly in the constant stream of laws of the late republic was swayed by personal dependence on members of the nobility. On the contrary, significant elements of the *popularis* legislation are explicitly anti-patronal in aim: the introduction of secret ballot by a series of laws in the 130s deliberately aimed to free the voter or juror from patronal pressure in registering his opinion - Cicero's indignant rejection of the principle of secret ballot on the grounds that it undermines *auctoritas* or social deference is a telling commentary (*de legibus* 3. 33f.). In particular, the distributions of land and corn initiated by the Gracchi constituted a frontal assault on patronal power, for dependence on the state for alleviation in times of poverty and crisis reduced the necessity of dependence on individuals. This may lie behind the perennial accusation of kingship levelled against popular legislators: for by making themselves through the distribution of public resources the equivalent of universal patrons, they usurped the function and social power of the pluralist patrons of the ruling class (Garnsey 1988, 197).

Thirdly, we must allow for the effect on social relationships of the influx of wealth and especially coin in the aftermath of the Punic Wars. Roman society underwent something of the transformation which Samuel Johnson observed in eighteenth century Scotland: the old relationships of dependence and protection between the highland chieftains and their clansmen became a new monetary relationship of landlord and tenant, as the chiefs sought to imitate and finance the lifestyle of the London-based aristocrat (Cregeen 1968). The effects of such 'monetisation' of social relationships are apparent in two spheres, the rewards of advocacy and the bribery of voters. Already in 204 BC the lex Cincia sought to keep money out of the patron-client relationship by banning 'gifts'. The ban was easily evaded, and we have seen above in Plautus concern over the pursuit of rich clients to the detriment of traditional patronal ties. Legacies in particular became a standard way of rewarding services, and it is arguable that the whole pattern of Roman inheritance was affected by the need to lubricate such patron-client obligations (Wallace-Hadrill 1981). The eventual modification of the lex Cincia by Claudius represents the admission that advocates had become 'patrons' only in name, and indeed even the name of *patronus* slips out of use for the advocate in the imperial period (Neuhauser 1958). Moreover, the massive advance of bribery in the late republic struck at the heart of the traditional patronage system. The dividing line between legitimate patronal rewards and the purchase of votes was a blurred one: and the purity of the traditional model was irreparably compromised. The very concept of bribery, as of debt (above), suggests a patronage system in crisis.

Such considerations have led some to deny patronage more than marginal significance in the political life of the late republic - and in view of the fact that we are enormously better informed about this period than about earlier ones, it becomes difficult to talk with confidence about the operation of political patronage at any period. Certainly, these arguments should be enough to deter us from taking a mechanistic view of patronage, as if it was a smoothly operating system following predictable and inevitable rules. The picture that emerges from the late republic is more dynamic: of social relationships in a state of flux and change, seen by participants to suffer from malfunction and abuse, subject to open challenge and attack. Rather than offering *the* key to Roman politics, patronage must be seen as one of several methods of generating power, a system actually in competition and conflict with other systems. But, once this is conceded, how are we to estimate its overall importance in Roman society and politics?

Patronage and social integration

The argument so far has tended to drive a wedge between ideal and reality. Patronage emerges as a distinctive and central element in Roman culture and ideology; yet when we look at its practical significance at precisely the point where it might be supposed to be most effective, in the politics of the late republic, major doubts arise. Some may be happy with such a dichotomy, particularly Roman historians in the positivist tradition which puts little faith in ideologies. The self-image of the Romans, it could be argued, was a survival inherited from their ancestors, which bore only a tenuous relationship to contemporary realities.

On the other hand, if we relegate Roman ideals and attitudes to a state of 'false consciousness', we ignore one of the most valuable contributions of the sociological and anthropological literature. One might expect to find in a value system the psychological underpinning of social structures, not a nebulous memory floating free from social realities. However distorted they may be, ideals and perceptions themselves play a vital role in constituting contemporary realities: for the Romans, their real world was fashioned of their perceptions of how it was and their ideals of how it ought to be. In what follows, I want to suggest that patronage was indeed as central to the Roman social system in reality as in ideology; and that though across the centuries diverse and varied relationships were seen by the Romans themselves as patronal, they all have in common a vital social function.

Dionysius of Halicarnassus saw in the patronage instituted by Romulus an instrument of social control, that kept the population in subjection to the ruling class. That is a plausible and, I want to argue, correct analysis; but what is less than plausible is his picture of how it worked. Even in the remotest Roman past, we may find difficulty in swallowing his rosy image of rich and poor competing to outdo each other in favours, and the rich studiously abstaining from the exploitation of the poor. It is in fact merely the reverse image of contemporary abuses; an attempt to explain social conflict of his own day in terms of the social relationships no longer pertaining. A more credible model of how patronage works as a system of social control in a relatively simple agrarian community is suggested by Silverman's study of nineteenth and twentieth century Umbria (1965 and 1967). Under the *mezzadria* system, the big landowners also acted as patrons to their peasant tenants. They provided them with access to certain services from which the peasants were otherwise cut off, particularly those located in the remote town: legal representation, intervention with the police, applications for jobs, medical facilities, loans. The patrons, because of their links with the central system of power, were able to act as mediators, between country and town, between locality and the state, channelling the requests for resources. The clients could not do without their patrons. Patronage thus serves as a mechanism for reproducing social power.

One of our problems in envisaging how Roman patronage worked is that of seeing how the patron was in a position to (let alone willing to) deliver the goods to large numbers of dependants. Yet the power of the patron may derive not from the ability to secure benefits for all who ask, but from the sheer impossibility of securing them for any but a minority. The secret of the game is the manipulation of scarce resources: where all need resources that are in short supply, it is easier for the patrons to secure control of the routes of access, so rendering access impossible except through a patron. Hence, Judith Chubb (1982) has argued, the control of the DC party in the impoverished Palermo and Naples; the scarcity of resources gives them power precisely over those poor people one might expect to be their natural enemies and vote socialist. A similar process is exposed by Juvenal (*Satire* 5): Clients themselves are the dupes, for the patrons have no intention of rewarding their services; a meal is all they get, and that not often; and when at last after two months the neglected client is invited, he is insulted with cheap and nasty fare while the patron gorges luxuriously. Here food may stand as the symbol of the resources a patron distributes: his power over the client derives not from generous and regular distribution, but from keeping him on tenterhooks with the prospect of access to resources which is in fact never fully granted. The client's only chance of breaking out of the system is to make the unacceptable admission that the resources are unavailable and in any case superfluous.

Here, then, may be a first step towards understanding the use by the Romans of patronage as an instrument of social control. The ruling nobility, priests, magistrates, judges, legal counsel, and generals rolled into one, stood astride all the major lines of communication with the centre of state power and the resources it had to distribute (cf. Sallust, *Jugurtha* 41). Their success in control lay as much in their power to refuse as in their readiness to deliver the goods. In this light, the inability of a few hundred to satisfy the needs of hundreds of thousands, their manifest failure to alleviate poverty, hunger and debt, indeed their exploitation of these circumstances to secure themselves advantage, all of which we have met in the case of the late republic, need not be seen as arguments for the inadequacy of patronage, so much as the conditions of its flourishing.

But we need to go a step further. The dominance of the republican nobility was, after all, identified, resented, and broken. In order to evolve a credible model of patronage which will stretch from Romulus' Rome to fourth century Gaul, we need to move away from the specific tie with the republican nobility. The model I wish to put forward is of patronage as a mechanism of social integration. Looking at Roman society over the *longue durée*, one of its most persistent defining characteristics is its ability to expand and absorb outsiders or newcomers. To attempt to explain how this constant assimilation and integration of outsiders was achieved would be to write a complete cultural history of Rome: for the absorption of outsiders involved not only their own acculturation, but the constant adaptation of Roman culture itself to accommodate the newcomers. In this context, however, it is enough to point to the role of patronage in the process of integration.

The problem of integration lies in the relationship between the centre and the peripheries. Rome expanded by constantly adding to its peripheries; yet peripheries are fissile, liable to split off and form separate entities unless united to the centre by strong bonds. They need access to the centre and the resources it controls. One model of access which the Romans did not use, but which was widespread in Greece, is the democratic model. Here the peripheries are afforded equality of access to the centre: thus the deme system of classical Attica allowed each component village regular and direct involvement in the political process at the centre (cf. Osborne 1985). This system, while egalitarian in its treatment of existing members, is not easily tolerant of expansion; the tendency is for the society to become more hedged about with rules of exclusion as access to the centre becomes more open. The Roman political system at all times avoided any sort of direct regional representation in government. Instead, access was mediated through individuals. It was this inaccessibility of the centre except through personal links that generated the power of patronage; and it was through the exercise of this power that patronage placed social integration within limits and so secured social control. At the same time, unlike the Attic democratic system, it was highly flexible, allowing continuing expansion.

Symmetrically corresponding with the Roman willingness to expand membership of its citizen body and incorporate outsiders, whether ex-slaves or foreigners, is a cautiousness about allowing the citizen unmediated access to power. The patron intervenes at both individual and corporate level. I shall look at the corporate level first, if only because here the relevance of the peripheries/centre model is more immediately apparent.

The patronage of subject communities, discussed in Badian's classic *Foreign Clientelae* (1958) and below by Braund and Rich, is probably the best documented form, and certainly a context in which the Romans themselves readily applied the terminology of *clientela*.

In law, the relationship of Rome to its subjects was complex and confused: they might be 'friends' and 'allies', 'free' cities bound to Rome by various treaties, directly governed non-citizen subjects, or half-citizens, or full citizens who nevertheless formed self-governing communities (*coloniae* and *municipia*). In practice, all these categories needed, from time to time, access to the decision-making centre in Rome, notably in the senate, and such access was virtually impossible without the personal intervention of a member of the ruling elite. In consequence, the component communities of the empire formed numerous personal links with members of the elite, often in highly formalised terms, expressed in honorific decrees and records (*tabulae patronatus*, cf. Nichols 1980a). Such relationships fall outside the standard modern definition of patronage in that one of the partners to the relationships was a community not an individual. But the important feature is that links between communities and the Roman state are mediated through individuals; and in fact the more formal links are supplemented by numerous informal patronal links between members of the local elites and members of the Roman elite. Typical is the spectacle presented by Sallust in his *Jugurtha* of the Numidian prince servicing his links with members of the elite with gifts and bribes in order to secure his position locally; or of the victims of Verres' government in Sicily establishing contact with patrons at Rome in order to secure redress.

Badian's interest in this phenomenon was primarily for its relevance to Roman internal politics: nobles with foreign *clientelae* enjoyed a power base in their competition with each other. But it also has relevance for the structure of Roman rule, as Badian notes in passing (p.165-6):

> It is mainly due to this solid structure of personal relationships that the Empire of the Roman People survived the storms of the last few generations of the Republic.

Patronage caused chaos as well as cohesion (as Braund argues); but the structure of Roman control relied heavily on it. The manipulation of scarce governmental resources by members of the elite kept the peripheries dependent on the ruling elite as a whole.

The patronage of foreign communities *as if* they were individuals was one of the techniques by which Rome managed to preserve the structure of a city-state while incorporating other city-states within its empire, and that despite what was by our standards a very weak system of communications. But in a closely parallel fashion, the patronage of individuals also served as a technique of integration and control. This was apparently the function they themselves attributed to patronage in the Rome of Romulus. They saw Rome as starting from a community of shepherds, rapidly expanding by absorbing rootless newcomers. Social organisation was based on the *gentes* under patrician control: patricians acted as patrons to the plebeian clients. Patronage thus operated as the mechanism by which newcomers were incorporated into the system. This picture may be historical fantasy (see Drummond below); but what is significant in this context is the myth itself. In attributing this sort of function to 'original' patronage, they provided a rationale for using patronage in similar ways in contemporary situations.

Certainly in the historical period Rome continued to expand by the admission of newcomers. The patron stood as sponsor to the new citizen, commonly providing him with his own gentile name. The patron was an essential channel for access to knowledge within Roman society. Republican Rome operated largely through a body of orally transmitted custom, *mos maiorum*, covering most areas of life including private law. The individual cannot operate a system without knowledge of how it works, and until in the late republic Greek influence transformed Roman knowledge, it was only through consultation of the patron that the newcomer could learn the Roman way.

One special type of newcomer is the freed slave. The *patronus-libertus* relationship is different from the *patronus-cliens* relationship in several crucial respects (Fabre 1981). It is not voluntary: the freedman neither has choice over whom to adopt as his patron, nor over whether to have one at all. The obligations of deference and service (*obsequium et officium*) were, unlike those of the client, enforcable in law. The freedman in fact is a special case, since the transition from slave to free is a special case of the transition from non-Roman to Roman. The obligatory nature of this patronage obviously protects the interests of the individual master; but it also has relevance for the relationship between the freedman and society at large. As a citizen, the ex-slave is a full member of Roman society; yet his membership is in some sense conditional, mediated through his patron who continues as a sort of sponsor. This patronal bond helps to account for the extraordinary ease with which slaves of diverse ethnic origins were assimilated into the fabric of Roman society.

The enfranchised foreigner or slave are only extreme cases of those on the periphery of Roman society. To understand the pervasiveness of patronage in Roman society, we need to think not only about relationships between those at opposite ends of the spectrum, but about the multifarious links which involved men of all social levels, rising to virtual social parity with the 'patron'. Nor is there always a clearcut distinction between patrons and clients, since one man's client is another man's patron. Such links are highly fluid and informal in character. There has been needless difficulty over the appropriateness of the term 'patronage' to such relationships. If Roman manners distinguished *amici* (friends) from *clientes*, it was not an objective analytical distinction: they applied the same language of friendship, trust and obligation to both indifferently (see Saller above). Of course there is a contrast between the friendship of social equals, and the dependent relationship of unequals; but what justifies describing the network as a whole as a patronage network is that it involves exchanges between those closer to the centre of power and those more distant from it, and has the effect of mediating state resources through personal relationships. This crisscrossing web of personal links is the system which Gelzer wanted to expose in *The Roman Nobility*.

The operation of such links is hard to document without numerous collections of letters. But all the collections of Roman letters we possess (Cicero from the republic, Horace, Seneca, Pliny, Fronto, Symmachus etc. from the empire) show letters of recommendation exchanged without embarrassment as a normal and proper part of public life (for documentary examples, see Cotton 1981). The small selection of Cicero's letters of recommendation which survives, mainly from the period 46-4 BC (*ad Familiares* 13), illustrate how frequent and diverse such correspondence was (de Ste. Croix 1954). In a single year (46) Cicero sends 13 letters to one friend alone (Servius Sulpicius Rufus) who is acting as governor of Achaea. Sulpicius and Cicero are social equals (not patron and client); but Sulpicius' position of authority enables him to distribute favours, particularly favourable judgments in legal cases, to those for whom Cicero acts as broker. Their social range is wide: a city (Sparta), a senator (Mescinius), local businessmen of citizen and non-citizen status, and on two occasions the freedmen of friends/clients.

Such networks must have, as Gelzer argued, implications for the
pattern of Roman politics; above all for election to senatorial office it
was necessary, as contemporary sources explicitly state, to activate
one's network of obligations. It was not the only element in political
life, but nestled among other techniques of winning support: Cicero
might count on the vote of a client defended in court, and of those
obliged to that client, but he could also hope to have made a
favourable impression on the jurors, the bystanders, and the readers of
his published speeches. The importance of the patronage network
does not best emerge from asking the question (which is in any case
unanswerable), How important was patronage for political success?
The revealing question is different: How effectively could any
individual or group gain access to the resources controlled by the
Roman state (of whatever sort, judgment, privilege, status, power,
money) except through personal links of patronage? Here, it seems to
me, Gelzer's conclusions remain valid:

> To maintain their rights citizens and subjects alike were
> constrained to seek the protection of powerful men ...

Pluralist and universal patronage

Republican patronage should not be seen as a stable and unchanging
set of relationships. On the contrary, it is because it was flexible and
dynamic and could be adapted to changing social circumstances that it
remained effective. Particularly in the last century of the republic, as
we have seen, a concatenation of changes placed traditional patterns of
patronage under strain: numerical explosion of the urban population
of Rome, new patterns of popular politics, and the influx of wealth
and monetisation. Traditional aristocratic patronage failed to cope
with problems of mob violence, starvation and land-hunger. The
Romans acknowledged their traditional system to be under attack and
collapsing. But alongside the decay of the old system, we can see the
growth of a new one.

The republican system was pluralist in its nature. A multiplicity
of patrons acted in competition with each other, offering alternative
routes of access to resources. Client choice guaranteed a measure of
freedom: by withholding the vote and transferring allegiance to
another patron the client (but not the freedman) could establish his
independence. It would appear axiomatic that if one patron achieves

monopoly control of resources, he destroys the system and becomes the state itself. That is exactly what seemed to Gelzer to have happened with the onset of autocratic rule. His essay concludes:

> At the end of the titanic conflict the opposition lay annihilated or utterly exhausted at the feet of a single victor, and the predominance of the nobility gave way to absolute monarchy.
>
> (1969, 139)

The key to republican patronage, at least for Gelzer, lies in the elections, for ultimately the only significant service the client can offer the patron in exchange for his protection is the vote. Even though Augustus initially restored the semblance (and perhaps more) of elections, he was evidently determined to break the powerbase of dependents of the nobility in the city of Rome. The mounting restrictions on aristocratic displays such as triumphs, gladiatorial games, public buildings in the city, even the striking of personal badges on coins, had done much to erode the traditional self-presentation of the nobility even before the end of the reign (Eck 1984). In AD 14 popular elections to senatorial office were reduced to a ceremony, leaving the reality of choice to the senate, guided as often as not by indications of imperial will. There seems small scope left for the operation of traditional patronage.

Yet, paradoxically, it was through patronage that the revolutionary leader achieved his power, and through the preservation of patronage that he maintained it. Just as Barrington Moore (1967) has shown that twentieth century dictatorships have relied on democratic structures to destroy democracy and generate their own power, Roman imperial power has at its root a transformation of the patronage structures of republican Rome. One of the most fruitful developments of patronage study was Anton von Premerstein's analysis of the sociological basis of imperial power, which saw the basis of Octavian's power in his position as universal patron. He saw as a forerunner of Octavian the tribune Livius Drusus, to whom also a great oath of loyalty was sworn. Indeed there is much about the behaviour of the popular leaders that is explicitly patronal in style: Livius Drusus built his house on the edge of the Palatine overlooking the forum 'so that everything he did could be visible to the whole people'; he is described at the time of his assassination as 'surrounded by the vast and chaotic mass which always accompanied him' (Velleius Paterculus 2.13-4). It is significant too that Gaius Gracchus is said to have been the first to have divided his friends into a first and second 'admission' (Seneca *de Beneficiis* 6.34). Such men evidently were playing the patron on a massive scale. The military dynasts of the period, through their control of wealth, rank and land, exercised equally a massive patronage that represented the other strand of Octavian's power.

One may object to the theory of 'universal' patronage on the grounds that it renders the concept vacuous. If patronage involves personal relationships, what relationship can there be between an emperor and a population of millions scattered across the Mediterranean? In practical terms, the oath of loyalty that has its origins in the oath of *tota Italia* before Actium, but was repeated for each emperor (Herrmann 1968), created no personal links between subject and emperor, but was merely an affirmation of obedience. Indeed one may speak of a special relationship between the emperor and his troops (Campbell 1984). Augustus and his successors also cultivated strong ties with the Roman plebs (Yavetz 1969), and one could argue that aristocratic patronage in the capital was partially extinguished by 'bread and circuses': thus Tacitus in a famous passage contrasts the minority of the city plebs bound to the noble houses by patronage with the rabble dependent on imperial handouts (*Histories* 1.4). But, the city of Rome perhaps apart, it is perfectly clear that the emperor in no sense diminished personal patronage as a general phenomenon in the Roman world. No reader of the letters of the younger Pliny can long remain in doubt of the continued importance, both ideologically and practically, of patronage in public life. After Saller's ample documentation and persuasive analysis (1982), the question can no longer be as to whether patronage continued; rather it is how and why it continued after the disappearance of elections.

The emperor then did not become universal patron in the sense of *sole* patron in the Roman world. Nevertheless, he brought about a profound transformation of the overall system of patronage. As a system, republican patronage was pluralist. Numerous patrons competed in the distribution of resources; ultimately the network converged on the *populus Romanus*, the sovereign body to which the resources belonged (*res publica populi Romani*). The clients themselves constituted the *populus Romanus*, and by their votes chose between and rewarded their patrons. The effect of imperial rule is to usurp the function of the *populus Romanus*. There is no longer a vote, and ultimate control of public resources passes *de facto* to the emperor. Thus the network of patronage realigns, and all strands converge on the emperor at the centre. The universal patron is not the only patron, nor is he powerful at the expense of others: on the contrary, they owe their power to him, and he exercises his patronage through them.

Autocracy and patronage

How then does the new system operate, and what is the payoff if not the vote? It is helpful to look sideways at the operation of patronage in other autocratic societies, and Sharon Kettering's analysis of seventeenth century France (1986) now offers a rewarding analogy.[1] Her argument is that in a nation with still relatively weak state control from the centre in the shape of the monarchy, patronage was deliberately exploited as a method of extending the tentacles of royal control into the loosely attached peripheries.

> The crown used royal officials to govern, but institutional procedures alone were insufficient because royal authority in the provinces was still too uncertain and its enforcement too weak ... So the crown had to supplement its authority with patron-broker-client ties that functioned inside and outside the institutional framework: they were used to manipulate political institutions from within, to operate across institutions, and to act in place of institutions. They were interstitial, supplementary, and parallel structures.(5)

Royal patronage and resources were channelled through ministers like Richelieu, Mazarin, Colbert to trusted clients who acted as 'brokers' in the provinces. A complicated web of mutual dependance built up.

> Brokers interceded for clients and mustered influence and resources on their behalf. They opened doors for them, secured offices for them, and provided patronage allowing them to build their own

---

[1] I am grateful to my former colleague, Professor Richard Bonney, of the History Department at Leicester for drawing this work to my attention.

> clienteles - creating a large client network was the first step in obtaining political power. Membership of a clientele was necessary for political advancement, and clientele hopping was essential to political preferment. (55-6)

Clients promised absolute loyalty and allegiance to their patrons, yet the patron was well aware that his own ability to command the loyalty of a client depended on his own political success. Clienteles evaporated at a whiff of failure.

> Government by patron-client ties is better understood as the utilization of changing interests and resources, motivating men to political action, than as tiers of fixed, immutable client loyalties.
>
> (39)

(This observation applies with equal force to the Roman republic, and undermines the picture put forward by the cruder exponents of prosopographical method.)

Finally, we should notice that this whole system operated not only from the top downwards (because the crown wanted it) but simultaneously from the bottom upwards. It worked because in the context of French society, a man's social standing depended on the respect in which he was held, and that respect was objectified in the strength and number of his clientele. There is no question of the vote here, but a more fluid estimate of the support he commanded.

> In order to act as broker, an individual needed *crédit* at home and at Paris ... *Crédit* was derived from personal reputation, rank, title and family name, wealth, officeholding, clients, and patrons ... A broker who had provincial credit did not owe everything to a Paris patron ... In fact, his provincial influence and clients, which made him independent, had probably secured him patronage in the first place and enabled him to act as a broker. (43-4)

Clients, in fact, were not merely the result of political success: they were the origin of political success. One could not achieve access to royal patronage, and distribute it to one's dependants unless one was seen to possess credit in commanding the loyalty of dependants. Ultimately the domestic power basis is crucial, for it is in the patron's house that many of the exchanges of clientage take place.

The size of a man's household indicated his rank and wealth. In order to keep his status and prestige and to display the wealth that promised generosity to his clients, thereby increasing his power, a great noble needed to maintain a large household. *Grands* or great nobles could easily have 100 salaried individuals on their staff, the majority stationed at one or perhaps two provincial châteaux ... Grands in high office also maintained entourages ... Great noble entourages were meant to impress, and they swelled with the occasion since they reflected the wealth and status of their patron.

(34-5)

Numerous features in this account of seventeenth century France are recognisable to the historian of the Roman empire. The network of obligations which spreads out from court, involving ministers and even the traditional nobility; the fluidity and multiplicity of ties, coupled with a constant cynical calculation of personal advantage; the collapse of credit of the fallen political favourite; the provincial power basis; the grand houses that both displayed and created power. But above all we should observe the superfluity of the vote. It is a confidence trick in which your standing depends on appearances, what people are seen to think of you; it is never put to the polls, and yet you are on trial every minute. The people below you estimate your standing in the eyes of those above you; and those above estimate your support from below. It is a jittery system like the stockmarket, not a system of occasional major tests like democratic elections.

Some of this is relevant even under the republic. Much of the value of *clientela* lay not in a solid and dependable block of votes, but in its contribution to appearances, by which the majority of voters themselves had to judge. In that sense the way for the imperial system had been prepared long before. The abolition of popular elections in AD 14 was not a violent revolution, but the removal of an element which had become superfluous to the working of the system, the voice of the city plebs of Rome. Rome was the special power base of the emperor; he could not afford to be seen to have rivals there. But he had no reason to discourage patronage in other contexts, provincial and domestic, for it provided structures of loyalty which he could manipulate to the benefit of his own power.

Fergus Millar (1977) has taught us to see the emperor not so much as an official controlling a system of bureaucratic government, but rather as a patron sitting at the centre of a vast web of resource distribution, granting or denying to individuals and communities status, privilege, favourable hearings and wealth. The French analogy suggests that these two images are not alternative but supplementary. The Roman emperor did govern through officials, on a scale not previously attempted; nevertheless, in comparison to modern bureaucratic systems, imperial government was exceedingly small and feeble (Garnsey and Saller 1987, 20ff.). The patronage network was an essential supplement, working in the interstices of bureaucracy, both inside and outside. Nor could the emperor operate this network alone, as Millar tends to envisage him, a solitary spider at the centre of the web. Elite brokers, as Saller (1982) shows, were essential to the structure, with the court at Rome operating as the first level of contact. Senators were indeed the emperor's potential rivals; but they were also his necessary collaborators, for they acted as focuses of loyalty which through the distribution of patronage he could keep loyal to himself.

The language of patronage tends to multiply and spread under the empire. Numerous inscriptions celebrate the election of patrons, by municipalities and bodies like the *collegia* of Ostia (Harmand 1957). These should not be dismissed as not 'true' patronage; on the contrary, the way they are recorded on stone or bronze reflects the need to make patronal links visible. Nor should the importance of local ties be underestimated (Nichols 1980b). The support of the people of Tifernum Tiberinum for Pliny, as their major local landowner, brought him no votes; but the care with which Pliny drew their enthusiastic support to the attention both of his friends and the emperor shows its value in enhancing his own standing (*Ep.* 4.1 and 10.8). Tifernum, or the college of bargemen at Ostia, may stand for thousands of communities and bodies round the empire. They needed patrons close to the centre of power to obtain access to resources, and protection from their enemies; reciprocally the patrons needed their support as the basis of their own political credibility.

Conclusion

The problem that emerged at the outset was of the relation between ideology and social reality. I moved from the image of the patron framed in the setting of his house, and the persistence of the patronal image in the self presentation of the Roman elite. I have argued that this self-image makes no sense except in the context of the real importance of patronage in the structure of Roman society. Patronage has not emerged from this survey as the only Roman system; rather as something operating alongside other systems, sometimes in competition with them, sometimes in collaboration. But throughout, I have suggested, it served one fundamental function, to provide a connection between the çentre of power and the peripheries which the centre sought to control. From the point of view of the society, patronage represented a flexible method of integration and simultaneously of social control; that is not to say that it was always effective, nor indeed a particularly attractive system to live in. From the point of view of the individual patron, the ability to persuade others of his power to secure access to benefits was the basis of social credibility. The ideology thus both results from and morally underpins the social system.

Bibliography

Badian, E. (1958), *Foreign Clientelae (264 - 70BC)*. Oxford.

Bek, L. (1980), *Towards Paradise on Earth*, (Analecta Romana vol. 9).

Brunt, P.A. (1988), 'Clientela', in *The Fall of the Roman Republic and Related Essays*, 382-442. Oxford.

Campbell, J.B. (1984), *The Emperor and the Roman Army 31BC - AD 235*. Oxford.

Chubb, J. (1982), *Patronage, power and poverty in southern Italy: a tale of two cities*. Cambridge.

Cotton, H. (1981), *Documentary Letters of Recommendation in Latin from the Roman Empire*, (Beiträge zur klassischen Philologie vol. 132). Königstein/Ts.

Cregeen, E.R. (1968), 'The changing role of the house of Argyll in the Scottish highlands', in I.M. Lewis (ed.), *History and Social Anthropology* (A.S.A. Monographs no. 7), 153-192. London.

Eck, W. (1984), 'Senatorial self-representation: developments in the Augustan period', in F. Millar and E. Segal (eds.), *Caesar Augustus. Seven aspects*, 129-167. Oxford.

Fabre, G. (1981), *Libertus. Recherches sur les rapports patron-affranchi à la fin de la république romaine*, (Coll. École Française à Rome vol. 50). Rome.

Finley, M.I. (1983), *Politics in the Ancient World*. Cambridge.

Friedländer, L. (1922), *Darstellungen aus der Sittengeschichte Roms* (10th ed.). Leipzig.

Fustel de Coulanges, N.D. (1890), *Histoire des institutions politiques de l'ancienne France, vol. 5: Les origines du système féodal*, 205-47. Paris.

Garnsey, P. and Saller, R.P. (1987), *The Roman Empire: Economy, Society and Culture*. London.

Garnsey P. (1988), *Famine and Food Supply in the Graeco-Roman World: Responses to Rish and Crisis*. Cambridge.

Gelzer, M. (1912), *Die Nobilität der römischen Republik*. Leipzig-Berlin.

Gelzer, M. (1969), *The Roman Nobility*, trans. R. Seager. Oxford.

Harmand, L. (1957), *Un aspect social et politique du monde romain: le patronat sur les collectivités publiques des origines au Bas-Empire*, (Publ. de Clermont, 2e Serie, Fasc. 2).

Herrmann, P. (1968), *Des römische Kaisereid: Untersuchungen zu seiner Herkunft und Entwicklung*, (Hypomnemata vol. 20). Göttingen.

Hopkins (1983), *Death and Renewal*. Cambridge.

Kettering, S. (1986), *Patrons, Brokers, and Clients in Seventeenth-Century France*. Oxford.

Millar, F. (1977), *The Emperor in the Roman World 31 BC - AD 337*. London.

Millar, F. (1984), 'The political character of the Classical Roman Republic, 200-151 BC', *Journal Roman Studies* 74, 1-19.

Millar, F. (1986), 'Politics, persuasion and the people before the Social war (150-90 BC)', *Journal Roman Studies* 76, 1-11/

Moore, Barrington (1967), *Social origins of dictatorship and democracy: lord and peasant in the making of the modern world*. Harmondsworth.

Neuhauser, W. (1958), *Patronus und Orator*. Innsbruck.

Nichols, J. (1980a), 'Tabulae Patronatus: a study of the agreement between patron and client-community', *Aufsteig und Niedergang der römischen Welt* (ed. H. Temporini), 2.13, 535-61.

Nichols, J. (1980b), 'Pliny and the patronage of communities', *Hermes* 108, 365-85.

Nippel, W. (1984), 'Policing Rome', *Journal Roman Studies* 74, 20-29.

Osborne, R. (1985), *Demos: the Discovery of Classical Attika*. Cambridge.

Premerstein, A. von (1937), *Vom Werden und Wesen des augusteischen Prinzipats*. Munich.

Rouland, N. (1979), *Pouvoir politique et dépendance personnelle dans l'antiquité romaine. Genèse et rôle des rapports de clientèle* (Coll. Latomus no. 166). Brussels.

Rouland, N. (1981), *Rome, démocratie impossible? Les acteures du pouvoir dans la cité romaine*. Paris.

Ste. Croix, G.E.M. de (1954), '*Suffragium*: from vote to patronage', *British Journal of Sociology* 5, 33-48.

Saller, R.P. (1982), *Personal Patronage under the Early Empire*. Cambridge.

Scullard, H.H. (1951), *Roman Politics, 220-150 BC*. Oxford.

Silverman, S. (1965), 'Patronage and community-nation relationships in central Italy', *Ethnology* 4.2, 172-89.

Silverman, S. (1967), 'The community-nation mediator in traditional central Italy' in J.M. Potter, M.N. Diaz and G.M. Foster (eds.), *Peasant Society: a Reader*, 279-93, Boston.

Silverman, S. (1977), 'Patronage as myth' in E. Gellner and J. Waterbury (eds.), *Patrons and Clients*, 7-19. London.

Van Dam, R. (1985), *Leadership and Community in Late Antique Gaul.*. California.

Wallace-Hadrill, A. (1981), 'Family and inheritance in the Augustan marriage laws', *Proceedings Cambridge Philological Society* 27, 58-80.

Wallace-Hadrill, A. (1986), 'Image and authority in the coinage of Augustus', *Journal Roman Studies* 76, 66-87.

Wallace-Hadrill, A. (1988), 'The social structure of the Roman house', *Papers British School Rome 56*, forthcoming.

Wiseman, T.P. (1982), '*Pete nobiles amicos*: poets and patrons in late republican Rome', in B.K. Gold (ed.), *Literary and Artistic Patronage in Ancient Rome*, 28-49. Austin, Texas.

Yavetz, Z. (1969), *Plebs and Princeps*. Oxford.

Chapter 4
Early Roman *clientes* [1]

Andrew Drummond

Early *clientela* in Dionysius and Livy

In the course of his artificial attempt to turn Romulus into the creator of Rome's basic social and political institutions in the Greek style,[2] the late first century BC historian Dionysius of Halicarnassus provides our only surviving general account of early clientship (*Antiquitates Romanae* 2.9f., see Appendix). According to this, Romulus, supposedly in the eighth century, divided the original population of Rome into two classes, the first an hereditary aristocracy, the patriciate, the second the ordinary free citizen populace, the plebs. Each plebeian selected a patrician as his patron and Romulus defined the obligations of the two parties to the relationship. Patrons were to expound the law to their clients, assist them in their contractual affairs,[3] and defend lawsuits on their behalf. A client was to provide financial assistance (should his patron need it) for a daughter's dowry, the expenses of office, fines or the ransom of

---

1 I am grateful to Professor P.A. Brunt for access to his forthcoming paper on Roman clientship.

2 For the compilation of this 'Constitution of Romulus' Dionysius himself may be largely responsible (Balsdon 1971). For his account of early clientship Varro and/or Valerius Antias are the most plausible sources (Balsdon 1971, 27; Ferenczy 1978-9, 168f.), as also perhaps for the additional or variant details in Plutarch's abbreviated version of Dionysius' account (*Romulus* 13). Cicero *De Republica* 2.16 suggests earlier emphasis on the topic and its significance.

3 A particular interest of Dionysius: 4.13.1; 43.1; 5.2.2.

his person.[1] Neither party was to take legal action, give evidence or vote against the other; if they did so, they were to be declared 'sacred to subterranean Zeus' (a form of outlawry). The relationship, Dionysius adds, became hereditary.

It has been argued that this account derives from a collection of authentic written 'regal laws' current in the late republic,[2] but the only law (*nomos*) which Dionysius cites is the provision for outlawry.[3] Even this need not have been a written statute, on Dionysius' own showing[4] and is certainly not of regal origin: for the 'subterranean Zeus' to whom transgressors are here declared sacred is Dis Pater, whose cult was introduced only in 249 BC.[5] Admittedly, the Vergilian commentator Servius ascribes a similar law to the Twelve Tables,[6] but on dubious authority, since outlawry does not otherwise appear as a penalty in that code and the penalty itself is both disproportionate and unenforceable. There is, therefore, little likelihood of a regal or early republican provision to this effect and this element in Dionysius' account must be rejected. For the rest of his account Dionysius nowhere claims that these were written regulations (or embodied in such a collection); indeed, for the most part they are explicitly customs (*ethe*) defined by Romulus (2.10.1). Nor is it likely that clientship would have been so precisely circumscribed and regulated from an early date: comparative data (and historical probability) suggest that such formal regulation is

---

[1] Dionysius assumes that assistance with dowries at least was expected only by indigent patrons, but so far as these contributions are at all historical, most relate to occasions where there was an unusual need for liquid capital and should perhaps be viewed in part as a strategy for raising the sums involved without recourse to the sale or mortgage of property.

[2] Watson (1972).

[3] On Dionysius' problematic phraseology here see Brecht (1938), 35-41.

[4] Cf. Dion.Hal. 2.24.1; 27.3.

[5] Latte (1960), 81f.; not refuted by Tondo (1963), 29 n.11.

[6] 'If a patron does mischief to a client, he shall be *sacer* (i.e. an outlaw)' (Serv. *Verg.Aen*.6.609 = Twelve Tables 8.21). Against authenticity cf. Schwegler (1853-8), I.640 n.1; Heinze (1929), 159 n.1.

normally a later development.[1] Moreover, it is commonly a result of pressure from the dependent, anxious to have his obligations clearly defined and thereby delimited, and for that there is no evidence at Rome. At best, therefore, Dionysius will be describing the rights and obligations of patrons and clients as they became established by custom, not as laid down by specific enactment.

If that is so and if, as a necessary corollary, Dionysius' account has no documentary basis, there must be a strong possibility that, like other elements in his schematic and idealising account of the Romulean constitution,[2] it is a later reconstruction. This supposition is reinforced by other characteristics of these chapters: their sentimental idealising, exemplified by the statement that patrons accepted no monetary gifts from clients; their manifest anachronisms (their references to the expenses of office and to voting and the general assumption of monetary exchanges); and the historical significance which Dionysius himself attributes to clientship as the determining factor in Rome's avoidance of violent internal conflict until the tribunates of C.Gracchus in 123-122.[3] Clearly Dionysius saw the political effects and presumably the substance of clientship as unchanged through to the late second century and his analysis may well, therefore, be based on aspects of the relationship as it was assumed to have operated in the mid republic.

The details of his account largely fit that hypothesis. The notion that neither patron nor client should act against each other in lawsuits was certainly current then,[4] as was that of the hereditary character of the relationship.[5] Patrons were expected to act as their clients' legal advisers and advocates;[6] they could not bring or defend suits on their

---

[1] Thus Pollock and Maitland (1898), 1.349f. (quoted by Watson 1972, 100f.): 'The duties implied in the relation between man and lord are but slowly developed and made legal duties. There long remains a fringe of vague obligations ... Gradually the occasions on which an aid of money may be demanded are determined.'

[2] Cf. Pohlenz (1924), esp. 174ff.

[3] For the idealisation of the relationship as it operated in earlier periods see also: Cicero, *Divinatio in Caecilium* 66; Aulus Gellius *Noctes Atticae* 20.1.40; cf. Cato, *Orat.* fr.41 Malcovati.

[4] Cf. Cato, *Orat.* fr. 41 Malc.; *lex repetundarum* 10; 33.

[5] See especially Plutarch *Marius* 5; cf. *lex repetundarum* 10.

[6] Plautus, *Menaechmi* 587ff. with Cuq (1919), 249ff.

behalf as Dionysius asserts of the Romulean period but that is probably a characteristic error by Dionysius who did not always properly understand Roman institutions[1] and who was presumably misled here by later practice when patrons effectively conducted their clients' cases.[2] Clients for their part may well have been expected to make occasional financial contributions in the later period[3] - at least the occasions cited by Dionysius for such assistance fit the mid-republican period much better than the monarchy.[4] Finally, Dionysius' assertion that all plebeians were originally clients of patrician patrons seems to belong to a more general idealising and paternalistic strain in historical writing about early Rome[5] and was prompted specifically by the etymological associations of the terms 'patronus' (patron) and 'patricius' (patrician); when Dionysius comes to fifth-century history, dependent *clientes* comprise only part of the plebeian element in the Roman state.

There is also a notable inconcinnity between Dionysius' account of the client's responsibilities and the role which they are ascribed in the literary narratives of the early republic (fifth-fourth centuries BC), including that of Dionysius himself. *Clientes* are largely conspicuous by their absence from accounts of the monarchy (although Dionysius already envisages them among the followings of major figures),[6] but in the early republic they appear as the patricians' loyal retainers, a

[1] Schwartz (1905), 939-43. The right to defend a suit on another's behalf was severely restricted under early civil procedure (Kaser 1966, 146f.).

[2] Even if patrons did so act for clients, this would not demonstrate the client's non-citizen status (as Magdelain 1971, 106) any more than that of others so represented. In any case, Dionysius does not state that clients were *obliged* to act through their patron and apparently envisages the theoretical possibility of clients bringing patrons to court (cf. also 11.28.5-37.6). His reference to their votes confirms that he saw them as full citizens.

[3] Whence in part the alleged preference for wealthy clients in Plaut. *Men.* 573ff.

[4] The only specific examples are the offer by clients to pay the fines imposed on Camillus (with *tribules*: Livy 5.32.8; with kinsmen: Dion. Hal. 13.5) and L. Scipio (with kinsmen and friends: Livy 38.60.9). Both narratives are late creations and suspect; that of L. Scipio at least derives from Valerius Antias.

[5] The notion recurs in Cic. *De Rep.* 2.16; Festus 262L. (also Plut. *Romulus* 13). Cf. also Livy 6.18.5.

[6] Dion. Hal. 2.46.3; 4.55.3.

crucial makeweight to the free plebs and used, for example, for political support, canvassing, intimidation and violence.[1] Even given the historians' preoccupation with politics, the loyalty and services of the *cliens* seem here to be freely at the patron's disposal, far beyond the obligations of occasional financial aid or refraining from mutual mischief rehearsed in Dionysius' earlier reconstruction.

At a very general level the historians' accounts have an obvious plausibility. There were at most some fifty patrician *gentes* (lineages)[2] and their assumption and retention of political power until the early/mid-fourth century would be difficult to explain without the adhesion of substantial followings. However, the picture offered of the size of client followings is wildly inflated. The notion that individual late-sixth-century aristocrats like Ap. Claudius or the members of a powerful lineage like the Fabii in the early fifth century might have several thousand clients[3] simply does not square with any plausible hypothesis on contemporary Roman manpower. It is unlikely that the territory of Rome in this period would have supported many more than 10,000 adult males (if indeed that).[4] Consequently, on the historians' own apparent assumptions that patronage was widespread among the aristocracy but that a substantial number of citizens was not subject to it, simple arithmetic shows that client numbers for individual patrons will have been counted at most in one or two hundreds. Indeed, they could well have been much smaller. For myself I would conjecture that twenty to thirty was the upper limit for all but the exceptionally powerful: if mass clientship ever existed, it was in a much later period.

On other elements in the historians' accounts judgement is more difficult. A crucial case is the notion, found in Dionysius, that clients served in the Roman army, at least to the extent of taking the field

[1] Rouland (1979), 140-7.

[2] E.g. Mommsen (1864-79), 1.107ff. Several recent hypotheses on the development of the patriciate would reduce Mommsen's figure substantially; for discussion cf. *CAH* VII.2 (ed.2, forthcoming), chap.5 I(c).

[3] Claudii: Dion.Hal. 5.40.3 (5,000 including clients). Fabii: Dion.Hal. 9.15.3 (clients and comrades a majority of the 4,000); Festus 450L., 451L. (5,000 clients). Cf. Dion. Hal. 10.14.1 (Ap. Herdonius).

[4] See Ampolo (1980), 27-30 with the discussion in *CAH* VII.2, chap. 4 II(e).

with their patrons when the plebeians refused to serve.[1] Is this merely a piece of guesswork, a reconstruction of the likely patrician response to the plebeians' political tactic of refusing military service until their demands were met? Or is it a genuine tradition which Dionysius' contemporary Livy has for some reason ignored or suppressed?[2]

Such issues cannot be determined simply by analysis of the historians' own narratives. Not merely is the detail of their accounts often clearly anachronistic, incoherent or inconsistent,[3] but even the *patterns* in the appearance and functions of clientship in the historians provide no reliable evidence for its varying role, prevalence or significance. Livy is bewilderingly haphazard in his references to an institution in which he is clearly little interested. Dionysius, in keeping with his general interest in the social basis of aristocratic power,[4] shows a more consistent and thorough concern, but that engagement itself may mean that much of the relevant material is his own work and in any case only fragments of his history are preserved for the period after 443 BC, a factor overlooked by those who draw sweeping conclusions from the comparative dearth of allusions to *clientes* thereafter.[5] In consequence, we should restrict ourselves to the broader outlines of the historians' picture(s) of clientship and its role in the early republican period; even then such outlines remain tantalisingly fragile.

---

[1] Dion. Hal. 6.47.1; 7.19.2;10.15.5; 27.3; 43.2. Cf. 6.51.1; 7.64.3; 9.15.3; also Festus 450L., 451L.

[2] In 2.64.2 Livy envisages clients as members of the army-based centuriate assembly. Cf. also 3.16.5.

[3] In particular Livy's notion (2.56.3) that from 471 the plebeian assembly was organised by tribes to prevent the patriciate using their clients' votes to control tribunician elections makes little sense, especially as clients still appear as voters in that assembly (5.32.8); and if (as this latter passage may suggest) Livy means that the patricians could not now direct their clients' votes, he fails either to express or justify that notion.

[4] Cf. the analyses in Pabst (1969); also Poma (1981).

[5] Rouland (1979), 127f., 156. The virtual absence of *clientes* from Livy Books 6-10 is more likely to reflect his own indifference or the use of different sources than a secure knowledge of a decline in their importance.

Modern theories of early *clientela*

Most accounts of early clientship depend not on an independent analysis of the literary tradition as such but on wider conceptions of early Roman society and its development, and of the place which clientship most plausibly occupies within that framework. In the nineteenth century it was generally supposed that patronage originated either as the power exercised by a conquering immigrant people over a subject population[1] or more generally as the authority enjoyed by the individual *gentes* over outsiders who sought to attach themselves to the community by securing the protection of one of these constituent kin-groups;[2] in more recent scholarship clientship has increasingly been regarded as first and foremost a basic source of dependent labour for the wealthy elite,[3] with sometimes a resultant assimilation of its character to that of serfdom, at least in its earliest phase.[4]

These theories (which are not mutually exclusive) all, to a greater or lesser extent, presuppose that clientship had in some, at best vaguely defined, 'original' phase a radically different character and/or function from those which it possessed in the mid/late republican periods. That possibility cannot be rejected out of hand. Given the progressive transformation of Rome from a primitive village community or communities (perhaps first tangible to us archaeologically in the tenth century BC) to a powerful city-state that was the dominant power in Italy by the early third century, her social structures cannot have remained static and parallels can readily be found in other societies for the forms and/or functions of clientship suggested. Thus in central Rwanda what could perhaps be regarded as quasi-ethnic differentiation was accompanied by economic

---

[1] So e.g. Schwegler (1853-8), 1.640f.

[2] So above all Mommsen (1864); cf. id. (1887-8), 3.54-88.

[3] So e.g. Zancan (1935), 13ff.; Ferenczy (1976), 18; (1978/9); De Martino (1980).

[4] Neumann (1900).

exploitation in the institution of (*u*)*buhake* by which the pastoralist Tutsi reinforced their supremacy over the agriculturalist Hutu.[1] Initiated by an exchange of gifts accompanied by customary formulae, (*u*)*buhake* created a personal dependent relationship between individual Tutsi and Hutu which was nominally voluntary but in fact a practical necessity for all Hutu, who needed the protection (including support in the king's court) and assistance (including an initial gift of cattle) from a Tutsi lord if they were to escape arbitrary exploitation. For the Tutsi the relationship both reinforced their power and provided them with agricultural produce since work in the lord's fields (along with personal attendance) comprised the dependent's principal obligation. Similarly, the possible integrating function of dependent relationships can be illustrated from the pastoralist Mandari of the southern Sudan as described by Buxton.[2] Here an outsider who has lost kin and family (e.g. through defeat in war) seeks the protection of a member of a land-owning clan. Such a *timit* (though it is degrading so to address him) becomes attached to his host's lineage; he and his children take its name and although he can change his allegiance, in practice the relationship usually becomes hereditary. The *timit* performs specified duties for his host, including personal attendance and work in the host's fields. In return, he is helped to acquire a wife and homestead and is afforded general aid and protection, including support in the chief's courts.

Taken simply as examples such comparisons demonstrate only possibilities. Not only is there no uniform parallel in either case with the suggested character and operation of early Roman clientship[3] but the most limited survey of comparative data demonstrates the very different form and functions which may characterise dependent relations even in neighbouring states with superficially similar social

---

[1]   Lemarchand (1970), 36ff.; Maquet (1970), 117ff. For Hutu and Tutsi as 'ethnic strata' cf. Mair (1974), 178ff. This predominance probably derived from the military superiority of the invading Tutsi (Maquet 1970, 106; Mair 1974, 168f.). In a modified form (with no obligation of agricultural labour) (*u*)*buhake* could also obtain between two Tutsi and here had different effects, including the definition and distribution of authority within the ruling stratum and perhaps a reinforcement of its internal solidarity.

[2]   Buxton (1967).

[3]   Note also that Mair (1964), 171ff. assigns yet other, political functions to dependent relations in 'agricultural' African states.

and economic structures or indeed within the same state.[1] Such evidence is valuable precisely because it illuminates the *range* of possible characteristics which these relationships may assume, but also because it may identify social, political or economic factors which influence or even determine their structure and role. Such insights are useful, however, only if we can identify securely the structures of the society with which we are primarily concerned. Yet our evidence for the earliest phases of Roman society remains fragmentary and uncertain, despite the new horizons opened up by study of the material remains.[2] Any reconstruction of those phases has to be highly speculative and cannot serve as a satisfactory starting-point for an enquiry into clientship: for hypothesis has simply to be piled upon hypothesis.

This becomes clear if we consider the theory that the earliest Roman community was exclusive in character, comprising a specified quota of lineages whose members alone enjoyed full citizen rights and which utilised clientship as a mechanism for the integration of outsiders.[3] Not only is this hypothesis at variance with Roman social institutions when these first become to any degree discernible (in the sixth and fifth centuries),[4] but it is itself based on the highly dubious assumption that later *gens* rights and activities represent the distant and enfeebled echo of a lost centrality in Roman social, political and economic structures.[5] It is simply a further consequence of this hypothesis that the *cliens* is seen as originally attached to the *gens*

---

[1] For the first cf. e.g. Maquet (1971), 191ff.; for the second p.96 n.1.

[2] See, e.g., Ampolo (1970-71). The possibilities and difficulties are illustrated by the seventh-century tombs from Acqua Acetosa near Rome in which less prestigious burials are grouped around a major central deposition (Bedini 1978, 32). The lord and his retainers is óne possible interpretative model but even then the form and functions of the relationship would elude us.

[3] Partly as a further consequence, the character of early clientship is often reconstructed from the later position of other 'outsiders', notably freedmen and those who make a formal surrender to a Roman commander. But although in both instances there is some overlap in language and concepts with the *cliens* relationship, a uniform correlation, which would permit inferences from one to the other, cannot be assumed and the reductionist methodology implied should be firmly rejected.

[4] Cf. Capogrosso Colognesi (1980).

[5] Against this cf. Meyer (1953-8), 3.471ff.; Botsford (1907).

(rather than the individual patron). Yet there is no valid evidence for clients being attached to the *gens* as such,[1] regularly taking the *gens* name,[2] participating in lineage cults,[3] being allocated *gens* land (itself a modern myth)[4] or being subject to *gens* inheritance rights.[5] So far as we know anything about it, clientship was and remained an individual and personal bond.

Similar difficulties apply to theories which assert a primary economic function to early clientship. It is commonly supposed, for example, that clients were allocated small pieces of land and in return surrendered a portion of their produce or worked on the patron's land. Appeal is often made here to the assertion, derived from the second century AD antiquarian Festus, that 'senators were called "fathers" (*patres*) because they had granted parcels (*partes*) of land to humbler individuals as if to their own children' (289L. cf. 288L.), for although Festus does not specify clients and patrons, he clearly has them in mind. But Festus' supposition of land allocations is based purely on the etymological jingle of *patres-partes* and his comparison of the recipients with children on the derivation of *patronus* from *pater*. To use this passage as serious evidence that clients regularly enjoyed land grants as revocable gifts, like a son's *peculium*, is absurd, still more so to combine it with Dionysius' account which knows nothing of such gifts but does envisage a separate class of hired labourers occasionally given land by individual rulers.[6] Undoubtedly dependent labour was in short supply until the development of large-scale

---

[1]   Even in the narratives of the migration to Rome of the Sabine Ap. Claudius with his clients in c.504 only Suetonius (*Tib.*1) might (but does not necessarily) imply that it was clients of the lineage who participated; in other sources the *clientes* are those of Appius himself. Similarly in the defeat of the Fabian *gens* in their campaign against neighbouring Veii in 477, the clients who accompanied them may be conceived as those of individual Fabii.

[2]   M.Claudius, the client of the tyrannous Appius Claudius (Livy 3.44.5; Dion.Hal. 11.28.5 (450 BC)), is fictitious and isolated.

[3]   Not shown by the (fictitious) narrative of a few clients *accompanying* their Fabian patrons in Dion.Hal.9.19.1.

[4]   The narrative of Ap.Claudius' arrival in Rome, even if historical in detail, shows only an individual securing allocations of public land for his *clientes*.

[5]   Cic. *De Orat.* 1.176 merely raises questions which we cannot answer (Watson 1971a, 182) and in any case concerns a freedman's son, to whom particular rules may have applied.

[6]   3.1.5; 4.9.8; 13.1; 6.51.1; 53.2; 9.44.7; cf. 8.87.5.

slavery, perhaps from the fourth century, but it was primarily *nexum* (debt-bondage) which met that need.[1] Whilst some clients may, for example, have been called on when additional temporary labour was needed, we should be wary of assuming even regular exactions from the generality of clients,[2] and certainly clientship was never comparable to serfdom. There is no evidence that *clientes* were ever bound to the land or restricted in the disposition of their persons or property or that patrons had rights of this kind over them. Moreover, whereas *nexum* caused considerable social and political tensions and was (significantly) abolished in 326 or 313 as greater resources of slave labour became available,[3] our sources contain no echo of similar disputes arising from the exaction of labour services or dues in kind; nor do we hear of the large-scale protests that on this hypothesis must have precipitated the transformation of the institution into its later, very different form. The conclusion must be that if the provision of such goods or services featured in the recompense offered by a client to his patron, such assistance was normally viewed as a voluntary prestation and for the *cliens* was not usually on a scale that caused serious difficulty or jeopardised his own viability.

More promising are hypotheses which see clients as forming the military retinue of individual aristocrats.[4] True, theories that cities like Rome owed their origin to the confraternisation of warrior associations, whose members supplied dependent outsiders with arms and land in return for (*inter alia*) military aid,[5] remain purely speculative. But in the sixth and early fifth centuries, we find in central Italy pre-eminent individuals apparently able to command followings of comrades (*sodales*) for independent military action. Our evidence centres principally on such legendary figures as Mastarna or Coriolanus but whilst some of it may be fiction, the social patterns implied are distinctive and plausible in the context of (sub-) archaic society[6] and may be reflected in the recently discovered fifth-century

---

[1] Weber (1968), 3.1355; Finley (1981).
[2] Cf. Weber (1924), 205; Richard (1978), 173.
[3] Cf. T.J. Cornell in *CAH* VII.2 (ed.2), chap. 8 II.
[4] See especially Alföldi (1967).
[5] Weber (1968), 3.1285ff.; 1356.
[6] Versnel (1980); (1982).

dedication at Satricum by comrades or associates of a P. Valerius;[1] whether he is Roman or Latin, Valerius appears here as the focus of a band of peer-group associates of the kind envisaged in the emperor Claudius' account of Mastarna.[2] It would be attractive to suppose that *clientes* also featured in such followings, but the limitations of our evidence must again be observed. On the one hand, we cannot assume that such followings enjoyed a long-term cohesion;[3] these military enterprises may have been occasional phenomena and increasingly subject to communal restrictions. On the other hand, even in societies where the military functions of a following are fundamental or at least semi-permanent, such bonds assume also a more general civil aspect, not least to preserve their solidarity and continuity.[4] Whilst, therefore, a military dimension to clientship cannot be excluded, it is not a sufficient explanation of either the institution as it operated in the archaic period or of its later survival into a period in which it ceased to fulfil such a role.

Clientela and archaic Roman society

If we cannot base our account of early clientship on either the literary tradition as such or on a reconstruction of primitive Roman society, we must adopt a different strategy and seek to isolate the most significant characteristics of the relationship in its mid/late republican form. Those basic features can then be assessed against what we know of Roman society in the sixth and fifth centuries, the earliest phase for which we can form a coherent and not entirely speculative picture of its essential social, political and economic structures. We can then determine whether a comparable character to clientship is credible also for that period. Inevitably such a procedure relies on a questionable argument from silence and by its own premises makes insufficient allowance for the possibility of major change. But if such change occurred, it now lies beyond recovery, and the limitations of

[1] De Simone (1980); Guarducci (1980).
[2] *ILS* 212; Versnel (1980); (1982).
[3] Cf. Bremmer (1982).
[4] Conceivably the *sodalitates* of Twelve Tables 8.27 represent a social expression of such peer-group associations.

method imposed by our evidence must be recognised but also acted upon.

In the mid/late republic, clientship was archetypally a dependent relationship between two citizens in which the difference in power (and status) between the two parties was clearly acknowledged and is probably already implicit in the term 'cliens'.[1] It was essentially a personal ('face to face'), and in principle a voluntary, relationship freely entered into, often on the initiative of the dependent and as the result of a specific benefaction. Like friendship (*amicitia*) and guest-friendship (*hospitium*), it could become hereditary but with no indication that this brought any stigma to the client. It found practical expression in mutual services, not unilateral impositions or exactions, and was multi-purpose rather than confined to specific specialist aid. Although certain services may have become customary, the reciprocal obligations involved, and the bond itself, were never prescribed by legislation and hence were potentially flexible according to the status and the needs of the parties concerned. It follows that the relationship was not sustained by legal sanction: even if it were historical, the provision on clientship in the Twelve Tables would be little more than a pious wish.[2] The fact that patron-client bonds were not legally enforceable, and more generally were neither formally regulated nor directly entailed by the institutional framework of Roman society, meant that potentially such bonds were particularly precarious in their attempt to link the provision of specific goods and services to a stable, long-term pattern of reciprocal exchange.[3] Hence, whilst patron-client bonds rested ultimately on the mutual self-interest of both parties and their peers, this was overlaid with norms of mutual obligation which considerations of honour (and more general social pressures) required the patron in particular to observe,[4] a feature also perhaps implied in the description of the *cliens* as 'in the *fides*' of his patron.[5]

---

[1] The etymology is disputed (see Rouland 1979, 19-22) but on all the principal modern theories the fact of dependence is implicit or explicit.

[2] Mommsen (1864), 385.

[3] Eisenstadt and Roniger (1980), 70f.; cf. Powell (1970), 424.

[4] Cf. Eisenstadt and Roniger (1980), 71f.

[5] On this see Rich below.

Further, clientship involved no formal ceremony[1] and conferred no legal rights or formal power over the client's person or property. There are no grounds, for example, for believing that patrons had rights of seizure or inheritance against their clients' property[2] or that the term 'patronus', as a derivative of 'pater' (father), signifies at any stage the exercise of paternal power over the *cliens* any more than it does for the freedman.[3] Such fictive use of (quasi-) kinship terminology is a recurrent feature of patron-client relations[4] and may here have served to signal the dependant's deference and his ranking of the patron and his protective or gubernatorial role on a level comparable to that of a father.[5] Certainly the *cliens*, though he may attend on his patron, remains in charge of his own affairs, with his own household, property and kin; he does not become formally part of his patron's lineage or *familia* (household); indeed, the fact that he did not (it seems) participate in the patron's family cult may show that the client had always stood outside the *familia*, given the inherent conservatism of religious practice.[6] What appears to emerge is a relationship which might (if circumstances so favoured it) be exploited by the patron but where the normal expectation was of the observance of customary obligations and mutual rights on both sides, a conception emphasised and reinforced by two pieces of late-third-century legislation, the *leges Cincia* and *Publicia*. These sought (it seems) to prevent the customary gifts from clients to their patrons

[1]   On the modern fiction of *applicatio* see Badian (1958), 7-9.

[2]   Cic. *De Orat.* 1.177 is too obscure to permit any such inference (cf. Watson 1971a, 187) and there is no evidence for the exercise of statute-based guardianship over the children of *clientes*, as we would expect if patrons enjoyed intestate inheritance rights to their property.

[3]   Cf. Cosentini (1948 and 1950); also Watson (1975), 98-110. Cosentini's emphasis on social norms rather than legal rules and on the social dependence rather than juridical subjection of freedmen in the archaic period runs parallel to the conception of clientship advanced here and illuminates the partial assimilation of the two relationships.

[4]   Scott (1972), 94.

[5]   Cf. also the comparison or ranking of the obligations to and of a client with those to and of kinsmen (Dion.Hal. 2.10.2; 4; Aulus Gellius *Noctes Atticae* 5.13.1ff. (quoting Cato, Masurius Sabinus and Caesar); 20.1.40).

[6]   Contrast Fustel de Coulanges (1980), 219. Similarly, there is no evidence that patrons could surrender a client to a third party he had injured, as heads of household could do with those subject to them.

from deteriorating into a mode of economic exploitation;[1] here the potential transformation to a more explicitly oppressive, even commercial relationship is both exemplified and nipped in the bud.

A patron-client relationship of this kind matches in virtually every particular the distinguishing characteristics attributed to such bonds by Eisenstadt and Roniger in their recent theoretical studies.[2] Can it be accommodated within what we know or can reasonably surmise of Rome under the later monarchy and in the early republic?[3] Rome in this period was a centrally organised city-state controlling a fitfully expanding but compact territory. All members of the community enjoyed citizen rights but for most these brought minimal political participation or power. For within the citizen body there was a considerable degree of economic and social stratification, which had already created a recognisable wealthy elite as far back as the eighth century. This elite by no means monopolised the primary productive resource (land) - indeed, land-ownership was probably quite widely dispersed among the citizen-body - but it had clearly established a position of pre-eminence which found overt expression in the emergence of a hereditary aristocracy, the patriciate, claiming under the early republic a monopoly of public office, power and privilege. Correspondingly, there was a clear concentration of political, military, judicial and religious power, authority and expertise in the hands of the king or chief magistrates, the aristocratic council and the priests.

The basic social unit, the nuclear family, was reinforced by its wider kinship ties, which, at least among the aristocracy, reached as far as the institutionalised recognition of *gentes*. Though some *gentes* had communal religious foci and their members enjoyed secondary rights of inheritance and guardianship, they do not in general appear to have acted as corporate social or economic units, and our scanty evidence suggests that they did not constitute closed communities in the sense that they discouraged their members from seeking assistance outside their own ranks. On the contrary, it is likely that the individual, at all social levels, sought to acquire and utilise the aid of

---

[1]   Livy 34.4.9 (Watson 1971b, 73f.); Macrobius, *Sat.* 1.7.33.

[2]   Eisenstadt and Roniger (1980), 49f.; (1981), 276f.; (1984), 48f.; cf. Scott (1972), 92f.

[3]   For what follows see *CAH* VII.2 (ed.2) chaps 4-5.

non-kin extensively and that at least before the fifth century Rome itself, like other central Italian communities, had an apparently 'open' character, enabling individuals to move freely from one community to another without serious difficulties of integration or (probably) immediate loss of contact with their own original kin-group.[1]

Eisenstadt and Roniger identify a number of societal characteristics that are typically associated with clientelism:[2] the relative incapacity of the central authority to impose its own norms, the internal weakness of the various societal units and their inability to achieve their objectives (political, social or economic) from their own resources, the comparative weakness of corporate kinship units (particularly among the lower social strata) and a set of clearly marked economic, social and political inequalities (usually with a close link between semi-ascriptive hierarchical status and access to power and public goods). In a fair measure archaic Rome fulfilled these criteria and provided conditions which would foster ties of dependency. For where power and knowledge were concentrated in the hands of a pre-eminent elite, the powerful could always offer a protection which the lesser man might often be unable to deploy from his own resources. That protection might take the form of economic aid, either through direct assistance or through influence on magisterial decisions; we have no reliable evidence for such aid but clearly cannot exclude it. It might certainly embrace legal advice and assistance. Our knowledge of Roman law and legal procedure, particularly before the Twelve Tables, is highly controversial but we are manifestly confronted with a society in which the individual had to secure redress for his own injuries and might encounter serious obstacles to such action,[3] including the fact that knowledge, creation and administration of the law were an aristocratic preserve. It would, however, be imprudent to assume that patronage was restricted to this sphere alone. The assistance and protection of a powerful man must often have been a valuable guarantee against more general abuse or exploitation, and

---

[1] Cf. Ampolo (1976-7); (1981); Sherwin-White (1973), 33-5; T.J. Cornell in *CAH* VII.2 (ed.2) chap. 6 II and III; also the discussion of *sodales* above. On the significance of such 'open' social and political structures cf. Wolf (1966).

[2] Eisenstadt and Roniger (1980), esp. 64ff.; (1981), esp. 284f.; (1984), 203f.; cf. Scott (1972), 101.

[3] von Ihering (1909).

beyond that the relationship could readily assume the function of multi-purpose assistance in a community where the central power was unable or reluctant to intervene actively to assist or protect the individual and where he was almost entirely reliant on the aid he could mobilise personally.

Equally, however, individual aristocrats needed all the support they could muster both for their own mutual rivalry and increasingly to preserve aristocratic power against outside challenge. At the individual level, of course, patronage above all defined and enhanced status, but that may also have found expression in particular services, in which occasional gifts and military attendance or assistance may have featured,[1] but not exclusively. Clients may also have acted as more general attendants and assistants with a concomitant range of personal services according to the occasion and needs of the individual patron. In this way a man's *clientes* could have formed something of a personal retinue[2] and a number of the rituals and expectations that later surround the relationship could be interpreted as attenuated survivals of this earlier character. The tradition of the morning greeting and of attendance on the *patronus* and the assimilation of the bond to that between kinsmen would all fit this hypothesis. So would the expectation of commensality. Communal feasting was an important and regular expression of the solidarity of the *curiae* (the earliest surviving division of the Roman people), probably already of the priestly colleges and perhaps among *sodales*. If it played a comparable role in patron-client relations, it is likely to have reinforced both the affective aspect of the bond and patronal control,[3] as well perhaps as encouraging a sense of communal identity among the man's clients themselves.[4]

If, therefore, it is not difficult to identify factors which encouraged such ties of dependence, nonetheless Rome in the archaic period only partially matches the societal conditions characteristic of a fully

---

[1] So the assignment of two horses to some of the early cavalry (Festus 247L.; Granius Licinianus 26.12, p.2 Criniti) will imply the use of 'squires', as in archaic Greece (Greenhalgh 1973, 59ff. etc.).

[2] Weber (1968), esp. 3.1355f.

[3] Cf. D'Arms (1984), 338; 344ff.

[4] This would be further reinforced if (as is possible) clientship in this period often had a strongly local character.

clientelistic society[1] and there are a number of countervailing factors, including a spasmodic capacity for autonomous community-wide action by strata outside the elite and, to a lesser extent, the competing effectiveness of other horizontal bonds, which could have limited the prevalence of clientship. Moreover, together with other characteristics (especially competition within the aristocracy itself), they would have tended also to moderate significantly the degree of subjection (and therefore exploitation) involved. As a result, they could have created the situation plausibly envisaged by the annalistic narratives of the early republic, in which many plebeians were not the clients of patrician patrons, and could have conferred on the relationship much of its later character as a voluntary social bond of mutual benefit to both parties:

(a)   Although those who are weak in kin are always most likely to need patronage, we cannot assume that clients in general fell into this category and for many *clientes* kinsmen, neighbours and friends may have continued to offer alternative or supplementary sources of aid.[2]

(b)   As a consequence of this and of aristocratic rivalry, there may well have been competition for the adhesion of dependants, a situation further complicated by the introduction of election to office in the early republic and by the fact that changes in the balance of power within the ranks of the aristocracy meant a varying and fluctuating ability to provide the protection and assistance required.

(c)   The probably restricted number of clients dependent on the individual patron[3] and the compact character of the early Roman community are not only likely to have made the patron-client bond inherently closer than in later times but they would also more clearly expose abuse and exploitation to public knowledge and disapprobation.

(d)   The introduction, in or by the mid-sixth century,[4] of 'hoplite' armour and tactics gave military primacy to the infantry phalanx. As a result, aristocrats could claim no monopoly or even pre-eminence in

[1]   Similarly, the cultural orientations associated by Eisenstadt and Roniger (1980), 68f.; (1981), 285f.; (1984), 206f. with clientelism seem at best only partially applicable to archaic Rome.

[2]   Cf. Millet and Garnsey and Woolf in this volume.

[3]   Cf. Scott (1972), 94f. with my (independently formulated) conjecture (above).

[4]   Stary (1981), 164.

their contribution to the defence and expansion of the Roman state. Moreover, the fact that troops provided their own equipment and the manner of 'phalanx' warfare reinforced the sense of common identity and importance and so far as *clientes* qualified for such service, that could only enhance their status and limit the demands which patrons could make of them individually or collectively.

(e)   Finally, the emergence of the plebeian movement in the fifth and fourth centuries BC must have strengthened the position of clients vis-à-vis their patrons. As already noted, the mere fact of the plebeian movement's survival and progressive successes seems to indicate that clientship, at least to a patrician patron, was far from universal. Of course, some clients may on occasion have actively supported plebeian demands and our sources' general (but not uniform: Livy 6.18.5) dichotomy between clients and free plebs may be a misleading stereotype, concealing a more fluid political situation. Nonetheless, in general the patriciate must have been able to rely on the loyalty of their clients to retain their hold on power, while for its part the vigorous leadership required by the plebeian movement (and its later demands for admission to office) imply a reservoir of support of relatively high status outside the patriciate. That in turn suggests the existence of a substantial element within the ranks of those who qualified for the heavy infantry with similar independence; indeed, the whole early history of the plebeian movement indicates that such 'yeomanry'[1] were a crucial factor in its creation and in many of its specific achievements.[2] And the existence of an independent 'popolo' with its own representatives opened up the possibility of oppressed clients seeking tribunician aid against their exploiters, a development which the aristocracy could clearly ill-afford.

A corollary of the account of clientship offered here, particularly the suggestion that *clientes* were in general able to avoid reduction to

---

[1]   Weber's term: (1922), 588.

[2]   Weber (1968), 3.1348f.; I have tried to argue the case in detail in *CAH* VII.2 (ed.2) chap.5. In contrast, Momigliano (1966), esp. 20-3; (1967), 211-19; (1969) sees the plebs as those who did not qualify for the heavy infantry, which was dominated by the patricians and their clients. In this perspective clientship served in part to reinforce the solidarity of the upper strata of Roman society and thereby their dominance over the poorer *plebeii* (cf. above p.96 n.1). This seems to me to over-simplify a more complex situation (Drummond 1970, 202).

a position of subjection, is that many clients may have come from the more prosperous levels of Roman society. That is in any case likely if *clientes* were an important factor in the patrician ability to resist plebeian demands. And so far as clients may have acted as a kind of retinue, reinforcing the individual's prestige and performing a variety of personal services, aristocratic self-interest would inevitably favour such dependants. However, since the relationship was presumably sufficiently flexible to be utilised at a variety of social levels, the possibility of much humbler *clientes* cannot be excluded[1] and it is obviously here, if anywhere, that we should seek dependants whose principal obligations (and advantages to the patron) included the provision of labour and/or produce. The mere existence and certainly the scale of patronage at such lower social levels is impossible to establish, but it was evidently not sufficiently prevalent (or efficacious to the dependant) to prevent numbers of individuals falling victim to debt-bondage and we should perhaps be sceptical of assumptions that it was widespread.

Conclusion

Dionysius saw clientship as an instrument of social and political concord, imposed from above. In fact such bonds may have first developed spontaneously from below but that does not preclude subsequent organisation and reinforcement of client ties by individual patrons or even the aristocracy as a whole.[2] And Dionysius' view of the socio-political function of clientship also admits of further development. What may be called the 'ideology' of clientship - and the character of the bond which that ideology presupposed - can be regarded as a crucial factor in its wider social role as a means of reconciling aristocratic pre-eminence with the requirements of a citizen community. For the notion that Rome comprised such a community, in which each member has certain basic rights at civil law and obligations of mutual assistance and defence, was already

---

[1] If the sanction in the Twelve Tables against patrons who 'did mischief' to a client were authentic (above), this might imply the existence of clients whose interests could more readily be sacrificed without significant social or personal repercussions for the patron.

[2] On the alternative possibilities in general cf. Flynn (1974), 148f.

fundamental.[1] In this context the character of the *patronus-cliens* relationship as a voluntary personal bond between full citizens can be seen as fulfilling an integrating role, reconciling the realities of power and its unequal distribution with the need to preserve the sense of common citizen identity in a way that the overtly exploitative debt-bondage signally failed to do.

Such functionalist analyses are open to criticism, however, for their neglect of the elements of tension and control inherent in or fostered by clientship.[2] Archaic Roman clientship as analysed here owes its form, prevalence and scope precisely to the interplay of conflicting political, social and economic forces within Roman society in that period. Moreover, although it lay outside the formal power structures of the Roman state and was never, so far as is known, employed as a mechanism for the determination or allocation of public authority, rights or obligations,[3] it is itself a product of the distribution of power in Roman society and in practice involves the client in at least a partial surrender of independent direct access to particular public goods (such as the assertion of his rights at law) which citizenship theoretically implies but which his situation makes it impossible for him to exercise effectively;[4] depending on the viable alternatives available, the formally voluntary character of the bond may in this context conceal a strong element of 'moral coercion'.[5] Furthermore, as Boissevain notes in his study of Sicilian patronage,[6] such relationships tend to perpetuate the conditions which fostered their initial development. Although it must remain doubtful whether patronage commonly made a major direct contribution to the patron's material advantage through the receipt of goods and services on a significant scale, it was an overt expression of his power and presumably brought public esteem for his readiness to lend aid and

[1]   Cf. *CAH* VII.2 (ed.2) chaps. 4-5.

[2]   Cf. Lemarchand (1981), 9f. for recent critiques.

[3]   So too there is no evidence that under the monarchy formal relations between the king and his subordinates constituted general dependency relations *per se* (as, for example, in Ankole: Oberg 1940).

[4]   For clientelism as a semi-institutionalised attempt to limit potential free access to particular goods and/or markets cf. Eisenstadt and Roniger (1980), 58f.; (1981), 280.

[5]   Flynn (1974).

[6]   Boissevain (1966), 30.

protection to those of lower status. And for the aristocracy collectively these arrangements embedded their power in the social fabric, made its exercise more acceptable and offered a means both of controlling those subject to it and of countering the claims of those outside it; as an instrument of social and political control, therefore, its importance was considerable.[1]

Nor was this position altered by the plebeian successes of the fourth century. We have no means of knowing how far leading plebeian families had succeeded in recruiting clients of their own[2] or of estimating the importance of such clients (or more general 'clientelistic' behaviour) in the plebeian agitation that culminated in regular tenure of state offices by a plebeian elite. What is clear, however, is that the plebeian movement did not challenge the socio-political order as such: the object of the plebeian elite was to secure a position of privilege and power, comparable to that enjoyed by the patriciate but within the existing framework. In consequence, if they did not already have followings of their own, they will rapidly have acquired them once they were admitted to office, as a symbol and reinforcement of their own pre-eminence. Hence clientship, and the expectations and outlook it fostered, remained a central instrument of Roman socio-political control; and Dionysius, for all his misplaced moral gloss and elitist viewpoint, must be correct in supposing that it was a major factor in the relative political stability which (rightly or wrongly) he regarded as so laudable a feature of Rome's earlier historical development.

[1]   As Cicero's discussion in the lost portion of the *De Republica* may have stressed (cf. ib.2.16). Cf. in general Flynn (1974).

[2]   This will be likely if economic assistance of the dependent was an important factor in some patron-client relationships since evidently (and perhaps increasingly) the patriciate did not enjoy a monopoly of wealth.

Bibliography

Alföldi, A. (1967), 'Zur Struktur des Römerstaates im 5. Jahrhundert v. Chr.', in *Les origines de la république romaine* (Entretiens Hardt 13), 223-78. Geneva.

Ampolo, C. (1970-1), 'Su alcuni mutamenti sociali nel Lazio tra l'VIII e il V secolo', *Dialoghi di Archeologia* 4-5, 37-68.

Ampolo, C. (1976-7), 'Demarato. Osservazioni sulla mobilità sociale arcaica', *Dialoghi di Archeologia* 9-10, 333-45.

Ampolo, C. (1980), 'Le condizioni materiali della produzione. Agricoltura e paesaggio agrario', *Dialoghia di Archeologia* n.s. 2, 15-46.

Ampolo, C. (1981), 'I gruppi etnici in Roma arcaica: posizione del problema e fonti', in *Gli Etruschi e Roma. Studi in onore di M. Pallottino*, 45-70. Rome.

Badian, E. (1958), *Foreign Clientelae (264-70 BC)*. Oxford.

Balsdon, J.P.V.D. (1971), 'Dionysius on Romulus: a political pamphlet?', *Journal of Roman Studies* 61, 18-27.

Bedini, A. (1978), 'Abitato protostorico in località Acqua Acetosa Laurentina', *Archeologia Laziale* 1, 30-4.

Boissevain, J. (1966), 'Patronage in Sicily', *Man* n.s. 1, 18-33.

Botsford, G.W. (1907), 'Some problems connected with the Roman *gens*', *Political Science Quarterly* 22, 663-92.

Brecht, Chr.H. (1938), *Perduellio. Eine Studie zu ihrer begrifflichen Abgrenzung im römischen Strafrecht bis zum Ausgang der Republik*. Munich.

Bremmer, J. (1982), 'The *suodales* of Poplios Valesios', *Zeitschrift für Papyrologie und Epigraphik* 47, 133-47.

Buxton, J. (1967), 'Clientship among the Mandari of the Southern Sudan', in R. Cohen and J. Middleton (eds.),*Comparative Political Systems: Studies on the Politics of Pre-Industrial Societies*, 229-45. New York.

Capogrossi Colognesi, L. (1980), 'Alcuni problemi di storia romana arcaica: *ager publicus*, *gentes* e clienti', *Bolletino dell' Instituto di Divitto romano* 83, 29-65.

Cosentini, C. (1948 and 1950), *Studi sui liberti: contributo allo studio della condizione giuridica dei liberti cittadini* (Università di Catania. Pubblicazioni della Facoltà di Giurisprudenza 11 and 14). 2 vols. Catania.

Cuq, E. (1919), 'La juridiction des édiles d'après *Men.* 590-3', *Revue des Études Anciennes* 21, 249-58.

D'Arms, J.H. (1984), 'Control, companionship and *clientela*: some social functions of the Roman communal meal', *Échos du Monde Classique/Classical Views* n.s. 3, 327-48.

Drummond, A. (1970), Review-discussion of *Les origines de la république romaine* (Entretiens Hardt 13) in *Journal of Roman Studies* 60, 199-202.

De Simone, C. (1980), 'L'aspetto linguistico', in C.M. Stibbe (ed.), *Lapis Satricanus* (Nederlands Instituut te Rome, Scripta Minora 5), 71-94. The Hague.

Eisenstadt, S.N. and Roniger, L. (1980), 'Patron-client relations as a model of structuring social exchange', *Comparative Studies in Society and History* 22, 42-77.

Eisenstadt, S.N. and Roniger, L. (1981), 'The study of patron-client relations and recent developments in sociological theory', in S.N. Eistenstadt and L. Roniger (eds.), *Political Clientelism, Patronage and Development*, 271-95. Beverly Hills-London.

Eisenstadt, S.N. and Roniger, L. (1984), *Patrons, Clients and Friends.* Cambridge.

Ferenczy E. (1976), *From the Patrician State to the Patricio-Plebeian State.* Budapest.

Ferenczy, E. (1978-9), 'Clientela e schiavitù nella repubblica romana primitiva', *Index* 8, 167-72.

Finley, M.I. (1981), 'Debt-bondage and the problem of slavery', in Finley, *Economy and Society in Ancient Greece* (ed. R.P. Saller and B.D. Shaw), 150-66. London.

Flynn, P. (1974), 'Class, clientelism and coercion: some mechanisms of internal dependency and control', *Journal of Commonwealth and Comparative Politics* 12, 133-56.

Fustel de Coulanges, N.D. (1890), *The Ancient City.* Baltimore-London.

Greenhalgh, P.A.L. (1973), *Early Greek Warfare.* Cambridge.

Guarducci, M. (1980), 'L'epigrafe arcaica di Satricum e Publio Valerio', *Rendiconti Accademia Lincei* ser. 8. 35, 479-89.

Heinze, R. (1929), 'Fides', *Hermes* 64, 140-66.

Ihering, R. von (1909), 'Reich und Arm im altrömischen Civilprozess', in id. *Scherz und Ernst in der Jurisprudenz* 175-232. 10th ed. Leipzig.

Kaser, M. (1966), *Das römische Zivilprozessrecht* (Handbuch der Altertumswissenschaft X. 3. 4). Munich.

Latte, K. (1960), *Römische Religionsgeschichte* (Handbuch der Altertumswissenschaft V. 4.). Munich.

Lemarchand, R. (1970), *Rwanda and Burundi.* London.

Lemarchand, R. (1981), 'Comparative political clientelism: structure, process and optic', in S.N. Eisenstadt and R. Lemarchand (eds.), *Political Clientelism, Patronage and Development*, 7-32. Beverly Hills-London.

Magdelain, A. (1971), 'Remarques sur la société romaine archaïque', *Revue des Études Latines* 49, 103-27.

Mair, L. (1964), *Primitive Government.* London.

Mair, L. (1974), *African Societies.* London.

Maquet, J. (1970), 'Rwanda castes', in A. Tuden and L. Plotnicov (eds.), *Social Stratification in Africa*, 93-124. New York-London.

Maquet, J. (1971), *Power and Society in Africa.* London.

Martino, F. De (1980), 'Clienti e condizioni materiali in Roma arcaica', in *Philias Charin. Miscellanea di studi classici in onore di Eugenio Manni* 2, 679-705. Rome.

Meyer, Ed. (1953-8),*Geschichte des Altertums*, 5 vols., 6th ed. Basle.

Momigliano, A. (1966), 'Procum patricium', *Journal of Roman Studies* 56, 16-24 = id. (1969),*Quarto contributo alla storia degli studi classici e del mondo antico*, 377-94. Rome.

Momigliano, A. (1967), 'Osservazioni sulla distinzione fra patrizi e plebei', in *Les origines de la république romaine* (Entretiens Hardt 13) 199-221. Geneva. = id. (1969), *Quarto contributo alla storia degli studi classici e del mondo antico*, 419-36. Rome.

Momigliano, A. (1969), 'The origins of the Roman republic', in C.S. Singleton (ed.), *Interpretation: Theory and Practice*, 1-34. Baltimore. = id. (1975), *Quinto contributo alla storia degli studi classici e del mondo antico*, 293-332. Rome.

Mommsen, Th. (1864), 'Die römische Clientel', in id. *Römische Forschungen*, I, 355-85. Berlin.

Mommsen, Th. (1864-79), *Römische Forschungen*, 2 vols. Berlin.

Mommsen, Th. (1887-8), *Römisches Staatsrecht*, 3 vols. 3rd ed. Leipzig.

Neumann, K.J. (1900), *Die Grundherrschaft der römischen Republik, die Bauernbefreiung und die Entstehung der servianischen Verfassung.* Strasbourg.

Oberg, K. (1940), 'The kingdom of Ankole in Uganda', in M. Forte and E.E. Evans-Pritchard (eds.), *African Political Systems*, 121-62. London.

Pabst, W. (1969), *Quellenkritische Studien zur inneren römischen Geschichte der älteren Zeit bei T. Livius und Dionys von Halikarnass* (diss. Innsbruck).

Pohlenz, M. (1924), 'Eine politische Tendenzschrift aus Caesars Zeit', *Hermes* 59, 157-89.

Pollock, F. and Maitland, F.W. (1898), *The History of English Law before the Time of Edward I*, 2nd ed. Cambridge (reprinted Cambridge, 1968).

Poma, G. (1981), 'Schiavi e schiavitù in Dionigi di Alicarnasso', *Rivista storia dell' Antichità* 11, 69-101.

Powell, J.D. (1970), 'Peasant society and clientelistic politics', *American Political Science Review* 64, 411-25.

Richard, J.-Cl. (1978), *Les origines de la plèbe romaine* (Bibliothèque des Écoles Françaises d'Athènes et de Rome 232). Paris.

Rouland, N. (1979), *Pouvoir politique et dépendance personelle dans l'antiquité romaine. Genèse et rôle des rapports de clientèle* (Collection Latomus 166). Brussels.

Schwartz, E. (1905), 'Dionysius von Halikarnassos', Pauly-Wissowa, *Real-Encyklopädie* 5, 934-61.

Schwegler, A. (1853-8), *Römische Geschichte*, 3 vols. Tübingen.

Scott, J.C. (1972), 'Patron-client politics and political change in SE Asia', *American Political Science Review* 66, 91-113.

Sherwin-White, A.N. (1973), *The Roman Citizenship*, 2nd ed. Oxford.

Stary, P.F. (1981), *Zur eisenzeitlichen Bewaffnung und Kampfesweise in Mittelitalien*. Mainz.

Tondo, S. (1963), 'Il "sacramentum militiae" nell' ambiente culturale romano-italico', *Studia et Documenta Historiae et Iuris* 29, 1-131.

Versnel, H.S. (1980), 'Historical implications', in C.M. Stibbe (ed.), *Lapis Satricanus* (Nederlands Instituut te Rome, Scripta Minora 5), 95-150. The Hague.

Versnel, H.S. (1982), 'Die neue Inschrift von Satricum in historischer Sicht', *Gymnasium* 89, 193-235.

Watson, A. (1971a), *The Law of Succession in the Later Roman Republic*. Oxford.

Watson, A. (1971b), *Roman Private Law Around 200 BC*. Edinburgh.

Watson, A. (1972), 'Roman private law and the *leges regiae*', *Journal of Roman Studies* 62, 100-5.

Watson, A. (1975), *Rome of the Twelve Tables. Persons and Property*. Princeton.

Weber, M. (1922), *Wirtschaft und Gesellschaft* (Grundriss der Sozialökonomik Abt. III). Tübingen. Translated as:

Weber, M. (1968), *Economy and Society: An Outline of Interpretative Sociology*, 3 vols. New York.

Weber, M. (1924), *Gesammelte Aufsätze zur Social- und Wirtschaftsgeschichte*. Tübingen.

Wolf, E.R. (1966), 'Kinship, friendship and patron-client relations in complex societies', in M. Banton (ed.), *The Social Anthropology of Complex Societies*, 1-22. London.

Zancan, L. (1935), *Ager publicus. Ricerche di storia e di diritto romano*. Padua.

Chapter 5
Patronage and interstate relations in the Roman republic

John Rich

It has been widely held that many of Rome's relations with other states may be interpreted in terms of *clientela*. This doctrine has recently come under attack. In this paper I shall attempt to defend and reformulate it.

Theories of interstate *clientela*

Proculus, a jurist of the first century AD, in the course of a discussion of *postliminium*, maintained that peoples who had a treaty with Rome requiring them 'courteously to uphold the majesty of the Roman people' were still free, and illustrated the point by drawing an analogy between the Romans' relationship with such peoples and individual Romans' relationship with their clients:

> For this provision is added so that it should be understood that one of these peoples is superior, not that the other is not free: just as we understand that our clients are free, although they are not equal to us in influence, rank or power, so it is to be understood that those who are required courteously to uphold our majesty are free.[1]

---

[1]   *Dig.* 49.15.7.1: *hoc enim adicitur ut intellegatur alterum populum superiorem esse, non ut intellegatur alterum esse non liberum: et quemadmodum clientes nostros intellegimus liberos esse, etiamsi neque auctoritate neque dignitate neque viri[bus] nobis [par]es sunt, sic eos, qui maiestatem nostram comiter conservare debent, liberos esse intellegendum est.* Cf. Saller above.

In the sixteenth and seventeenth centuries some of the founding fathers of modern international law, like Bodin, Grotius and Zouche, used this passage in support of their view that an unequal alliance is not incompatible with sovereignty.[1] Grotius illustrated his discussion of the point from ancient history with, as usual, remarkable erudition and understanding.

It is, however, to the great nineteenth-century historian of Rome, Mommsen, that we must look for the origins of the modern interpretation of Rome's relations with other states in terms of *clientela*.[2] Mommsen's starting point was his conception of *clientela* itself. *Clientela*, he held, was originally a relationship between Romans and foreigners, whether as individuals or as communities. Juridically, there were only two types of relationship between Romans and foreigners: 'guest-friendship' (*hospitium*) and *clientela*. In the primitive Roman state only the patricians were citizens, and the plebeians were foreigners who had entered the Roman state as clients of the patricians either by leaving their home states for Rome as individuals or through their state's making an act of surrender (*deditio*) to Rome and so ceasing to exist. It was only by a later development, once the plebeians had acquired full citizenship, that *clientela* relations came to be formed between full citizens. Although *clientela* was a relationship of protection, the client was juridically in the patron's power, and it was only through the patron's choosing not to exercise his power that the relationship became one of trust, or, as Premerstein was to put it, '*potestas* modified by *fides*'. Thus a patron could revoke a grant of freedom to a freedman, and Rome's client states could lose their freedom at her whim. In the developed Roman empire there were two categories of subject: the 'autonomous subjects' or 'client states', who comprised the Italian allies, the 'free cities' and cities with treaties within the provinces, and the 'friendly' kings, and the 'non-autonomous subjects', that is, the provincials.

Mommsen's theory enjoyed great and long-lasting influence partly because of his own enormous prestige and partly through Premerstein's classic encyclopaedia article (1901), which differs from Mommsen only on a few details. However, the theory is

---

[1]   Bodin (1583) 1.7, p.105, cf. (1962), 72, A109; Grotius (1625) 1.3.21, pp.87-9, cf. (1925), 130-2; Zouche (1650) 2.2.4, p. 61. Cf. Harris (1979), 135 n.2.

[2]   Mommsen (1864), (1887-8), III. 54 ff., 645 ff.

fundamentally flawed. The claims that the plebeians were in origin outsiders and that *clientela*, which in historical times played such an important part in Roman social relationships, had at first been exclusively a relationship between Romans and foreigners find no support in the traditions about early Rome and seem inherently unlikely.[1] Mommsen's legalistic view of *clientela* is altogether mistaken: it was an essentially extra-legal relationship, imposing mutual obligations which were not legal but moral.

There was opposition to Mommsen's doctrine even within the German legalist school of which he was the principal exponent. Thus Täubler, rightly reacting against Mommsen's claim that even juridically the status of states with treaties on equal terms was no more favourable than that of those with unequal treaties, maintained that only unequal treaties created *clientela*.[2] He appealed to the authority of Proculus, wrongly, for Proculus did not say that an unequal alliance established *clientela*, but just drew a parallel between them.

It was, however, in Britain that a new way forward was found, adumbrated briefly by Sherwin-White[3] and developed fully by Badian in the first part of his *Foreign Clientelae*, a masterly work which has had a profound influence on the study of Roman republican history.[4] The basis for Badian's work was the conception of *clientela* in the middle and late republic which had been developed by Fustel de Coulanges and Gelzer.[5] This view stressed the central importance of *clientela* in Roman society and in the political power structure and rightly insisted on its extra-legal character. Badian set out to show that relationships of the same kind had played a very important part in Roman interstate relations. He maintained that Rome's 'friends' and 'allies' were in a position like that of a client vis-à-vis his patron and that the parallel was particularly close in the case of states which did not have a treaty with Rome. Both were unequal relationships, in

---

[1] See further Drummond above.

[2] Täubler (1913), 6ff., etc. His term 'clientela-treaty' (*Klientelvertrag*) s still used by Dahlheim (1968).

[3] Sherwin-White (1939), 161-2 = (1973), 187-8.

[4] Badian (1958), 1-153; for a recent restatement of his views see Badian (1984), 408ff.

[5] Fustel de Coulanges (1890), 205-25; Gelzer (1912), 50ff. = (1969), 62ff.

which the weaker party looked to the stronger for protection and the stronger expected the weaker to show gratitude, loyalty and respect. In the case of states with treaties of alliance there were mutual legal obligations too, but the mutual obligations of Rome and her 'friends' without treaties were, like those of patron and client, exclusively extra-legal. Such relationships thus 'fitted into the Roman habits of social thought which we know as "clientela"'.[1] Badian did not hesitate to speak of such states as Rome's clients and criticised Sherwin-White for asserting that 'to speak of "client states" is to use a metaphor'.[2]

On this foundation Badian constructed a subtle interpretation of the history and character of the status of free, treatyless friend of Rome, which he saw as a theme of central significance in the history of Roman imperialism in the third and second centuries BC. This status was evolved, he held, in the Romans' dealings overseas in the later third century, being granted to various communities in Sicily and Illyria as a result of the First Punic and First and Second Illyrian Wars, and to Saguntum c.224-1. Following these precedents, it was given to the Greeks in the settlement after the Second Macedonian War. Although 'the pomp and grandiloquence' of Flamininus' declaration of the freedom of the Greeks may be ascribed to his 'knowledge of Greek history and ideas', 'the idea itself is thoroughly Roman'.[3] The elasticity of the obligations created by the relationship worked to the Romans' advantage, 'for the interpretation of the client's obligations rest(ed) largely - as in private *clientela* - with the patron'.[4] Their free friends did not have such a binding claim to Roman assistance as treaty allies, as the Saguntines found to their cost, but they were expected to show gratitude and loyalty to the Romans, who were prepared to act against those they deemed ungrateful. Unfortunately, their Greek friends, being unfamiliar with the Roman *clientela*, often failed to understand what the Romans expected of them, and this was an important factor in the collapse of the Romans' first settlements in the Greek East.

---

[1]   Badian (1958), 68; his fullest statements of his overall view are to be found here and at 41-2, 53-4.

[2]   Sherwin-White, cited n.6; Badian (1958), 42 n.2.

[3]   Badian (1958), 74.

[4]   Badian (1958), 54.

Badian's views have had wide influence,[1] but there have always been sceptics[2] and the reaction is now in full swing. Several scholars have recently insisted that 'client' and related terms are only metaphors when used of Roman interstate relations, and, since they were seldom so used by the Romans themselves, best avoided.[3] The first part of Gruen's massive and important book *The Hellenistic World and the Coming of Rome* is devoted to 'the instruments of diplomacy' and offers a sustained critique of Badian's doctrine. Gruen contends that the Romans did not seek to impose on the Greeks a pattern of interstate relations of their own devising but merely adopted the Greeks' own diplomatic practices, and in a chapter devoted to '*Patrocinium* and *Clientela*' he argues that 'the idea that Rome transplanted her *clientela* system to the East misconceives both the direction and the structure of Graeco-Roman relations'.[4]

I would agree that Badian was wrong to claim that the settlement of Greece in 196-4 was essentially Roman in character and followed precedents set in Sicily and Illyria. The origin of the status of 'free cities immune from taxation' (*civitates liberae et immunes*) held by certain Sicilian cities remains obscure (it is uncertain what sort of presence, if any, the Romans maintained in Sicily between the expulsion of the Carthaginians in 241 and 227, when the number of praetors was increased to allow for the despatch of military commanders to Sicily and Sardinia every year),[5] and there is, in any case, little in common between the position of these communities as 'free cities' within a Roman province and the settlement of Greece by which the Romans proclaimed all the Greeks free and withdrew all their personnel. Contemporary treaties show that the states in Illyria which were linked to the Romans after 229 were regarded not as their

[1] His most notable follower is Errington (1969), (1971). Edlund (1977) largely agrees with Badian, though stressing the extent to which Polybius and Greeks generally were able to interpret *clientela* in terms of their own concepts of friendship and euergetism.

[2] Bleicken (1964) is an important early attack.

[3] Harris (1979), 135 n.2; Lintott (1981), 61-2; Braund (1984), 23, 29-30. Cf. Ste. Croix (1981), 341-2.

[4] Gruen (1984), 13-200, especially 158-200.

[5] Cf. Dahlheim (1977), 28-53; Richardson (1986), 7-9; Eckstein (1987), 103-15.

free friends but as their subjects by the Romans themselves.[1] When the Romans declared the Greeks free they were not extending to the Greeks a policy which they had already implemented elsewhere, but doing something which was for them entirely new. Their motive is clear: they could ensure their hegemony in Greece much more effectively if they could stand forth as the liberators of the Greeks rather than lay themselves open to the charge of having brought them into subjection.

No less clear is the model they were following: not Roman precedents, but the long Greek tradition of exploiting the slogan of 'the freedom of the Greeks' for propaganda purposes, which had been a diplomatic commonplace throughout the Hellenistic period.[2] When the Romans subsequently laid claim to the Greeks' gratitude for their liberation, they were not playing a game whose rules only they understood. The obligation of gratitude to benefactors had always figured prominently in the Greeks' own diplomatic exchanges.[3] Friends of Rome who quarrelled with her, like Demetrius of Pharos in 221-19 and the Achaean Philopoemen in the 180s, were not unclear what Rome wanted but seeing how much they could get away with.

Gruen is, in my view, right to insist that the Romans in their dealings with the Greeks never sought to impose an alien, Italian system, but he carries his reaction too far when he maintains that throughout they merely accommodated themselves to the Greeks' ways. The instruments of diplomacy which Rome employed in the Greek East were an amalgam, of which some elements, like

[1]   In the treaty of alliance concluded in 215 between Hannibal and Philip V the Romans were referred to as *kurioi* ('masters') of these states (Polybius 7.9.13). Under the Peace of Phoenice concluded at the end of the First Macedonian War, Rome's friends were 'adscripted' as parties to the treaty but the treaty terms specified which places in Illyria should belong to Rome and which to Philip (Livy 29.12.13-4). (I owe this point to J.-L. Ferrary.) The juridical position of these states is unclear. They could have been simply deemed to be Rome's subjects but in practice left to run their own affairs (perhaps like the majority of the Sicilian cities immediately after 241). Alternatively, Rome may have concluded treaties of alliance with them, as they did with Pharos, either when they captured it in 219 or later (*SEG* 23.489, on which see Braccesi 1971, 205-220).

[2]   Gruen (1984), 133-42.

[3]   Gruen (1984), 172ff.

'friendship', were the common currency of diplomatic exchange throughout the Mediterranean world, some, like the slogan of the 'freedom of the Greeks', were distinctively Greek, and some, like the treaty requirement to respect the majesty of the Roman people which they imposed on the Aetolians in 188, were the Romans' own contribution.[1]

Various aspects of Badian's complex thesis are thus open to question. However, his critics go much further, appearing to deny that there is any validity in interpreting Roman interstate relations in terms of *clientela*. In what follows I shall try to show that this is mistaken.

The language of patronage

The term 'client state' is now commonly used to denote a state which, without losing sovereignty and becoming formally a subject, is bound in a relation of dependence to a stronger state. Other terms for such a relationship are 'hegemony' and the euphemistic 'protectorate'. The degree of dependence varies widely. So too does the nature of the connection: in some cases it is purely informal, in others it is solemnized by treaties of alliance, whose terms are sometimes equal, sometimes not. It is appropriate to use the word 'client' in this way because this type of interstate relationship has much in common with the patron-client relationship between individuals. Both are asymmetrical relationships involving an exchange of services; in both the weaker party looks to the stronger for protection and must show him respect.

Relationships of this kind formed an important part of the structure of the Roman empire in every phase of its history. Much of Italy remained until the first century BC a mosaic of nominally independent states. In the Greek East the Romans at first preferred hegemony and imposed direct rule only when events obliged them to do so. In the developed imperial system the provinces constituted the largest part of the empire, but there remained many states which were nominally independent but under Roman hegemony. Within the provinces there were numerous cities which were held to be free,

---

[1] See further Rich (1985), 90-2.

some enjoying treaties of alliance with Rome (*civitates foederatae*), some simply grants of 'freedom' (*civitates liberae*), although in practice this meant merely that their status was privileged by comparison with that of the other cities of the province. Outside the provinces there were states (chiefly kingdoms) which were regarded as free and Rome's friends.

Those who hold that we should avoid speaking of other states as Rome's clients rest their case on the fact that the Romans themselves seldom used their patron/client terminology in this way. In the same way it has sometimes been claimed that we should only speak of patron/client relationships between individual Romans where our sources themselves use this terminology, but this line of argument has been effectively rebutted by Saller.[1] Politeness often led Romans to use words like *amicus* ('friend') rather than *patronus* and *cliens* of what were in fact patronage relationships between individuals. For us to insist on using 'friendship' where that is the term used in the sources would be to obscure both the function and the inequality of these relationships. The point holds good for interstate relations as well. Client kings, for example, were usually called by the Romans 'friendly and allied kings' (*reges socii et amici*), never *clientes*. Yet it is best for us to continue to use the traditional term 'client king', which accurately reflects the character of the relationship. To speak instead of 'friendly kings', as Braund does in his excellent recent study, gives a misleading impression of equality.

It has been claimed that when the Romans did use the terminology of *clientela* of their interstate relations they did so metaphorically. This is a misconception. The Romans did not conceive of states as abstract entities, as we do, but as people, whether individuals (King Philip, King Masinissa) or groups (the Romans, the Athenians - not Rome, Athens), and thus *clientela*, like friendship, could subsist as well between them as between private persons.

The number of passages in our sources in which patron/client terminology is used of Roman interstate relations is certainly very small. We have already noticed the Proculus passage: as we saw, Proculus did not describe other states as clients of the Romans, but simply drew an analogy between the patronage relationship between individuals and the relationship to the Romans of peoples whose

[1] Saller (1982), 7ff. and above.

inequality had been formalized by treaty. The only instance in Latin literature of the republic or early empire where another state may be spoken of as a client of Rome is a passage in Cicero's *De Republica* where Scipio is made to speak of the people of Massilia (Marseilles) as 'our clients',[1] and even this is not certain, for some suppose that the reference is to an otherwise unattested personal patronage of Scipio over Massilia.[2] No passage applies the term 'patron' to the Roman people, but there are three in which *patrocinium* is used of them, a term which denotes the exercise of the functions of a *patronus* and for which words like 'protectorate' or 'championship' are often more suitable translations than 'patronage'. Cicero in the *De Officiis* draws a quite unhistorical contrast between Roman rule in his own day and in earlier times, when, he claims, 'the empire of the Roman people was maintained by benefactions, not injuries', and asserts that then it 'could more truthfully be called a protectorate (*patrocinium*) of the world than an empire'.[3]

The other two passages come from speeches in Livy and concern Rome's liberation of the Greeks after the Second Macedonian War and its implications for the Greeks of Asia ruled or claimed by Antiochus III. In the first Flamininus tells the envoys of Antiochus that the Roman people cannot desert 'the championship (*patrocinium*) of the freedom of the Greeks which it has undertaken'.[4] In the second the Rhodians, urging the senate to liberate the Asian Greeks after the victory over Antiochus, say that 'you have undertaken to defend against enslavement to a king the liberty of a people of the highest antiquity and renown ...; it behoves you to maintain for all time this *patrocinium* of a people received into your protection (*fides*) and *clientela*'.[5] The first passage speaks merely of a *patrocinium* of Greek freedom, but the second does actually attribute to the Romans a

---

[1] Cicero *de Rep*. 1.43.

[2] So Gelzer (1912), 71 = (1969), 88; Harris (1979), 135 n.2.

[3] Cicero *de Officiis* 2.26-7: ... *imperium populi Romani beneficiis tenebatur, non iniuriis ...; itaque illud patrocinium orbis terrae verius quam imperium poterat nominari*. Cicero also uses *patrocinium* ironically of the Roman empire in his own day at *De Domo Sua* 20, unless the text is corrupt.

[4] Livy 34.58.11: *susceptum patrocinium libertatis Graecorum*.

[5] Livy 37.54.17: *gentis vetustissimae nobilissimaeque ... tuendam ab servitio regio libertatem suscepistis; hoc patrocinium receptae in fidem et clientelam vestram universae gentis perpetuum vos praestare decet*.

patronage over the Greeks. In this Livy was departing from his source Polybius, who in the corresponding passage speaks simply of the Romans' liberation of the Greeks.[1] Finally, some later texts must be noticed. Florus, writing in the second century AD, says that, when Jugurtha began his crimes, the kingdom of Numidia was 'in the protection (*fides*) and *clientela* of the Roman senate and people'.[2] Two centuries later Ammianus shows greater readiness to use the terminology of *clientela* of Rome's relations with other states than any earlier writer: he speaks of the Sarmatae as 'always Roman clients' and the Alamannic king Vadomarius as 'having been received into the *clientela* of the Roman state by the emperor'.[3]

The infrequency with which the Romans used patron/client terminology of their interstate relations is a fact of some interest which requires explanation. The answer cannot be that they felt any difficulty about using this terminology of relations between states, for Caesar freely speaks of certain Gallic tribes as clients of others.[4] The traditional explanation is that politeness led the Romans to avoid using this language of their interstate relations just as it often did in their individual patronage relationships.[5] I do not find this convincing. A crucial factor in determining how patronage relationships between individuals were described was the social distance between patron and client. A humble man might acquiesce or

---

[1]   Polybius 21.23.10: 'The noblest of your achievements was the liberation of the Greeks. If you now thus supplement it, your glorious record will be complete; but if you neglect to do so, the glory you have already gained will be patently diminished.' On Livy's expansion of Polybius' speech see Tränkle (1977), 125-6; Gruen (1984), 176. There is no need to suppose that Livy also departed significantly from Polybius at 34.58.11 (so Gruen). Polybius could well have spoken of Roman 'championship' of Greek freedom, using *prostasia* or its cognates. He does not do so in the extant fragments, but makes Perseus speak of the Rhodians as 'championing' (*prostatountes*) Greek freedom (27.4.7).

[2]   Florus 1.36.3. No earlier writer explicitly uses *clientela* terminology of Numidia, though the kings are represented as stressing their dependent position vis-à-vis Rome when it suits them: Livy 45.13.15-6; Sallust *Jugurtha* 14,24. Cf. Timpe (1962), 336-345; Gruen (1984), 159-60.

[3]   Ammianus 17.12.12 *semper Romanorum clientes*; 18.2.16 *ab Augusto in clientelam rei Romanae susceptus*.

[4]   Caesar *BG* 1.31.6, 4.6.4, 5.39.3, 6.12.2, 4.

[5]   Mommsen (1864), 355; Badian (1958), 7, 11-13.

even rejoice in being called the client of a great man, while someone of higher status might 'think it like death to have accepted a patron or be called a client'.[1] There was no risk of rudeness when in the nature of things there could be no question of the client aspiring to his patron's status, and thus we find the patron-client terminology being freely used of the relationships between individual members of the Roman elite and municipalities and foreign communities.[2] If foreign peoples were happy to be called the clients of individual Romans, men cannot have feared that they would be offended at being spoken of as the clients of the Roman people.

I would suggest that the terminology may have been avoided because it was only felt to be appropriate in a world where there could be a multiplicity of patrons. This was the case within the state, where a patron might help his clients against other patrons or in their dealings with the government, and in an international community like that of the Gallic tribes, but if Rome was the patron there could be no other. The states under their hegemony were formally known as their friends and allies. When Romans spoke of the political realities, they used the language of empire. The passages where Cicero and Livy speak of *patrocinium* are idealising, and it should be noticed that Cicero's words imply that empire, not *patrocinium*, is what Roman rule actually was called. It may be no accident that Ammianus, who lived at a time when Roman primacy was no longer unquestioned, is the first writer whom we know to have spoken freely of other states as clients of Rome.

Saller has shown that to study patronage within Roman society it is necessary to examine a considerably wider vocabulary than the terms *patronus* and *cliens* and their cognates. The same is true for the present enquiry, and, once the narrow focus on the Romans' own patron-client terminology is abandoned, the similarities between the relationships of the Roman state and the patronage relationships of individual Romans become readily apparent.

[1] Cicero *de Officiis* 2.69.
[2] Cf. Saller (1982), 7-11; Braund below.

The Romans' chief terms for states with which they had links were *amicus* ('friend') and *socius* ('ally'). Both words were also used of relationships between individuals (the basic meaning of *socius* is 'associate', 'partner').[1] There were necessarily differences in the procedures followed by the Roman people and by individual Romans in their dealings with their friends (we do not, for example, hear of individuals keeping written lists of their friends),[2] but there were also similarities: thus, when quarrels occurred, the Roman people renounced its friendship, just as individual Romans did.[3] In their ideology the similarities between these friendships were even greater. The Roman people's friendships, like so many of those of individual Romans, were essentially instrumental, resting on a reciprocal exchange and expectation of services (*beneficia, officia*) and the consequent obligation of gratitude (*gratia*).[4] Between individuals of unequal status such friendships were relationships of patronage, whether or not the terms *patronus* and *cliens* were applied to them. From the late fourth century BC the Romans were the stronger partner in most of their friendships and alliances, and from the early second century they had no equals. From then on all their 'friends' were in effect their clients.

Nothing shows more clearly how close the links were between patronage relationships within Roman society and the Roman state's relationships with its friends than the word *fides*. In one of the most important of its many uses *fides* means 'protection'.[5] The weaker party is said 'to be in the *fides*' of the stronger. At the formation of such a relationship, the weaker party is said to give himself into or entrust himself to the *fides* of the stronger and the stronger to receive the weaker into his *fides*. Used in this way of a relationship in which an individual is the protector of another individual or a community,

---

[1] On *socius* see Wegner (1969).

[2] On the *formula sociorum/amicorum* see Marshall (1968); Gruen (1984), 89 n.202. Against Gruen's view that it included only individuals, not states, see Rich (1985), 91.

[3] E.g. Livy 36.3.8-10, 45.20.8, 25.4; Polybius 31.20.3. 33.12.5.

[4] Saller (1982), 11ff.

[5] *TLL* VI.1.664-5. In general on the word *fides* see *TLL* VI.1.663-91; Fraenkel (1916); Heinze (1929); Freyburger (1986). Heinze and Freyburger seem to me right to reject Fraenkel's view that its original sense was 'guarantee' and did not imply a moral obligation.

fides is virtually synonymous with *clientela*, and the two words are often bracketed together. 'To be in X's *fides*' in effect means to be his client. *Fides* is also used in this way of the relations between states.

Thus Caesar speaks of Gallic tribes 'in the *fides* of the Aedui'[1] and in a number of passages other states are spoken of as in the Romans' *fides*.[2] The usage occurs most frequently in connection with acts of surrender (*deditio*): surrendering states are said to give themselves into or to be received into the *fides* of the Roman people and/or of the Roman commander to whom they are surrendering.[3] The significance of this has been much discussed.[4]

On the most probable view, to make an act of surrender to Rome always meant to put oneself completely into the Romans' power, but the Romans normally regarded themselves as under an obligation to treat those who surrendered leniently and so they could be spoken of as taken into the Roman *fides*. It was not only states which were under threat from the Romans which entrusted themselves to their *fides*: states also did this voluntarily to secure their own protection. Badian held that being in the Roman *fides* as a result of a *deditio* was merely a temporary condition pending a permanent settlement,[5] but this seems unduly legalistic, and it is more likely that the Romans envisaged that, unless it defected, a community which entered their *fides* remained there for ever.[6]

---

[1] Caesar *BG* 2.14.2, 6.4.2, 7.5.2; cf. p.126 n.4.

[2] Polybius 3.15.5; *SIG* 675.11; Cicero *Verr.* 2.5.83; Livy 8.1.10, 25.16.14; Florus 1.36.3.

[3] For instances *TLL*, cited p.128 n.5. Claims that the surrender was always into the *fides* of the commander (Premerstein 1901, 26-8) or always into the *fides* of the Roman people (Badian 1958, 6, 156) fail to take account of the frequency with which both formulations occur in the sources.

[4] See e.g. Dahlheim (1968), 5-67; Gruen (1982); Freyburger (1986), 108ff., 142ff.

[5] Badian (1958), 6, 157.

[6] Cf. Polybius on Saguntum: Polybius evidently held that in 220/19 the Saguntines were in the Roman *fides* as a result of having given themselves into the Roman *fides* some years earlier (3.15.5, 30.1), and the possibility that he may have been wrong in supposing that Saguntum made a *deditio* (Astin 1967, 589-93) does not invalidate this as evidence for his conception of *deditio* and *fides*.

Another common use of *fides* is to denote the faithfulness or loyalty which friends should show each other.[1] 'A mind without *fides* cannot be relied on by friends',[2] and no word occurs more frequently than *fides* in Roman discourse about friendships, whether those of individuals or of states. The way in which *fides* was used in respect of the Roman people's friendships generally reflects their inequality. Their friends are praised for their *fides*, loyalty, to the Romans, while the Romans show their *fides* by helping their friends in their need and treating them fairly. The proud claims which, from at least the third century BC, were made for *Fides Romana* played a central part in the ideology of Roman imperialism.[3] In this way not just those who surrendered into the Roman *fides* but every state which entered into relations with Rome could be said to have, as Augustus put it, 'experienced the *fides* of the Roman people'.[4]

Conclusion

Badian's critics, then, were wrong to conclude from the infrequency with which the Romans used their patron-client terminology of their interstate relations that it is not valid to interpret those relations in terms of *clientela*. There is much in common between the patronage relationships of individual Romans and the relationships of the Roman people with other states, and we may continue to speak of other states as Rome's clients. My own disagreement with Badian is confined to some aspects of the theory which he built on this foundation, and I would like in conclusion to draw attention to two of these.

First, I cannot accept Badian's view that the Greeks' inexperience of the Roman *clientela* led to a failure of understanding between them and the Romans. The features which Roman interstate relations had in common with their domestic patronage relationships were just as much a part of the Greeks' own tradition of interstate relations. There

[1] *TLL* VI.1.675-7. On *fides* and *amicitia* see Hellegouarc'h (1963), 23ff.; Freyburger (1986), 177ff.

[2] Cicero *de inventione* 1.47; cf. *de amicitia* 65.

[3] Cf. Boyancé (1972), 91-152; Gruen (1982), 59-60.

[4] *Res Gestae* 32.3.

philos ('friend') was used in much the same way as *amicus*, and the ideology of reciprocal service and obligation was no less prominent.[1] The way in which the Romans exploited the Greeks' obligation of gratitude in the years after the declaration of Greek freedom provides a good illustration of this. The declaration of freedom itself followed a Greek model, but in demanding that the Greeks show gratitude the Romans were behaving in a way that was common to both cultures. The same holds good for *fides*. As Gruen has shown, the corresponding Greek word *pistis* was used in very similar ways.[2] Greek communities can be spoken of as surrendering into the *pistis* of another, and *pistis* can denote the fidelity and loyalty which two states linked in a relationship of unequal friendship should show each other. It is among Greek states that we find some of the earliest celebrations of Roman *fides*: a Locrian coin of the early third century depicts Roma crowned by a personified *Pistis*, and at Chalcis c.190 a hymn was sung in praise of Flamininus and the *pistis* of the Romans.[3] All this may seem to be contradicted by the famous episode in 191 when according to Polybius a misunderstanding occurred between the Aetolians and the Romans about the implications of the word *pistis*: the Aetolians surrendered into the Roman *pistis*, not realizing that 'with the Romans to commit oneself to the *pistis* of a victor is equivalent to surrendering at discretion'.[4] However, Gruen has argued convincingly that Polybius has misinterpreted and generalized misleadingly from this incident: all our other evidence makes it clear that the Romans did acknowledge a moral obligation towards those whom they accepted into their *fides*.[5]

Secondly, Badian seems to me to set too much store by the presence or absence of a treaty of alliance. In his view, the free, treatyless friends of Rome were her clients *par excellence* because the obligations between them and Rome were, like those between patrons and clients, exclusively extra-legal. There is an important difference between the Romans' relations with their Italian allies, with all of whom they had treaties and from whom they demanded military

---

[1]   Cf. Gruen (1984), 69ff., 172ff.

[2]   Gruen (1982), 64-66; cf. Frederiksen (1984), 190.

[3]   *BMC Italy* 365.15; Plutarch *Flamininus* 16.4.

[4]   Polybius 20.9-10, especially 9.12.

[5]   Gruen (1982).

assistance every year, and their relations with their friends and allies overseas, only some of whom had treaties and who were asked for military aid only occasionally. However, among their overseas friends it was a matter of relatively small importance which had treaties and which did not. For all of them the obligations which carried most weight were moral. The Romans sought respect from all of their friends, whether bound to them by treaty or not, demanded help from all of them alike when occasion arose, and in their turn acknowledged a responsibility to protect them all. In practice they did not always live up to that responsibility, but there is no reason to think that whether or not it derived from a treaty made any difference to their conduct: Badian may well be right that the Saguntines did not possess a treaty, but the Romans would surely not have done any more to help them if they had.[1]

Another distinction which modern scholars make more sharply than the Romans themselves did is that between the provincials and those under indirect hegemony. The terms *amici* and *socii* were used of both categories and the same ideology of service and obligation was applied to both. Although it is convenient for us to speak of those under indirect rule as the Romans' clients, their relationship with all their subjects was in a sense patronal, and this may have helped to facilitate their eventual assimilation to citizenship and membership of the ruling elite.[2]

[1] The failure to relieve Saguntum can be explained without supposing that the Romans were in doubt about their obligation to send help: see Rich (1976), 38-44; Welwei (1977).

[2] I owe this point to Andrew Wallace-Hadrill: cf. his remarks above. I am very grateful to him and also to David Braund, Tim Cornell, John Davies and other members of the Seminar for their comments on earlier versions of this paper.

Bibliography

Astin, A.E. (1967), 'Saguntum and the origins of the Second Punic War', *Latomus* 26, 577-96.
Badian, E. (1958), *Foreign Clientelae (264-70 BC)*. Oxford.
Badian, E. (1984), 'Hegemony and independence. Prolegomena to a study of the relations of Rome and the hellenistic states in the second century BC', in J. Harmatta (ed.), *Proceedings of the VIIth Congress of the International Federation of Classical Studies.* Budapest, I. 397-414.
Bleicken, J. (1964), Review of Badian (1958), *Gnomon* 36, 176-87.
Bodin, J. (1583), *Les Six Livres de la République*, 4th ed. Paris.
Bodin, J. (1962), *The Six Books of a Commonweale*, reprint of the 1606 translation, (ed.) K.D. McRae. Cambridge, Mass.
Boyancé, P. (1972), *Études sur la religion romaine*. Rome.
Braccesi, L. (1971), *Grecità adriatica: un capitolo della colonizzazione greca in occidente*. Bologna.
Braund, D.C. (1984), *Rome and the Friendly King: the Character of the Client Kingship*. London.
Dahlheim, W. (1968), *Struktur und Entwicklung des römischen Völkerrechts im dritten und zweiten Jahrhundert v. Chr.* Munich.
Dahlheim, W. (1977), *Gewalt und Herrschaft: Das provinziale Herrschaftssystem der römischen Republik*. Berlin.
Eckstein, A.M. (1987), *Senate and General. Individual Decision Making and Roman Foreign Relations, 264-194 BC*. Berkeley.
Edlund, I.E.M. (1977), 'Invisible bonds: clients and patrons through the eyes of Polybios', *Klio* 59, 129-36.
Errington, R.M. (1969), *Philopoemen*. Oxford.
Errington, R.M. (1971), *The Dawn of Empire: Rome's Rise to World Power*. London.
Fraenkel, E. (1916), 'Zur Geschichte des Wortes *fides*', *Rheinisches Museum für Philogie* 71, 187-99, reprinted (1964) in his *Kleine Beiträge zur klassischen Philologie*, I, 15-26. Rome.
Frederiksen, M. W. (1984), *Campania*. London.
Freyburger, G. (1986), *Fides. Étude sémantique et religieuse depuis les origines jusqu'à l'époque augustéenne*. Paris.
Fustel de Coulanges, N.D. (1890), *Histoire des institutions politiques de l'ancienne France*, vol. V: *Les origines du système féodal*. Paris.

Gelzer, M. (1912), *Die Nobilität der römischen Republik*. Leipzig-Berlin.

Gelzer, M. (1969), *The Roman Nobility*, trans. R. Seager. Oxford.

Grotius, H. (1625), *De Jure Belli ac Pacis Libri Tres*. Paris.

Grotius, H. (1925), *De Jure Belli ac Pacis Libri Tres*, trans. F.W. Kelsey. Oxford.

Gruen, E.S. (1982), 'Greek *pistis* and Roman *fides*', *Athenaeum* 60, 50-68.

Gruen, E.S. (1984), *The Hellenistic World and the Coming of Rome*, 2 vols. Berkeley.

Harris, W.V. (1979), *War and Imperialism in Republican Rome 327-70 B.C.* Oxford.

Heinze, R. (1929), 'Fides', *Hermes* 64, 140-66.

Hellegouarc'h, J. (1963), *Le vocabulaire latin des relations et des partis politiques sous la république*. Paris.

Lintott, A.W. (1981), 'What was the "Imperium Romanum"?', *Greece and Rome* 28, 53-67.

Marshall, A.J. (1968), 'Friends of the Roman People', *American Journal of Philology* 89, 39-55.

Mommsen, Th. (1864), 'Das römische Gastrecht und die römische Clientel', *Römische Forschungen* I.319-90. Berlin.

Mommsen, Th. (1887-8), *Römisches Staatsrecht*, 3 vols. 3rd. ed. Leipzig.

Premerstein, A.von (1901), 'Clientes', in Pauly-Wissowa, *Real-Encyclopädie* IV. 23-55. Stuttgart.

Richardson, J.S. (1986), *Hispaniae. Spain and the Development of Roman Imperialism, 218-82 B.C.* Cambridge.

Rich, J.W. (1976), *Declaring War in the Roman Republic in the Period of Transmarine Expansion*. Brussels.

Rich, J.W. (1985), Review of Gruen (1984), *Liverpool Classical Monthly* 10.6, 90-6.

Ste. Croix, G.E.M. de. (1981), *The Class Struggle in the Ancient Greek World*. London.

Saller, R.P. (1982), *Personal Patronage under the Early Empire*. Cambridge.

Sherwin-White, A.N. (1939), (1973), *The Roman Citizenship*. Oxford. First and second editions.

Täubler, E. (1913), *Imperium Romanum*. Leipzig.

Timpe, D. (1962), 'Herrschaftsidee und Klientelstaatenpolitik in Sallusts Bellum Jugurthinum', *Hermes* 90, 334-75.

Tränkle, H. (1977), *Livius und Polybios*. Basle-Stuttgart.
Wegner, M. (1969), *Untersuchungen zu den lateinischen Begriffen socius und societas*. Göttingen.
Welwei, K.W. (1977), 'Die Belagerung Sagunts und die römische Passivität im Westen 219 v. Chr.', *Talanta* 8/9, 156-73.
Zouche, R. (1650), *Iuris et Iudicii Fecialis sive Iuris inter Gentes et Quaestionum de eodem Explicatio*. Oxford.

Chapter 6
Function and dysfunction: personal patronage in Roman imperialism

David Braund

Since personal patronage was all-pervasive in Roman society, it is hardly surprising that it played a leading role in what was perhaps the greatest issue of that society - namely, the creation, retention, administration and expansion of Rome's empire.

In what follows I shall consider first the many ways in which Roman imperial activities were facilitated and structured by personal patronage. Thereafter, I shall proceed to examine tensions and conflicts, actual and potential, between personal patronage and the interests of the Roman imperial state at large.

Patronage and imperialism: function

Probably about 167/6 BC the city of Abdera issued a decree honouring envoys to Rome: the envoys were Teans, acting for Abdera. At Rome the envoys took a full and conspicuous part in the rituals of patronage in order to advance their case:

> Undertaking an embassy to Rome on the [sc.Abderan] people's behalf they endured hardship to body and spirit alike, meeting the foremost Romans and forming bonds with them by doing obeisance day after day, and having enlisted their country's patrons (*patronas*) to give help to our people, and by presentation of the facts and by daily attendance in their *atria*, they won over those who looked to and championed (*prostatountas*) our opponent [sc.King Cotys of Thrace].
>
> (*Sylloge* [3].656; cf. Gruen 1984, 166 n.56).

Similarly in 167 BC King Prusias II of Bithynia came to Rome with his son and a large retinue. He made a grand entrance:

> Entering the city with a large train he proceeded from the gate to the Forum and the judgment-seat of Quintus Cassius the praetor. A crowd gathered from all sides: Prusias announced that he had come to bring greetings to the gods who inhabited the city of Rome, and to the Senate and the Roman people and to congratulate them on their victory over King Perseus and King Gentius, and on the extension of their empire by placing the Macedonians and Illyrians under their sway. When the praetor offered to call a session of the Senate for him on that very day, if he pleased, Prusias asked for a two-day interval, during which he might visit the temples of the gods, the city and his friends and guest-friends. (Livy 45.44)

In the Senate he congratulated Rome on her victory at Pydna, formally presented his son and made a number of detailed requests. The essential success of Prusias in the Senate was, according to Livy, due at least in part to the favour shown him by the generals who had fought in Macedonia. No doubt these were among the friends whom he had taken care to visit before his audience in the Senate. It seems most probable that, like the envoys of Abdera, Prusias was concerned to drum up support for the requests which he was subsequently to present to the Senate by calling upon his patrons (cf. Braund 1984, 9-10). Both cases tell against Gruen's wish to argue that patronage was of little significance in Roman decision-making before the late republic - though it must be acknowledged that patrons might fail clients, as the Abderan text serves to indicate (Gruen 1984, 164, observing the shortage of hard evidence on his point; cf. Rich 1985).

More than a century later, Caesar is made to denounce the Spanish town of Hispalis for its ingratitude towards him in supporting the Pompeian forces in Spain. In the course of this denunciation Caesar is represented as giving a valuable description of the benefits which a Roman patron might bestow upon a provincial community:

> He reminded them that at the outset of his quaestorship he had made that province above all others his own special concern, and had liberally bestowed upon it such benefits as lay in his power at that time; that when subsequently he had been promoted to the

praetorship he had asked the Senate to rescind the taxes which Metellus had imposed, and had secured the province immunity from paying the money in question; that having once taken it upon himself to champion the province (*patrocinio suscepto*) he had defended it, not only introducing numerous deputations into the Senate, but also undertaking legal actions both public and private, and thereby incurring the enmity of many men. Similarly during the period of his consulship he had bestowed on the province in his absence such advantages as lay in his power. Yet both in the present war and in the period before it he was well aware that they had been unmindful of all these advantages and ungrateful for them, both towards himself and towards the Roman people. (*Bellum Hispanicum* 42; cf. *Bellum Alexandrinum* 67-8)

These were the sort of benefits which Abdera and Prusias stood to gain. To a very great extent, when a provincial individual or state or a king had dealings with the Roman state, he dealt with and through patrons like Caesar. Patronage was a principal channel by means of which foreign relations and provincial administration were conducted. On the view presented in the *Bellum Hispanicum* it was entirely understood that the good patron might use his high public position and offices in order to benefit his particular favourites, who should respond with proper gratitude.

Provincial communities and kings evidently needed powerful patrons at Rome very badly indeed. Small wonder then that one of the first acts of the city of Cyrene after the death of its last king in 96 BC was to erect a statue in honour of the consul Gaius Claudius Pulcher in 92 BC: Pulcher is described as patron and benefactor. His support would have been most valuable in the difficult years which followed the king's death and bequest to Rome (Gasperini 1967, 53-7 with Braund 1985, 322).

Cicero tells how equestrian statues of the Marcelli stood in most of the market-places of the towns of Sicily, over which the family exercised long-standing patronage. Cicero expresses particular outrage that (allegedly) Verres stripped one worthy burgher and forced him to sit naked astride one of these statues (in bronze) on a very cold day. This, says Cicero, was a flagrant affront to the patronage of the Marcelli (*In Verrem* 2.4.86-7). Personal patronage like that of the Marcelli over Sicilian communities was no covert deal or unspoken understanding. Rather it was proudly and loudly proclaimed by the contracting parties, not least by means of statues and honorific inscriptions. And Roman public officials in the provinces were expected to respect the symbols and functioning of personal and familial patronage there.

The conspiracy of Catiline indicates further ways in which Roman foreign relations were channelled through patrons. When the conspirators first approached envoys of the Allobroges of Gaul for help, they did so through Publius Umbrenus 'because he had been engaged in business in Gaul and had come to know and be known by many of the leading men of the Gallic communities' (Sallust, *Catiline* 40). When the Allobroges decided to reject Umbrenus' advances, they reported the whole matter not to the consul Cicero but to Quintus Fabius Sanga, 'whose patronage their community most used' (*cuius patrocinio civitas plurimum utebatur*). It was Sanga who reported the matter to Cicero (ibid. 41).

Patronage was no less useful to the Roman governor or general in the field. Indeed such public offices tended to generate patronage (Gruen 1984, 163; cf. Aviola below). When Caesar wished to negotiate with Ariovistus, he sent as his envoys Gaius Valerius Procillus, who had a common language with the king, and Marcus Mettius, who enjoyed guest-friendship with him (*qui hospitio Ariovisti utebatur* : Caesar *Bellum Gallicum* 1.47). Though their mission failed, the mechanism is clear enough - and Mettius' personal connection seems to have brought him better treatment than Procillus received from Ariovistus (ibid. 1.53). As governor in Cilicia, Cicero deposited his son and nephew with the son of his old friend King Deiotarus of Galatia. Cicero was later to defend that king before Caesar. As Caesar is made to say in the *Bellum Hispanicum*, quoted above, speeches were part of the patron's duties (Cicero *ad Atticum* 5.17.3; *pro rege Deiotaro*).

To a great extent the personal patronage of individuals could accord well with the patronage which Rome claimed to exercise as a state. It was all too easy for Roman imperialists to stress the positive features of their power - Rome gave laws to her subjects, gave protection, saved them from their own local regimes (Brunt 1978, 186). Local disputes and enmities among subjects further encouraged Roman self-righteousness (e.g. Cicero *ad Quintum fratrum* 1.1.33). And over all this lay notions of the gods' special favour for Rome, which gave divine sanction to her rule. Cicero could use patronage (*patrocinium*) as a metaphor for the morally 'proper' imperialism of the past, which he contrasts with that of his own day (*De Officiis* 2.26-7 with Rich in this volume). Roman legislation against extortion and for such propriety could be described accordingly:

> Since that very law on extortion is the patron of the friends and allies of the Roman people ... (*cum lex ipsa de pecuniis repetundis sociorum atque amicorum populi Romani patrona sit*)
> (Cicero *Divinatio in Caecilium* 65)

On one view of Roman imperialism, therefore, personal patronage in the provinces and kingdoms could be seen as functioning in the context of a beneficent state-patronage.

At the same time, Cicero's correspondence shows vividly how a Roman provincial governor was enmeshed in a complex web of personal patronage which reached to Rome itself. A persistent minor irritant for Cicero was the repeated request of his friend Caelius for the capture and despatch to him of panthers to enhance his aedilician games. Caelius also makes a quite detailed request of Cicero on behalf of M. Feridius:

> I recommend to you M. Feridius, a Roman knight, the son of a friend of mine, a worthy and hard-working young man, who has come to Cilicia on business. I ask you to treat him as one of your friends. He wants you to grant him the favour of freeing from tax certain lands which pay rent to the cities - a thing which you may easily and honourably do and which will put some grateful and sound men under an obligation to you. (*ad Familiares* 8.9.4)

A runaway slave of Atticus seems to have been a factor encouraging Cicero to war with the chieftain Moeragenes (*ad Atticum* 5.15.3).Cicero writes to Crassipes, quaestor of Bithynia, to recommend the *publicani* of Bithynia and urge him to assist them (*ad Familiares* 13.9). He writes to Thermus, propraetor of Asia, to recommend his friend L. Genucilius Curvus and urge him to support his interests on the Hellespont (*ibid.* 13.53). He writes again to Thermus in support of his legate M. Anneius in his dispute with the people of Sardis: Thermus was to give judgment in that dispute (*ibid.* 13.55). Again to Thermus, Cicero writes calling upon him to ensure the payment of debts of M. Cluvius of Puteoli by various cities and individuals of the province of Asia (*ibid.* 13.56). He writes to Nerva, propraetor of Bithynia-Pontus, asking him to ensure the payment of outstanding sums by the people of Nicaea to the son of T. Pinnius (under whose will Cicero was both trustee and beneficiary: *ibid.* 13.61). To Nerva also he writes in furtherance of the relationship between that governor and Quintus Cicero, his brother (*ibid.* 13.62). In a particularly forthright letter, Cicero writes again to Nerva and urges him to help Ti. Claudius Nero:

> ... regard the Nysaeans as warmly recommended to you, for Nero regards them as his particular friends and supports and protects them with the utmost devotion. Do this so that this community may learn that its main defence lies in the patronage of Nero (*ut intellegat illa civitas sibi in Neronis patrocinio summum esse praesidium*). Servilius Strabo I have often recommended to you: I do so now all the more strongly because Nero has taken up his case. All I ask of you is to press the matter on so as not to leave an innocent man to the mercies of some avaricious governor unlike yourself. Not only will that be a favour to me, but I shall also consider that you have exhibited your customary kindness. The whole point of this letter is that you should promote Nero's honour in every respect... If he has your patronage (*si te fautore usus erit*) ... he will be able to strengthen the massive clientele which he has inherited from his ancestors and to obligate them by his own acts of beneficence (*amplissimas clientelas acceptas a maioribus confirmare poterit et beneficiis suis obligare*).
>
> (*ad Familiares* 13.65)

Public and private are scarcely distinguishable as the complex of patronage is deepened and extended. In particular, Cicero feels able to ask the governor of Asia, quite bluntly, to help Nero build his personal patronage in the province by showing favour to the Nysaeans. In this way the governor will reinforce his own relationship with both Cicero and Nero and will at the same time advance that between Cicero and Nero.

Evident in Cicero's correspondence is a tension and potential conflict between the claims of patronage and the high reputation for 'proper' administration which Cicero so prized. In writing letters of recommendation Cicero sometimes hints at that tension. On Curvus, for example, Cicero writes to Thermus:

I introduce him to you first of all in order that you may serve him
in every respect, so far as your honour and position permit - and
they will permit you in every respect: for there is no demand that
he will ever make of you that is incompatible with your character
- and I may add, with his own. (*ad Familiares* 13.53; cf.61)

Between such 'gentlemen', it is implied, malpractice simply cannot
be an issue, though it may be elsewhere. Yet Cicero's
recommendations are evidently intended to win special favour for his
friends with the likes of Thermus. Degrees of propriety and
malpractice can only have varied significantly from case to case, as
Cicero himself discovered as governor of Cilicia, as we shall see.

Patronage and imperialism: dysfunction

Having sketched ways in which personal patronage was central to the
functioning of the Roman empire, we may now proceed to consider
dysfunction. Personal patronage could be constructive, but it could
also be destructive.

The people of Salamis on Cyprus owed money to Brutus. Brutus'
agent, Scaptius, called upon Cicero to have the debt paid, for Cyprus
was part of his Cilician province. Cicero refused to give Scaptius
troops so that he could use force, but he did summon the Salaminians
to meet with him and Scaptius at Tarsus. There Cicero told them to
pay, but the people of Salamis complained about Scaptius' past
conduct and the terms of the loan. As Cicero himself states, he
refused to hear their case, harangued them and asked them to repay his
kindnesses to their city by settling the debt. To that extent patronage
became the very currency of government. Finally, Cicero threatened
compulsion. The Salaminians gave way, but could not agree the
amount due to Scaptius. After some discussion, confesses Cicero:

Scaptius took me aside and asked me to leave the matter in the air.
I granted this disgraceful request and when the Greeks [sc. of
Salamis] protested and demanded permission to deposit the money
in a temple I refused. Everyone who was there shouted that
nothing could be more shocking than Scaptius' refusal to be

satisfied with 12% compound interest. Others said nothing could be more stupid. But I thought he was outrageous rather than stupid   ...   (*ad Atticum* 5.21.12)

The reason for Cicero's reluctant connivance is made clearer in another letter to Atticus (*ad Atticum* 6.1). There Cicero says that in the course of these negotiations Scaptius showed him a letter which revealed that Scaptius was acting for Brutus, with whom Cicero had contracted friendship, as he says, at the prompting of Atticus himself. It was on account of his connection with Brutus that Cicero refused the Salaminians' reasonable request:

> The Salaminians wanted to deposit the money; I got them to keep quiet. They agreed as a favour to me, but what will become of them if Paulus comes out here? But I did this entirely as a concession to Brutus. And Brutus, who writes about me so kindly to you, is apt in his letters to me to take a brusque, ungracious tone even when he is asking a favour. I should be glad if you would write to him about these matters so that I know how he reacts - you will inform me. In my last letter I gave you a detailed account of all this, but I wanted you fully to realise that I have not forgotten the remark in one of yours that if I bring nothing back from this province but Brutus' good-will I may be well satisfied. So be it, since you will have it so, but with the proviso surely that I keep my hands clean. (*ad Atticum* 6.1.7)

Cicero's dilemma is evident: the claims of personal patronage pulled him in one direction, while the claims of proper administration and his reputation pulled him in another. He struggled for a compromise, concerned not to offend Brutus. It should also be noted that Cicero had no confidence that his successor would be as scrupulous. Evidently his predecessor had not been, for he had given Scaptius a cavalry-command and had allowed him to besiege the council-house of Salamis, so that five Salaminian councillors were actually starved to death (*ibid.* 6.1.6).

And Cicero was himself apparently rather less concerned with propriety when it came to debt-collection from the neighbouring king of Cappadocia, Ariobarzanes III. Cicero had a special commission to protect the king, but the king owed money to Brutus and to Pompey. Cicero sanctioned the activities of their agents in the kingdom and bombarded the king with exhortations to pay. King Deiotarus too had sent envoys to Ariobarzanes on Brutus' behalf. Ariobarzanes, striving to pay, instituted a harsh tax-regime within his kingdom. Even so, he could hardly raise enough to pay Pompey's interest. Ariobarzanes' position, already most insecure, was being further undermined by his need to satisfy his Roman creditors (*ibid.* 6.1.3-4). And these men, particularly Pompey, were his patrons. Similarly, the Salaminians who suffered so badly at the hands of Brutus' men were in fact in Brutus' patronage (*ibid.* 6.1.5). After all, the contracting of debts, financial and other, was and is the very essence of patronage.

But the ill-treatment of the Salaminians would do nothing to win the 'hearts and minds' of Rome's subjects. Moreover, the further destabilisation of the kingdom of Cappadocia at a time when a major war with Parthia seemed imminent ran in flat contradiction to the aims of the Roman imperial state at large. Nor were these isolated instances. Comparable is the contemporary case of Ptolemy Auletes, king of Egypt. In order to secure his throne by obtaining formal recognition from Rome, Auletes had to incur vast debts to Roman patrons. To satisfy his patron-creditors, Auletes was forced to exploit his own subjects more than ever. That exploitation led directly to his expulsion. Auletes returned to Rome and incurred still more debts in a quest for reinstatement. In due course the governor of Syria returned him to his throne at a great price. He died shortly after, still heavily in debt. Personal patronage had thrown the kingdom of Egypt into a turmoil which could hardly be to the advantage of the Roman state (see Braund 1984, 59-60).

Personal patronage could undermine the functioning of the imperial state in other ways. A provincial might use his connections at Rome to strike at his governor. Cicero says that Verres prosecuted a certain Diodorus because he wished to seize his property. Diodorus' response was to rush off to Rome. There he did the rounds of his *patroni* and *hospites*, telling them his story and seeking their support against Verres. Verres' father got wind of Diodorus' activities and wrote to his son that he should leave Diodorus alone. Verres did just that (*In Verrem* 2.4.41). The details of this story are not beyond suspicion, but its outline is meant to be credible - even normal. An individual subject-client could use his patrons at Rome to subvert the authority of his provincial governor. This is the application of the practice of Prusias and Abdera (above) to conflicts with Roman officials. And Cicero approves it, since (allegedly) Diodorus was morally right. Later he proceeds to denounce Verres' failure to pay sufficient respect to personal patronage; he expresses the greatest outrage that:

> ... the *imperium* of a disreputable governor on the spot had more force than the *patrocinium* of good men not on the spot.
>
> (*In Verrem* 2.4.89)

Cicero perceives the conflict between *patrocinium* and *imperium* and takes it for granted that personal patronage should override the power invested in an officer of the state when the patrons are 'good' and the officer is not. The principle is a dangerous one for the proper functioning of the state. How far were Roman patrons restricted by concern for morality? Whose morality? As Cicero's letters show, the wise governor would do his best to avoid offence to powerful Romans - even when that governor was relatively scrupulous and was faced with unjust requests. Personal patronage gave power to Rome's subjects. Insofar as that power was used to check maladministration, it could be a positive force. But its use was not, of course, so restricted. According to Sallust, Gauda, a royal Numidian, having been thwarted in his unreasonable ambitions by the Roman general Metellus, used his friends at Rome to assist in the replacement of Metellus by Marius (*Bellum Jugurthinum* 65).

As Cicero's letters suggest, a governor's concern for his reputation could restrict the abuses which personal patronage could encourage. Yet patronage could even remove that restriction, for it could win a governor eulogies which were not deserved: the bad governor might thus gain the reputation of a good governor thanks to provincial clients. Tacitus reports that under Nero one Claudius Timarchus of Crete had boasted that he decided which governors of that island received public thanks and which did not. Timarchus' boast was taken to be an insult to the Senate. The speech which Tacitus gives to Thrasea Paetus, denouncing Timarchus and proposing the abolition of such eulogies, displays a full comprehension of the problem:

> Let us, then, meet this new development of provincial arrogance by framing a decision consonant with Roman honour and firmness: a decision which, without detriment to the protection we owe to our allies, shall disabuse us of the idea that the reputation of a Roman may be settled elsewhere than in the judgment of his

countrymen. There was a day, indeed, when ... nations awaited in
trepidation the verdict of individual Romans. But now we court
foreigners; we flatter them; and, as at the nod of one or other
among them, there is decreed a vote of thanks, so - with more
alacrity - is decreed an impeachment. And let it be decreed! Leave
the provincials the right to advertise their power in that fashion;
but see that these hollow compliments, elicited by the entreaties
of the receiver, are repressed as sternly as knavery or cruelty.

(Tacitus *Annals* 15.20.21)

Tacitus' Thrasea perceives that eulogies might seem to protect the
provincials against maladministration. But he also sees how personal
patronage could invalidate the eulogy and give provincials a power
over their governors which he finds abhorrent. Such use of patronage
threatened to undermine the prestige of the Senate and the proper
administration of the provinces. There was little new about this,
however, except perhaps Timarchus' tactlessness.

In the *Verrines* Cicero offers an analysis similar to that of Tacitus'
Thrasea, for he is concerned to discredit the eulogy awarded to the
allegedly dreadful Verres by Messana, a city in his province. Cicero
argues that the eulogy was given because Verres had made that city
his special favourite and partner in crime, to the considerable
detriment of the Roman state and the rest of the province - *non sine
magno quidem rei publicae provinciaeque Siciliae detrimento* (*In
Verrem* 2.4.17ff., esp. 20). Verres, says Cicero, was the *amicus* of
the people of Messana (*ibid*. 2.4.25).

Yet Cicero attempts to show that Verres robbed Gaius Heius,
perhaps the most important man in Messana and the leader of the
delegation which came to deliver his eulogy (*ibid*. 2.4.3ff.). We have
insufficient evidence to deny Cicero's claim, but we may at least be
sceptical. Cicero fails to explain how Verres could have so ill-treated
the important Heius and yet retained the friendship of his city.
Moreover, at least some of the alleged robbery resembles - and was, it
seems, taken by Heius to be - the sort of loan of valuable artefacts
which was often agreed between patron and client (*ibid*. 2.4.27).
Indeed, Cicero approves such loans (*ibid*. 2.4.6). Nor can we tell how
many of Verres' alleged robberies from Heius and others were in fact
gifts or sweeteners to a patron-governor. The eulogy from Messana
would be much more comprehensible if Verres had, *pace* Cicero, built

strong ties of patronage not only with Messana at large (which is not in dispute), but also with the important Heius.

At any rate, provincials could not fail to grasp the importance of their eulogies. Indeed, Cicero mentions in passing that there was a move in the council-chamber of Syracuse to confer a eulogy upon a previous governor of Sicily specifically in order to help him in his present troubles at Rome (*ibid.* 2.4.142). Some further indication of the importance attached to such eulogies may be gained from the anger of Cicero's predecessor in Cilicia, Appius, when Cicero prevented the delivery of his eulogies, albeit indirectly. We should note that a governor like Appius, who was so undeserving (on Cicero's account) could receive eulogies - no doubt thanks to his provincial friends (*ad Familiares* 3.8). Cicero's claim to be surprised that Appius took such eulogies so seriously is disingenuous, as is shown by his persistent attempts to discredit Verres' eulogy from Messana and by Appius' evident anger.

Just as personal patronage in the provinces was bound up with relationships and politics at the centre of power, so the destructive potential of that patronage also manifested itself at Rome. Competition and rivalry were dominant features of the ideology and behaviour of the Roman elite (see Wiseman 1985). In that competition, personal patronage was both a means and an end. Members of the Roman elite could even compete for particular clients. When King Eumenes of Pergamum came to Rome in the late 170s BC, the great men of the city vied with each other in their eagerness to win his favour, much to the disgust of the elder Cato (Plutarch, *Cato Maior* 8). Cicero was similarly hostile to a member of the elite who was, in his view, too eager to offer hospitality to important foreign visitors. Yet, at the very same time, he expresses his own eagerness to receive Ariarathes, a royal visitor from Cappadocia. Cicero's main objection to his rival's conduct seems to be that his rival strove to receive all such visitors and thereby gain an undue share of the available patronage connections (*ad Atticum* 13.2a).

Royalty were especially desirable. Kings might be frowned upon at times and by the likes of Cato, but their high status was broadly acknowledged (Rawson 1975). And, as we have seen with Prusias and Eumenes, their arrival in Rome made a great impact. Their prestige redounded to the credit of the Roman patrons whom they visited. It is for that reason that Augustus says so much about his dealings with kings in the *Res Gestae*. There too Augustus boasts of his reception of envoys from exotic parts of the world (*Res Gestae* 31). For the republican elite, no doubt, the éclat of some envoys was greater than that of others, but all foreign visitors, such as the envoys of Abdera, will have contributed to the standing of their Roman patrons by their very presence.

Sallust, after the manner of Cicero (*ad Atticum* 13.2a), presents complaints about the domination of personal patronage by a few. In so doing, he contrasts private interests (the interests of a few) and public interests (the interests of the whole Roman people). Scipio Aemilianus is made to advise the young Jugurtha:

> ... to cultivate the friendship of the Roman people publicly rather than privately and not to become accustomed to bribery: he said that it was dangerous to buy from a few what belonged to many.
>
> (Sallust, *Bellum Jugurthinum* 8.2).

Sallust proceeds to describe how Jugurtha ignored this advice and used private friendships at Rome to achieve his ends. Throughout, Sallust stresses Jugurtha's use of bribery. A more sympathetic interpretation might call these bribes 'gifts' - a common terminological dilemma for the student of patronage. At Rome Jugurtha's envoys did the rounds of his old friends and gave them presents; they also tried to make new friends for him (*Bellum Jugurthinum* 13.6). According to Sallust, Jugurtha's Roman friends fought for him vigorously and effectively in the Senate (*ibid.* 15.2ff.). And the pattern was repeated when Roman commissioners and generals visited Numidia (*ibid.* 16; 29.1ff.). Sallust observes that the public good was conquered by private favour (*bonum publicum ... privata gratia devictum*: *ibid.* 25.3). And he makes Jugurtha's rival, Adherbal, denounce the influence of Jugurtha's private friendships (*privata amicitia* : *ibid.* 14.20) in the decision-making of the Senate. He makes Gaius Memmius deliver a similar denunciation in rather stronger terms (*ibid.* 31.18-20).

Sallust's *Bellum Jugurthinum* displays a conception of personal patronage as a threat to the state. It is said to have strengthened the few who monopolise it (cf. also *ibid.* 31.9; 85.4), but to have damaged the interests of the state. Patronage over kings and provincials should, argues Sallust, be shared throughout the state. For all that, Tacitus looks back at the republic as a period of relatively widespread patronage in contrast to the situation under the principate:

> Once, noble families which were wealthy or outstandingly famous used to fall through their eagerness for magnificence. For then, too, it was permitted to cultivate and be cultivated by the plebs, provincials and kingdoms. A man was held more illustrious, through his name and clients, in proportion to his wealth, house and establishment. But after savage slaughtering, once great fame meant death, those left alive turned to wiser pursuits.
>
> (Tacitus, *Annals* 3.55)

Much of the elite had opted out of personal patronage through fear, Tacitus implies. Indeed, Suetonius says that Claudius degraded a man for accompanying a king in his province (Suetonius, *Claudius* 16.2). Nero is said to have executed a man for renting out part of his establishment near the Forum as a base for foreign states (Suetonius, *Nero* 37.1). On the face of it, both instances are rather extreme - it is for that reason that Suetonius mentions them. But it remains the case that the emperor had to be on his guard against powerful Romans who enjoyed strong personal patronage in the provinces and kingdoms. The civil wars from 49 to 31 BC had shown repeatedly how important were the troops and resources at the disposal of cities and monarchs like Juba I and Cleopatra. In AD 69 Vespasian drew much of his support from such sources (Tacitus, *Histories* 2.81).

That is not to say, of course, that only the emperor and those close to him enjoyed personal patronage in the provinces and kingdoms. For example, one Gaius Silius Aviola seems to have had a residence near Brixia in northern Italy, wherein he displayed patronage agreements contracted with small towns in Africa (*ILS* 6099-6100). These agreements were evidently the fruits of Aviola's service in Africa as an officer in legion III Augusta in AD 28. The emperor had nothing to fear from personal patronage on this level. On the contrary, Aviola's connections had doubtless facilitated the local administration of Africa, which had probably given rise to them in the first place.

The emperor needed to excel in patronage as he needed to excel in all else so as to justify his position. This did not mean an imperial monopoly of patronage, as Saller has recently stressed (Saller 1982). Nor did the emperor need to try very hard to excel in patronage, for the foremost man in the state would tend to attract the more prestigious clients in large numbers. A comparison of the activities of Ptolemy Auletes under the republic with those of the future Agrippa I under the principate shows well enough the way in which the emperor and his household had taken over, effortlessly, much of the role of the republican elite in exercising personal patronage outside Rome (Braund 1984, 59-62).

Conclusion

Under the republic personal patronage constituted much of the framework of empire: it was, to a great extent, through the medium and processes of personal patronage that the empire functioned. But personal patronage in the provinces and kingdoms could also promote dysfunction - local maladministration and destabilisation and, at the centre of power, schism. Under the principate personal patronage in the provinces and kingdoms remained both functional and dysfunctional. Yet its capacity to promote dysfunction may have been limited to the extent that the greatest patron and the state came to be identified in the person of the emperor. Conflict between the interests of the state and the interests of the patron became more difficult where the emperor became at once both state and patron. Symptomatic of the change is the fact that, in contrast to the republic, bribery by kings is simply not an issue under the principate (Braund 1984, 62). But even under the principate personal patronage remained all-pervasive: it continued to be vital to the functioning of the empire and could still generate dysfunction, as the case of Timarchus and the complaints of Tacitus' Thrasea serve to indicate.

Bibliography

Braund, D.C. (1984), *Rome and the Friendly King : the Character of the Client Kingship*. London.

Braund, D.C. (1985), 'The social and economic context of the Roman annexation of Cyrenaica', in G. Barker, J. Lloyd and J. Reynolds (eds.),*Cyrenaica in Antiquity*, BAR, 319-25. Oxford.

Brunt, P.A. (1978), 'Laus imperii', in P. Garnsey and C.R. Whittaker (eds.), *Imperialism in the Ancient World*, 159-91. Cambridge.

Gasperini, L. (1967), 'Due nuovi apporti epigrafici alla storia di Cirene romana', *Quaderni di Archeologia della Libia* 5, 53-64.

Gruen, E.S. (1984), *The Hellenistic World and the Coming of Rome*. Berkeley.

Rawson, E. (1975), 'Caesar's heritage: hellenistic kings and their Roman equals', *Journal of Roman Studies* 65, 148-59.

Rich, J.W. (1985), Review of Gruen (1984), *Liverpool Classical Monthly* 10.6, 90-96.

Saller, R.P. (1982), *Personal Patronage under the Early Empire*. Cambridge.

Wiseman, T.P. (1985), 'Competition and co-operation', in T.P. Wiseman (ed.), *Roman Political Life 90 BC to AD 69*, 3-19. Exeter.

Chapter 7
Patronage of the rural poor in the Roman world

Peter Garnsey and Greg Woolf

Definitions

We begin with two paradoxes. The first is to do with the existence of the poor in antiquity, the second with their survival. The poor were ubiquitous but are more or less invisible. 'The poor you will have always with you' are words spoken by an unusually sympathetic observer. The regular spokesmen for ancient society, the standard-bearers of Greco-Roman urban culture, were less concerned with the poor and disinclined to broadcast their presence.

Secondly, the poor survived (though doubtless for a shorter time span than their social superiors), but we are not told how. We know neither what they could do to help themselves nor what help was available from outside. It might be suspected that patronage played a crucial role in their survival, but we would be hard put to it to show it.

In contrast there is no difficulty in demonstrating that communities and social organisations, upwardly mobile members of the Roman or provincial propertied classes, and even 'respectable' plebeians were caught up in patronal networks; in some cases they have received monographic treatment from modern historians (Harmand 1957; Saller 1982). There is the additional problem of deciding whether vertical links, insofar as they can be isolated, can be legitimately considered as patronage, by their definition or by ours.

For our purposes a working definition of the poor along the following lines will suffice. The poor are those living at or near subsistence level, whose prime concern is to obtain the minimum food, shelter and clothing necessary to sustain life, whose lives are dominated by the struggle for physical survival (Sen 1981; cf. Rein 1971; Townsend 1984). Patronage is defined, as elsewhere in this volume, as an enduring bond between two persons of unequal social and economic status, which implies and is maintained by periodic exchanges of goods and services, and also has social and affective dimensions.

The survival chances of the poor in antiquity, as in all historical periods, depended to a significant degree on the quality of their relationships with more fortunate members of their own society. From time to time they were thrown back on their social and economic superiors for the satisfaction of vital needs, whether security against violence (of barbarians, bandits or tax collectors), or food, clothing and shelter. Our concern is to ask how important patronage was to the poor in comparison with other ways of coping with insecurity and deprivation.

Patronage offered one way of securing protection against violence and hunger, but it was only one option. Any study of patronage, as is conceded by specialists in the field (Waterbury 1977; Saller 1982, 205-8), runs the risk that it will overrate the significance of that one institution. Patronage is 'a way of doing things, amongst others' (Gellner 1977, 3). It is an alternative way of doing things because it is voluntary, an option which an actor may (but need not) take up, because he thinks it offers some advantage over the 'official system', over the 'normal' status quo. It is a gap filler, doing what the open and established order cannot do or does less efficiently.

Patronage coexists with charity and euergetism (philanthropy or public benefaction), and support provided by other members of the poor man's family, village or town. There was also the market, through which he might try to exchange his produce or his labour in return for greater security, at least in the short term. Few individuals can ever have had access to more than a few of these options. However, the importance of patronage to the poor of the ancient world can only be assessed by setting it against this background. Only in this way can we hope to answer the broad question, how did the poor survive?

Kin, village and patron

Most of the freeborn population of the empire were peasants or agricultural producers - perhaps 80% of the population were occupied on the land. But we know very little about ancient peasants. They did not leave inscriptions or monuments behind them, and their dwellings, constructed for the most part out of perishable materials, have largely disappeared. Nor, obviously, did they compose literature. The members of the urban cultured elite who did compose literature largely ignored them. Even the writers of agricultural treatises more or less leave them out of account: they were writing for a public which employed slaves as a permanent labour force, and, more often than not, slaves as estate managers as well. The nearest we can get to an observer of lower-class society is, rather surprisingly, a doctor/philosopher of the mid-2nd century AD, Galen of Pergamum. In the *de alimentorum facultatibus, On the Properties of Foodstuffs,* he provides a catalogue of the foods and drinks consumed in the Roman empire, with particular attention to those consumed by ordinary rustics. But Galen gives inadequate coverage of social relationships, merely illustrating, on the side, the collective exploitation of rural producers by rich urbanites, or the exercise of peasant ingenuity and cunning at the expense of merchants, bakers and consumers in general.

In general, then, the ancient evidence is not very informative about the needs and deficiencies of the peasants of the Roman empire. At the same time, it is not difficult, with the aid of comparative material from better-known peasant societies, to reconstruct the situation of the rural poor. The life of subsistence peasants in the Mediterranean was a struggle for survival. Peasants strove to provide enough food for their immediate needs, and indeed to set aside something to spare, but these efforts might be thwarted by harvest failures or other disasters.

Peasants faced with both occasional crises and regular deficiencies could have recourse to a number of survival strategies. They were bound to turn first to kinsmen, neighbours and fellow villagers. Papyri from Egypt show claims made on the solidarity of the kin-group. Peasants commonly invested in children whom they raised in the expectation of being supported by them in old age. Of course not all children would have satisfied these expectations, as this letter, written in the pre-Roman period, shows:

To King Ptolemy greeting from Ctesicles. I am being wronged by Dionysius and my daughter Nike. For though I had nurtured her, being my own daughter, and educated her and brought her up to womanhood, when I was stricken with bodily infirmity and my

eyesight became enfeebled she would not furnish me with the necessities of life. And when I wished to obtain justice from her in Alexandria ... she gave me a written oath by the king that she would pay me twenty drachmae every month by means of her own bodily labour ... Now, however, corrupted by that bugger (*sic*) Dionysius, she is not keeping any of her engagements to me, in contempt of my old age and my present infirmity.
(Select Papyri II, 268, tr. Bowman (1986) p.58)

A more optimistic picture of the operation of links within the family is presented by Dio Chrysostom, in an oration which is part of a literary/philosophical tradition in which the dignity and freedom of the poor are compared favourably to the onerous duties and worries that attached to membership of the social and economic elite of the ancient world. Dio relates a conversation with a group of subsistence peasants who rescued him after he was shipwrecked in Euboea, and are now entertaining him.

'That daughter', he [sc., the peasant father] said, 'was married long ago, and her children are already grown up. Her husband is a rich man living in the village.'
'So they are able to help you out with anything you lack, are they?' I asked.
'We aren't short of anything.' his wife answered. 'They get game from us, whenever we catch anything, and fruit and vegetables. (They don't have a garden, you see.) Last year we borrowed some grain, just for seed, but we paid it back to them as soon as the harvest was in.' (Dio *Oration* 7.68-9)

Between fellow villagers, reciprocal exchanges of labour or food could even out the year-to-year imbalances of fortune. The peasant who helped his neighbour one year might expect a fair return another year when his own crop failed or he fell ill (cf. Millett above). For peasants existing at the margins of subsistence, even a small-scale disaster - damage caused to a growing crop by animals, for example - could make the difference between a good year and a bad one. Reciprocity could operate at a number of different levels, from groups of families, perhaps linked by marriage ties or friendships, to whole villages acting as a community to protect their members.

There is debate as to whether peasant households in the modern world have characteristically acted in accordance with this communal ethic or rather have put their own interests before those of the community (Popkin 1979; cf. Wolf 1966b). The possibility of a real variation in the relative strengths of communal and individualistic ideologies in different peasantries must surely be countenanced (Silverman 1968). It is not difficult to imagine that the strength of village solidarity in any given area in antiquity will have varied, and that, while some peasants will have been able to rely on substantial help from their fellow villagers in time of crisis, others elsewhere will have fallen foul of a more opportunistic ethic.

The origins of such extreme individualism are likely to be complex, but it has frequently been observed that the power of patronage is in opposition to that of horizontal associations in society, and that the vertical bondings that it creates undermine the solidarity of individual status groups, especially those of the clients (e.g. Eisenstadt and Roniger 1980, 50). Patronage works by distributing resources and services preferentially to some of the poor but not others, and the ideal rural client (from the patron's perspective) is concerned with his own interests to the exclusion of those of his fellows. It may be that we should see the ideology of patronage as supplementing and subverting village solidarity in some areas of the ancient world.

Patronage provides an alternative or a supplement to reciprocity within kinship groups and between status equals. In fact, it is hard to imagine a peasant society surviving without both lateral and vertical support systems (Wolf 1966a, 82-3). Few peasant societies have been capable of defending themselves against rural violence whether at the hands of bandits, landlords or government officials sent to collect taxes or enforce law and order (and these categories must often have overlapped). Peasants have at times chosen to live together in fortified settlements in an effort to make the odds a little less uneven, but these measures are no substitute for a powerful defender. Similar considerations apply to protection against hunger. In bad years, when shortages affect an entire community, peasants must seek help from the wealthy and powerful. Apart from risk insurance of this kind, many peasants need regular access to equipment which represents too great a capital investment for any one family: in pre-industrial societies this included teams of draught animals, olive and wine presses and threshing floors. Seed corn and even land might also be lacking.

The kinship group, the village, the patron: the list is not complete. An individual in dire straits would have made claims on as many people as possible, through all the ideological frameworks available. In desperation he might even appeal, as a beggar, to complete strangers, basing his claim on common humanity. Nor were these ideologies always alternatives. It may be analytically helpful to treat patronage as one of a number of options, but in reality these strategies might intersect and complement each other. Access to work and even the market might be in the gift of a powerful man and a peasant might make overtures to a kinsman to gain access to *his* patron or might represent his village to a rich man whose client he already was.

Dependency and patronage

Vertical linkages of one sort or another are well attested in a number of areas. There were systems of rural dependancy in the East and in Africa, Gaul and Spain (Whittaker 1980; Adrados 1946). Garlan (1980) has argued that some form or other of rural dependancy must be presumed in all areas where agricultural production was not managed through the slave economy.

Dependancy and clientage are not the same thing, although there are obvious points of contact and real similarity. Dependancy relations are links between members of different status groups (Finley 1985, 66-9), but unlike clientage they are not entered into voluntarily and are backed up by legal and extra-legal sanctions. In pre-conquest and post-conquest Gaul, the literary sources mention a number of lower-class status groups, described variously as *servi*, *plebs*, *clientes*, *obaerati* and *ambacti*. Caesar found the situation of one group, which he terms the *plebs* (commoners), not far removed from slavery:

> The situation of the *plebs* is almost one of slavery. They do nothing on their own initiative and have no role in decision making. Oppressed by debt, the great weight of taxes or the violent acts of more powerful men, many of them commit

themselves in slavery to the nobles, who then have all the same
rights over them which masters have over slaves.

(Caesar, *Bellum Gallicum*, 6.13)

Patron-client relations do not come into sharp focus in the sources. In
particular, the economic roles and occupations of the various lower-
class groups are not specified. We know that some groups formed
part of the regular escort and entourage of a chieftain in peace and in
war. It is a plausible hypothesis that within Gallic society a wide
range of statuses co-existed, ranging from patronage to slavery (cf.
Drinkwater below).

Optimal conditions for patron-client relations have in modern
times been provided by an environment wherein free smallholders
have lived in close proximity to, and in socio-economic
interdependance with, powerful men. In antiquity, even in the areas of
Italy where slave estates were at their strongest, we can find a setting
of this sort. Calculations based on research in the Ager Cosanus in
modern Tuscany have shown that the poorest of the colonists
established at Cosa in the middle republican period probably
supplemented their income by providing casual labour at peak times
on the large estates, and that the estate owners were dependant on the
availability of free labour at harvest time to run their own properties
economically (Rathbone 1981).

Horace tells a story that suggests how patronage may have enabled
urban landlords to manage distant farms through clients (*Epistles*
1.7.46-82). Philippus, a Roman senator, recruits an auctioneer,
Mena, by inviting him to dinner. Mena eventually joins Philippus'
other clients at the early morning *salutatio*, and becomes a regular
dinner guest. One day,

> he was asked to accompany his patron, during the Latin Festival,
> on a trip to the nearby countryside. Riding in the carriage, Mena
> sang the praises of the Sabine soil and climate again and again,
> while Philippus watched and smiled, and since he was used to
> seeking entertainment wherever it was offered, he gave Mena seven
> thousand sesterces, promised him a loan of another seven and
> persuaded him to buy a little plot. (*Epistles* 1.7.75-80)

The story goes on to relate how Mena becomes a peasant and a bore,
his vineyard and corn are spoiled and his livestock sicken or are

stolen: the moral is that he would have been better off remaining independant, 'with no powerful friends but the master of his own house' (line 58). This story cannot provide an archetype of how patron-client relations were regularly established. Both characters are satirised, their eccentricities are emphasised, and the transaction is portrayed as extraordinary. But it is likely enough that absentee landlords settled urban clients on small estates. *Popularis* politicians who offered land distributions, and *generalissimi* who carried them out, by force if necessary, were seeking to set up patronage networks extending into the countryside on a large scale.

Tenancy is also fertile ground for patronage. The position of a landless peasant who cultivates a plot owned by his social superior is close to that of a client and may become that. To the extent that his tenurial position is defined by law and his obligations are limited to a range of economic payments directly related to their joint exploitation of that land, he is not a client, but in practice some tenants and landlords entered into the less clearly limited social relationships with which we are dealing.

In Italy tenancies were well established as early as the last century BC (de Neeve 1984). During the civil wars at the end of the republic both Pompey and Ahenobarbus raised private armies from the tenants of their own estates, but we are ignorant of their precise status (Plutarch, *Pompey* 6, Caesar, *Bellum Civile* 1.34 and 56). Patronage is not the only possibility. Pre-Roman systems of dependancy may have lasted into the imperial period in Tuscany and among the Celtic tribes of the Po valley, and the dynasts of the late republic may have made use of them.

Pliny the Younger's relationships with his tenant farmers in Tuscany and the Po valley give us a glimpse of social relations in rural Italy. Pliny discusses the respective merits of fixed rents and share cropping (9.37), the mechanics of contracting out a grape harvest (8.2) and other detailed matters of farm management. But he has little to say about the social and affective aspects (if any) of his relations with his tenants. His willingness to shift over to a system of share cropping, so as to ease the burden on his tenants in bad years, may be as much as we can expect from a landlord who rarely visited his estates. Perhaps he did, during his seasonal sojourns, intervene at law, arrange marriages, receive services when resident on his property and honour in the community, but if so we do not hear about it. It is a reasonable argument that Pliny disqualified himself, through absenteeism, from being able to offer *effective* patronage to the countryfolk with whom he had economic dealings. Resident landlords were in a better position to engage in such relationships. It does not follow that they regularly did so.

Absentee landowners like Pliny *did* act as patrons in the sphere of municipal benefaction. Modern definitions of patronage focus on relationships between individuals, but Roman ideas differed from ours in this respect. Patronage of a community was treated as analogous to personal patronage: it was described in similar vocabulary, was equally heritable, and also involved reciprocal services.

Municipal patronage is generally thought of as an urban phenomenon in the ancient world, and the inscriptions which honour patrons and the gifts dispensed by them were focussed on the urban centres of communities. But the urban/rural distinction was not clear cut in the smaller towns of Italy and the empire at large, where many of the population were peasants, their farming plots not far from the city limits. Besides, access to patronal benefactions was not restricted to those who lived in the cities. Dio's Euboean peasant relates how his father had once visited a town, and chancing to be there when there was a distribution of money, he had taken his share alongside all the other citizens (*Oration* 7.49). We might expect a slightly greater distinction between town and country to have operated in Roman communities than in Greek ones, but some villagers certainly did benefit from 'famine relief' provided for their community by municipal patrons (CIL XI 337, 339). We may presume they also shared in banquets, and in distributions of food and cash.

One type of benefit which became popular in Italy, from the end of the first century AD, was the 'alimentary scheme' (*alimenta*). This entailed fixing loans to properties, the income from which provided subsistence for children. The main promoter of the *alimenta* was the emperor Trajan, but some schemes were also established by lesser individuals. The normal view is that the children of the poor were specifically intended to benefit from the alimentary distributions (Duncan-Jones 1982, ch.7; Patterson 1987). If so, they differed from other distributions in the cities of classical antiquity, in which the main criterion of eligibility was citizenship, not poverty, and which commonly gave more to privileged groups than to ordinary citizens. The matter requires more extensive treatment than can be given here: the only visible distinctions among recipients at Veleia (near Piacenza) are those of sex and legitimacy of birth.

Competing systems of patronage in the late empire

We are much better informed about personal patronage of the poor in the late empire. Libanius of Antioch in Syria describes one such set of relations between himself and some Jewish tenants on his land in the second half of the fourth century AD. Libanius was concerned with new developments in rural patronage (to which he was hostile) and which we will discuss below, but at one point he harks back to an idealised presentation of how things used to be in the good old days. Libanius' family had had these Jewish tenants on their land for four generations. His present complaint deals with their attempt to bring in outsiders to help them. After attacking the conduct of the outsiders, Libanius goes on to provide a fascinating insight into the ideology of patronage, from the patron's point of view:

> Well, I may be asked on behalf of the peasants, aren't they allowed to get help for themselves? Certainly, would be my reply, provided that it is not illegal but never any that is evil. First there is that from the gods, which may be gained by prayers and acts of worship. Then there is that from water: if it does harm it is shut off, but if it is likely to be of assistance it is let in. They can even make their masters (*kyrious*) more kindly disposed towards them, so as either to allow a remission of debts, or even to offer a grant and again, if they ever have need to have recourse to law between each other, they should approach the owner ...
> ... 'Well,' it may be said, 'what happens if the landlord is incapable of doing the job, and some more powerful personage is needed?' Then let the peasant tell the master, and he tell this other. You, my man, make your request to him, and let him pass it on. You could get help in this way, and he would suffer no harm since the proper order of precedence in such matters remains firmly fixed.
> (Libanius, *Oration* 47.19 and 22 tr. Norman (Loeb))

Libanius here provides a model of how he thought rural social relations ought to be organised. The landlord assumes the role of protector, monopolising the dual functions of a patron, as a provider of protection and resources and as a broker controlling access to the outside world.

Libanius' model for landlord-tenant relations was constructed in explicit opposition to contemporary practice. We have several complaints about the operation of 'illicit' patronage systems from the late fourth and early fifth centuries AD, relating to Gaul, Egypt, Palestine and Syria. The systems criticised differ from each other considerably in detail, but most scholars have seen them all as part of a single development.

The Syrian example is attacked by Libanius in the oration we quoted from above. He accused peasant villagers of allying with military personnel against their neighbours and against the tax-collectors from the city of Antioch. The military provided protection against rival villagers, city officials and tax-collectors. In the case of Libanius' own tenants, ostensibly mentioned only as an example of a general problem, the military exerted their influence on the governor to deny Libanius justice in the courts. In another oration (39), Libanius introduces Mixidemus, a civilian patron who was an *honoratus*, an ex-official. He took over the patronage of some villagers from men on the governor's staff, and proceeded to exact a payment in grain and other produce from the peasants and to use their wives as household servants. His intention, according to Libanius' admittedly hostile account, was to take over entire villages, not a forlorn hope in view of the peasants' need for protection. Similar events are alluded to in some of Libanius' other orations (cf. Liebeschuetz 1972, 192-208).

The general pattern is clear: military and civilian potentates were persuaded (with material inducements) to assist peasants to achieve a variety of goals. The authority and prerogatives of the class who both were the landlords and made up the local government (the *curiales)* could now be bypassed. When taxes were successfully evaded, the fiscal obligations were passed on to the *curiales* as a group. So the interventions of the peasants' protectors were very often at the expense of the *curiales*.

The situation in Egypt seems to have been similar. Our sources here are a series of laws in the Theodosian Code under the title *de Patrociniis Vicorum* (CTh 11.24. 1-6). The main preoccupation of the central government was to ensure that the taxes were paid and public offices were performed. In some circumstances the rights of patrons were recognised on condition that they assumed the obligations attached to the land they had taken into their protection. Again the picture is one of powerful individuals, exempt from civic duties by means of imperial service or favour, taking villages under their protection, in exchange for rights over and often possession of the land.

To turn to Gaul: Salvian, Bishop of Marseilles, tells us that the poor, oppressed by heavy taxes, were handing themselves over to powerful men for protection, in exchange for the loss of the freehold over their lands. The impoverished children were forced to become tied peasants working on the lands of the rich. They became *inquilini*, losing the *ius libertatis*, and were converted into slaves (*de Gubernatione Dei* 5.38-45). Salvian's account is at the heart of the controversies surrounding the origins of the colonate, the system of tied labour that appears in the late empire. This paper is not concerned with that debate. But even in Salvian's account it is a two-stage process, and in the first generation at least, it is a case of rich men sheltering the poor against tax-collectors, while taking over their lands. This is the same situation visible in the laws from Egypt, and similar complaints are made against landowners in Palestine, also by religious authorities (Sperber 1971).

We began by considering patronage as one option among many, and patron-client relations as the product of choices made by the participants. Late imperial peasants could choose not only whether to become clients but also *between* several kinds of potential patrons. Under the principate, in the urbanised societies of the Mediterranean, there was, generally speaking, no alternative to the absentee landlord as patron. Central government was more remote and made few demands on local government officials, the *decuriones* or *curiales*, who were in effect the representatives of the landowning classes. There was no developed bureaucracy to supervise their activities, and the military were concentrated in frontier zones. With the later empire came important changes: greater dispersal of the military within the empire, and increasing demands made by central government on the communities. *Curiales* were more harassed and were increasingly overshadowed in the localities by active or retired members of the imperial elite. A gap opened up between local and imperial aristocracies, and the two groups came into competition for power and privileges (Millar 1983). The elites competed ultimately before the emperor, each alleging public advantage in their own case. The advantage in the contest lay with those with superior influence and connections who were at the same time less remote from the rural community.

The poor were able to exploit this competition between the two elites. This is the context of Libanius' problems with his tenants. Alternatively, they might persuade *curiales* to represent them against the imperial elite. Libanius' 45th and 50th orations are made on behalf of the poor, defending them against imprisonment by the military and against demands for corvée labour. While they had the choice, peasants might be promiscuous in their relationships with their social superiors.

So far we have considered only secular power as a focus of patronage relationships. Late antique society saw the emergence of individuals whose miracles, prophecies, wisdom or asceticism had given them great *acquired* status. These 'holy men' inhabited the margins of society, acting as arbitrators in disputes, and as defenders of the poor against the rich (Brown 1971, 1976). The social role of the holy men often put them at odds not only with the tax-collectors and other representatives of central and local government, but also with the leaders of the ecclesiastical hierarchy, the bishops, invested by the church with *ascribed* status, *ex officio* authority. The most successful bishops, men like Augustine and Ambrose, capitalised on both sources of power, and were able to lead their communities against, or in default of, the secular authorities. The complaints against landowner patrons, made both by Salvian and in the rabbinical tradition, can be seen in this context. The rabbis explicitly contrasted the arrogance of the Jewish 'men-of-the-arm', their precarious position and their shortcomings as protectors, with the immediate and dependable help offered by Jehovah (Sperber 1971). But many bishops managed to combine religious authority and more traditional secular power.

Sidonius Apollinaris became bishop of the Arverni, at Clermont Ferrand, in the mid-fifth century AD (Stevens 1933). His authority seems to be based in at least three traditions. As a bishop he was in a position, as one correspondent put it (*Ep.* 4.2), to 'lavish your wealth upon the poor'. He was a kind of universal patron, in a loose sense, but to the extent that his activities are to be seen as charitable, his disbursements come perhaps into a different category. Secondly, he was a Roman aristocrat, educated in the classical literary traditions, intermarrying with the great families of the western empire, a great landowner and devoting a good deal of his letters to promoting the interests of his immediate social inferiors and juniors, just as Cicero, Pliny and Fronto had done in earlier generations. Finally there is also a case to be made that Sidonius and his peers were in some sense heirs to a Celtic tradition of social relationships (cf. Wightman 1978). Without committing ourselves on this issue, we could cite a number of possible examples of social continuity. Sidonius' brother-in-law, Ecdicius, organised his dependants into an army to repel Gothic invaders. Sidonius had *clientes*, and they were poor and of low but probably free status: they are coupled with but distinct from *pueri*, slaves (*Ep.* 1.5.24). They are once referred to as a *comitatus*, which might mean they formed an entourage like that of a traditional Celtic noble. At all events, they seem quite distinct from the friends, the *amici*, who shared Sidonius' table.

How did individuals combine these roles and make sense of the combination? The career of another Gallic bishop, Caesarius of Arles, suggests one answer. He devoted a great deal of energy to ransoming prisoners of war, so increasing his own clientele and standing in the community. But his sermons set this activity firmly within the ideological framework of Christian charity. There is a distinction to be made between the ideological element of patronage and the exchanges of goods to which it gives social meaning. Caesarius was able to exploit a single activity, which had meaning in two complementary ideologies, and so to act simultaneously as a patron and out of charitable motives (Klingshirn 1985). Such examples allow us to envisage how Sidonius and his kind managed to combine their roles.

Conclusion

The presence of patronage can be surmised in widely separated parts of the Roman empire, operating alongside systems of rural dependancy or more strictly economic and legal relationships. While its outward form varied according to place, time and social context, the context of the patronage relationship will have remained essentially the same. Patronage was voluntary and reciprocal, and it offered the client, at the least, basic subsistence and physical protection.

However, patronage could be more or less operational or effective. Patronage made its most substantial contribution to the survival strategies of the *rural* poor, supplementing the horizontal links between kinsmen and fellow villagers, where the patrons were rooted in the rural communities. It was least efficacious where the patronal class was remote, caught up in the political, social and cultural life of the cities.

This leads us to the paradox with which we began. Why the relative silence of the sources? The poor, themselves mute, were generally passed over by the elite as unworthy of attention. And besides, to literate urbanites, the countryside was another world (MacMullen 1974, 30). Where the rural poor were actively patronised, this was both a fact of life and not a proper subject for literature. The 'moans of the countryfolk' (*querelae rusticorum*) that Pliny complains about had no place in an 'ideology of amateurism' that affected to despise the mundane affairs of the soil (Patterson 1987). Higher up the social scale, at least, it was not good manners for a Roman to allude to his clients' status openly. No Roman noble ever addressed any of the upper-class clients, about whom we *are* well informed, except as *amici*, and the rule extended even to relations with foreign monarchs (Saller 1982; Braund 1984).

The more pertinent question is why patronage was talked about at all. Patronage of the poor became a topic of debate only in the context of the late antique competition for power and economic resources. Traditional patrons found themselves supplanted as patrons, but also impeded as landlords - and as tax-collectors - by men with local authority, secular or religious. Their protests were echoed in legislation representing the fiscal interests of the central government. Our period ends with the strange spectacle of urban *rentiers*, who were the natural and traditional patron class, and high-ranking officials, the status-equals of the new and 'illegitimate' patrons, joining forces to condemn patronage.[1]

[1] We would like to thank John Patterson for help and advice in preparing this paper, and Nicholas Purcell, whose unpublished paper 'Studying the poor in antiquity', read at a seminar in Oxford in 1987, was a source of many stimulating ideas.

168 *Garnsey and Woolf*

Bibliography

Adrados, F.R. (1946), 'La "Fides" Iberica', *Emerita* 14, 128-209.

Bowman, A.K. (1986), *Egypt after the Pharaohs*. London.

Braund, D.C. (1984), *Rome and the Friendly King: the Character of the Client Kingship*. London.

Brown, P. (1971), 'The rise and function of the holy man in late antiquity', *Journal of Roman Studies* 61, 80-101.

Brown, P. (1976), 'Town, village and holy men: the case of Syria', in *Assimilation et Résistance. (VI cong.int.études class.*, Madrid), 213-20.

Brunt, P.A. (1965), ' "Amicitia" in the late republic', *Proceedings of the Cambridge Philological Society* n.s. 11, 1-20.

Duncan-Jones, R. (1982), *The Economy of the Roman Empire: Quantitative Studies*. 2nd ed. Cambridge.

Eisenstadt, S.N. and Roniger L. (1980), 'Patron client relations as a model of structuring social exchange',*Comparative Studies in Sociology and History* 22:1, 42-77.

Finley, M.I. (1985), *The Ancient Economy*. 2nd ed. London.

Garlan, Y. (1980), 'Le travail libre en Grèce antique', in Garnsey (ed.) (1980), 6-22.

Garnsey, P. (1979), 'Where did Italian peasants live?', *Proceedings of the Cambridge Philological Society* n.s. 25, 1-25.

Garnsey, P. (ed.) (1980), *Non-Slave Labour in the Greco-Roman World* (Cambridge Philological Soceity, supp. vol. 6). Cambridge.

Garnsey, P. (1988), *Famine and Food Supply in the Graeco-Roman World: Responses to Risk and Crisis*. Cambridge.

Gellner, E. (1977), 'Patrons and clients', introduction to Gellner and Waterbury (eds.) (1977), 1-6.

Gellner, E. and Waterbury, J. (eds.) (1977), *Patrons and Clients in Mediterranean Societies*. London.

Harmand, L. (1957), *Le Patronat sur les collectivités publiques des origines au Bas-Empire* (Publ. de ... Clermont, 2e Serie, Fasc.2).

Hobsbawn, E. (1968), s.v. 'Poverty' in the *International Encyclopaedia of the Social Sciences*. New York.

Klingshirn, W. (1985), 'Charity and power: Caesarius of Arles and the ransoming of captives in Sub-Roman Gaul', *Journal of Roman Studies* 75, 183-203.

Liebeschuetz, J.H.W.G. (1972), *Antioch. City and Imperial Administration in the Later Roman Empire*. Oxford.

MacMullen, R. (1974), *Roman Social Relations, 50 BC to AD 284*. New Haven.

Millar, F.G.B. (1983), 'Empire and city, Augustus to Julian: obligations, excuses and status', *Journal of Roman Studies* 73, 76-96.

Neeve, P.W. de (1984), *Colonus: Private Farm Tenancy in Roman Italy during the Republic and Early Principate*. Amsterdam.

Patterson, J.R. (1987), 'Crisis, what crisis? Rural change and urban development in imperial Appennine Italy', *Papers British School Rome* LV, 115-46.

Popkin, S.L. (1979), *The Rational Peasant: the Political Economy of Rural Society in Vietnam*. Berkeley.

Rathbone, D.W. (1981), 'The development of agriculture in the "Ager Cosanus" during the Roman Republic: problems of evidence and interpretation', *Journal of Roman Studies* 71, 10-23.

Rein, M. (1971), 'Problems in the definition and measurement of poverty', in Townsend (ed.) (1971), 46-63.

Ste Croix, G.E.M. de (1954), 'Suffragium: from vote to patronage', *British Joural of Sociology*. 5, 33-48.

Saller, R.P. (1982), *Personal Patronage under the Early Empire*. Cambridge.

Scott, J. (1977), 'Patronage or exploitation?', in Gellner and Waterbury (eds.) (1977), 21-39.

Sen, A. (1981), *Poverty and Famines. An Essay on Entitlement and Deprivation*. Oxford.

Silverman, S. (1968), 'Agricultural organisation, social structure and values in Italy. Amoral familism reconsidered', *American Anthropology* 70, 1-20.

Silverman, S. (1977), 'Patronage as myth', in Gellner and Waterbury (eds.) (1977), 7-19.

Sperber, D. (1971), 'Patronage in Palestine (c.220-400): causes and effects', *Journal of Economic and Social History of the Orient* 14, 227-52.

Stevens, C.E. (1933), *Sidonius Apollinaris and his Age*. Oxford.

Townsend, P. (ed.) (1971), *The Concept of Poverty*. London.

Townsend, P. (1984) 'Understanding poverty and inegality in Europe', in Walker et al. (eds.) (1984), 1-27.

Walker, R. et al. (eds.) (1984), *Responses to Poverty: Lessons from Europe*. London.

Waterbury, J. (1977), 'An attempt to put patrons and clients in their place', in Gellner and Waterbury (eds.) (1977), 329-42.

Whittaker, C.R. (1980), 'Rural labour in three Roman provinces', in Garnsey (ed.) (1980), 73-99.

Wightman, E.M. (1978), 'Peasants and potentates in Roman Gaul', *American Journal of Ancient History* 3, 43-63.

Wolf, E.R. (1966a), 'Kinship, friendship and patron-client relations in complex societies' in M. Banton (ed.), *The Social Anthropology of Complex Societies*, 1-22. London.

Wolf, E.R. (1966b), *Peasants*. New Jersey.

Chapter 8
Bandits, elites and rural order[1]

Keith Hopwood

One of the major problems facing the ancient historian is the lack of evidence at his disposal for many of the basic questions of the day-to-day organization of life in the ancient world.[2] Consequently he is continually forced to construct models to describe and explain ancient social structures and modes of behaviour, models which are in need of constant refinement.

Let me pose a problem, which I believe has not been answered adequately in the past. How did the city magistrates ensure that the hinterland of the city remained quiet and supplied the necessary surplus to feed the city's population and finance their own competitive spending in providing baths, gymnasia, theatres, temples and all the necessary features of a city which aspired to the manners of the Hellenized way of life?

I should like to examine an area where such problems occurred in a particularly extreme form, Rough Cilicia/Isauria on the south coast of Asia Minor, where I myself have conducted fieldwork over the last four Easters. I make no apology for choosing an extreme case, for I believe that the problems posed by such an area cast into sharper focus the same or similar problems faced by less 'wild' areas such as, say, the hinterlands of Carian Aphrodisias.

The area of study is the eastern end of the horse-shoe of the Taurus Mountains. Between Alanya (ancient Coracesium) and Silifke

---

[1] I should like to thank all members of the seminar to which I read an earlier draft of this paper for their advice and constructive comments. None of them, of course, can be responsible for errors or any mistaken views which I express here.

[2] A point ably expressed in Professor Sir Moses Finley's book *Ancient History. Evidence and Models* (London, 1985).

(ancient Seleuceia) they rise directly from the sea, leaving a coastal plain only in the estuaries of the rivers that drain from the High Taurus. By these embayments there developed the cities of Coracesium, Laertes, Syedra, Iotape, Selinus, Cestrus, Antiocheia-ad-Cragum, Anemurium, Celenderis and Seleuceia itself. The slopes are more gradual to the east behind Seleuceia, where the land rises by a series of limestone plateaux to the Taurus proper. Routes to the interior take either the western valleys, or the Calycadnus valley in the East.

In antiquity, as today, the settlements large and small are located where depressions in the limestone allow the accumulation of sufficient topsoil for arable farming. Today, every possible square metre of the ground is utilized, terraces being cut into the valley slopes close to the settlement. A considerable number of disused terraces associated with ancient sites suggests that a similar pattern existed in antiquity also, with each plot possibly consisting of several separated fields.

Within such an environment, the lot of the peasant is very hard. It is an impressive feat of exploitation that a sufficient surplus was extracted from such a territory to finance large-scale public building works at private expense in the cities, when even to provide a surplus for urban consumption must have been difficult. A famous passage in Galen sums up the possibilities for rural suffering:

> When summer was over, those who lived in the cities, in accordance with their universal practice of collecting a sufficient supply of corn to last a whole year, took from the fields all the wheat, barley, beans and lentils, and left to the rustics only those annual products which are called pulses and leguminous fruits: they even took away a good part of these to the city. So the people in the countryside, after consuming during the winter what had been left, were compelled to use unhealthy forms of nourishment ... I myself saw some of them at the end of the spring, and almost all of them at the beginning of summer, afflicted with numerous ulcers covering their skin, not of the same kind in every case, for some suffered from erysipelas, others from inflamed tumours, others from spreading boils, others had an eruption resembling lichen and scabs and leprosy.
>
> (*Peri Euchumias kai Kakochumias* 1, trans. de Ste. Croix)

In an agriculturally unproviding area like Cilicia, these sufferings must have fallen harshly on the peasantry, where even today peasants have to diversify to make a living. A farmer I interviewed in 1982 in the hinterland of Syedra at Gevinde had been forced to develop silk manufacture and turn his wives and daughters to carpet manufacture in order to obtain the capital for his seed-corn. In antiquity the safety valve was either legitimate soldiering in the army, or illegitimate soldiering: banditry.[1]

Throughout the period of Roman rule Cilicia was famed for banditry; so much so that by the second century AD Lucian's list of national stereotypes includes 'Cilicians robbing, Phoenicians trading, Egyptians farming, Athenians litigating and Spartans whipping each other' (*Icaromenippos* 16. 771). In addition to endemic violence major revolts broke out in AD 6, 36, 51, possibly two more under Gallienus and Probus in the third century, others in 354, 359, 367-8, 375, 403 and 469.[2] The system of control had on these occasions broken down.

It is time to consider the bandits themselves. In AD 51 the Cietae, who normally lived in the coastal plain near Selinus, withdrew into the Taurus and began to attack the cities. They laid siege to Anemurium where, according to Tacitus, their targets were 'farmers, townsmen and particularly the merchants and the shippers' (*Annales* 12. 55). When we next hear of a specific target, in 354, it is the Metropolis of the Diocletianic province of Isauria, Seleuceia (Ammianus 14. 2). Was banditry simply the countryside's revenge on the town for its economic exploitation and, if so, are bandits to be considered as primitive protesters, proto-revolutionaries, or as freedom-fighters against Roman rule?

---

[1] The closeness between soldiering and banditry was frequently emphasised in the Roman imperial period. Livy (8.34.7-11) saw disobedience by rankers (however highly connected) of officers' commands as the beginning of the descent to banditry. Dio (52.27; 75.2) emphasises how easy is the drift from regular soldiering to banditry.

[2] AD 6: Dio 55.28.3; AD 36: Tac. *Ann.* 6.41; AD 51: *Ann.* 12.55; Gallienus and Probus: S.H.A. *Trig. Tyr.* 26; *Vit. Probi* 16.4; Zosimus 1.69.2, cf. Rouge (1966) Syme (1968) ch. 9; AD 354: Ammianus 14.2; AD 359... Ammianus 19.13; AD 367-8: Ammianus 27.9.6ff.; AD 375: Zosimus 4.20; AD 403: Zosimus 5.25; Sozomen 8.25; Philostorgius 9.8; John Chrysostom *Ep.* 9.4; Jerome *Ep.* 114: AD 469: John of Antioch fr. 206.

We must consider the nature of the targets more closely. The cities were not only centres which extracted the peasants' surplus. They were centres of Hellenic culture and civilisation which, in Strabo's words 'stood far apart from Cilician and Pamphylian customs' (14. 5.4, 670c). The local ruling classes under Roman rule diverted much of their resources to acquiring for their cities the appurtenances of Greco-Roman life, as well as the Greek language. In the countryside Luwian survived well into the fifth century.[1] The city elites distanced themselves considerably from the local peasantry in their language and social habits like bathing and attendance at the gymnasium, many of which activities were only open to the elite. The peasants' surplus was extracted to procure for the local elites an alienating lifestyle. It can hardly be a matter for surprise that cities were a major target of the 'bandits'.

At this point it is necessary to assess to what extent such activity can still be called 'banditry'. Primitive forms of rebellion in underprivileged areas are hardly rare (although today they find their purest expression in riots in areas of urban deprivation), and 'bandit' seems to have been a pejorative term in the Roman political vocabulary for movements to which the writer/speaker is opposed.[2] Yet Hobsbawm has documented cases in which bandit groups form the nucleus of a rebellion (1985, 99). Such a process seems to be implied by Dio's account of a rebellion in AD 6: 'they began from banditry and then moved on to a very dreadful war' (55.28.3). The bandit bands seem to have grown and escalated their activity into a full scale revolt.

But we must consider how much of a protest such a rebellion might have been. For G. Rudé criminal activity can only class as protest if it takes place 'in pursuit of common political goals' (1978, 2). If so, then this rebellion was hardly a protest. This raises a major methodological problem: how does the historian categorize and analyse crime in past societies? A preliminary answer must suffice here. I believe that Rudé's analysis is insufficient, for it would exclude all social rebellions in antiquity. We must accept Hobsbawm's terminology, when he describes such movements as those of 'pre-political people who have not yet found, or only begun

[1] Holl (1908), 240; MacMullen (1966), 1.
[2] For a preliminary discussion cf. MacMullen (1963), 3ff.

to find, a specific language to express their aspirations about the world ...' (1985, 2). The movements we have been considering represent the basic level of protest: for the Cietae (just as with the Handsworth and Brixton rioters today) the simple satisfaction of destruction and looting, a craving well-attested among primitive rebels, must have been sufficient.[1]

The local strong men who formed the nucleus of these movements seem to have held an ambivalent status in their communities, as men to be both loved and feared.[2] An example of local support for such bandits can be seen in the events of 354. In the words of Ammianus Marcellinus:

> (The Isaurians) were now especially exasperated, they declared, by the indignity of some of their associates, who had been taken prisoner, having been thrown to beasts of prey in the shows of the ampitheatre at Iconium, a town of Pisidia - an outrage without precedent. (Ammianus 14.2.1, trans. J.C. Rolfe)

The execution of bandits by this means was prescribed by the Law Codes and is attested by numerous references in the literary sources.[3] Clearly it was not 'an outrage without precedent' in terms of the Roman state. That it was to the Isaurians, who embarked on a large scale revolt as a result of this, is illuminating. Bandits seem to have enjoyed considerable support in their local communities, a fact recognized by the Roman lawyers who realised that such support was essential for the bandits to survive and enjoined local officials to do

---

[1] Hobsbawm (1985 ch. 4) classifies one type of bandit as 'The Avenger'. However the examples he gives all appear under other categories. It is clear, I think, that this is not a type of bandit, but a phase which bandits may go through in the course of their career.

[2] Such indeed are the emotions which Yasar Kemal sees as essential for bandits to arouse: 'Brigands live by love and fear. When they inspire only love, it is a weakness. When they inspire fear, they are hated and have no supporters.' (*Memed My Hawk* ch.7).

[3] Literary sources: e.g. Lucian *Toxaris* 59; Inscriptions collected in L. Robert, *Les Gladiateurs dans L'Orient Grec*, Paris, 1940, esp. 59; 201; 222; 235. For a recent analysis cf. Hopkins (1983), ch.1.

the best they could to erode popular support for bandits and ensure support for the agents of law and order.[1]

Bandits could also reflect local values. Unfortunately, one of the greatest gaps in our knowledge is that we do not have any good evidence for the views of the majority of the population of the Greco-Roman world. On this question there are, however, hints. Tales which surface in the Christian literature (particularly in the Egyptian *Historia Lausiaca*)[2] suggest that as in medieval legend, bandits were seen as 'righters of wrongs'. Such a view adds a particular motive for the harbouring of bandits and anger at the loss of local heroes.

Consequently, bandits could function within their communities, dispensing a local form of law and order which, although not that of the cities and the Roman world, would appear 'just' to the locals.[3]

Under pressure they could retire to the mountains. Here was a different world from the city and its immediate farmland. It was a haunt of wild beasts - as late as the 1890s Vital Cuinet noticed bear, wolf, leopard and hyena in these mountains. A specially tough kind of man was needed to live here. Shepherds looked after the flocks of local landowners and in the course of their annual migrations spent the summer in the mountains. Here they had to fight off attacks by human and animal predators. In 399 a local landowner raised a troop from among his dependants who had been 'trained in many battles with neighbouring bandits' (Zosimus 5.15). Such men carried arms and were distinct in appearance from the town dweller. Lucian described one as 'a rough and hairy fellow, his body showing much exposure to the sun' (*Ignorant Book Collector* 3). In the common man's view, as reflected in Firmicus Maternus' Astrological handbook, shepherds were subverters of established order (*Mathesis* 8.6.6).

In the mountains, what sort of order was maintained? When M. Aurelius recruited Dalmatian hill-tribes to cope with the military emergency of the 160s, the Scriptores Historiae Augustae claim that

[1] *Cod. Iust.* 9.39.2.3.

[2] Available in Migne, *Patrologia Latina* vol. 73, trans. by R.T. Meyer, *Ancient Christian Writers* 34. Cf. col. 1170ff. for a 'Robin Hood' type story (and 1159ff. for a Friar Tuck).

[3] For the early modern period - England, cf. Wrightson (1980).

he recruited 'bandits'.[1] Indeed, to the townsman, those living in the haunts of beasts and lawless men could hardly be otherwise.

In such an environment, the 'outsiders' would associate closely with one another. Ammianus's account of the revolt of 354 indicates that the insurgents used the transhumance routes along the Melas valley still used by semi-nomads today. Parallels for such collaboration between shepherds and bandits or outlaws are not difficult to find. Le Roy Ladurie (1978) has shown how the shepherds of the Pyrenees aided the activities of Albigensian heretics (necessarily peripatetic!) in medieval France and Spain.

Consequently we must consider an area in which the cards are very much in the hands of the forces of disorder. How did the cities retain control?

Policing such territories is a difficult and hazardous operation, even for modern armies and police forces equipped with sophisticated equipment. Ancient 'police forces' suffered from two disadvantages: they had purely local jurisdiction and they were amateurish.

Let us deal with these topics in order. The 'police forces' of ancient cities were constrained to function only within the territories of their individual cities. Needless to say, the bandits did not labour under this impediment. Hobsbawm has described such circumstances as ideal for banditry (1985, 21).

All ancient government was 'amateurish' in the sense that the government was in the hands of landed gentlemen who derived their income from their property. As in senates (*boulai*, *curiae*) throughout the empire, the deliberative bodies of the cities of Rough Cilicia were composed of the wealthiest locals, who were expected to hold high administrative office and finance it, or donate wealth to their communities in the form of hand-outs or building projects. Policing was a task handed out like any other. Libanius (*Oration* 25.43) gives almost comic pictures of city gentlemen called out of their beds to chase bandits. Yet we must not denigrate these police chiefs, called eirenarchs or paraphylaces according to the constitution of the different cities.[2] It is clear from rescripts of Hadrian and Antoninus Pius that such officials were carefully briefed (*Digest* 48.3.6), and the selection process, which Aelius Aristeides managed (with

[1] S.H.A. *M. Aur.* 21.7, cf. Mócsy (1968), 351-4.
[2] For policing in this area, cf. Hopwood (1983) and (1984).

considerable effort) to evade,[1] shows the care with which the provincial governor oversaw appointments.

Even so, the scope of such forces would have been extremely limited. Their assistants seem to have been recruited from the urbanised sections of the population,[2] and evidence suggests that 'preventive policing' as we know it was non-existent. Votive inscriptions set up by police chiefs and their men from Phrygia and Caria suggest the insecurity felt by such men acting outside the city and its immediate environs.[3] The uselessness of such forces is made manifest by the annihilation of Musonius' force of assistant policemen by Isaurian insurgents (Ammianus 27.9.6).

Another point arises: effective policing depends upon a close relationship between the police and the policed. If the police chief comes from the upper classes and exists in a different cultural and linguistic world; if the policemen are drawn from an urban environment and look down on those they police, the efficacy of preventive policing must be minimal. The scenario is one of 'military' policing[4] (to use the modern jargon): alienation of the police from the community and forceful response by the police after a disturbance has occurred.

The laws themselves lay open to misinterpretation and evasion. A prime example is the *Lex Iulia de Vi Publica*, which supposedly ensured the security of the inhabitants of the Roman world from the illegitimate use of violence, and apparently prohibited the possession of weapons. Yet there are exceptions: weapons may be needed for one's livelihood, or bequeathed to one in a will; the possession of such weapons is not an offence. However, the final clause provides us with the greatest difficulty:

> those who carry weapons for the sake of protecting their own
> safety do not appear to carry weapons for the sake of killing men.
> *(Digest* 48.6.1-11)

---

[1]   Aristeides, *Sacred Discourse* 4.31.601. (= Dindorf p.523.)

[2]   M.A.M.A. 3. 305 firmly roots a diogmites in Corycian urban society. Pay suits such a background (Libanius *Or.* 48.9).

[3]   Reinach (1908), 499f.

[4]   Cf. Lea and Young (1984); Bowden (1978).

This law seems to probe into the intentions of the possessor of the weapons. How could it have been enforced? Clearly the arresting officer must have grounds for suspecting a felonious intent.[1] If not, the arrest is purely on the grounds of suspicion. We have seen earlier how shepherds as well as bandits would appear different from town-dwellers and they carried weapons for their self-protection. Perhaps a man known to the arresting officer might have a better chance of avoiding arrest and interrogation. More likely a fellow town councillor or a member of the urban culture would not be arrested, while an outsider would. The laws were written so as to be differentially enforced.

The bias of such differential enforcement was strengthened by the process of arrest and trial. Eirenarchs were instructed to conduct the preliminary hearing and then send the accused with a written account of proceedings to the provincial governor (*Digest* 48.3.6). It seems from what little we know of the introductory hearing that the eirenarch had much scope for the exercise of his initiative. The eirenarch, Herodes, in Smyrna gently chides St Polycarp until he realizes that the martyr is resolved on death (*Acta Polycarpi* 8). On the other hand, a fragmentary papyrus transcript of a hearing in Egypt suggests that torture was used to extract a confession from the accused (Antinoöpolis Papyri 87).

It is clear that torture was a process which the provincial governor could deploy. A child's bilingual school-book gives the following account of everyday things in the forum:[2]

> The defendant, a bandit, stands. He is interrogated according to his
> deserts. He is tortured: the torturer beats him, his chest is
> constricted, he is hung up, racked, beaten with clubs, he goes
> through the whole gamut of tortures and still he denies. He is to
> be punished ... he is led to the sword.

---

[1] Assuming, of course, that the arrest is not *in flagrante delicto*. It has been pointed out to me by Professor Crook that the initiative to decide whether an action is being committed with felonious intent or not always lies with the arresting officer. I agree, but stress that within such initiative, prejudice, bias and social discrimination may well turn the apparently unbiased and legal decision of the officer into an expression of the dominant ideology: in this case the city's.

[2] Published by Dionisotti (1982), at p. 105.

A further law enjoins magistrates to torture bandits and Isaurians even over Easter (*Codex Theodosianus* 9.35.7).

Polycarp presumably is treated leniently because he is the social equal of Herodes. His crime of Christianity may have been seen as less dangerous than banditry: but these incidents still emphasize the discretion available at a later stage of proceedings.

Today we tend to distrust torture as we believe that the suspect will confess what is not the 'truth' to save himself from further pain.[1] This is based on our belief that we need to find the 'true' or 'real' culprit. Early legal systems did not fetter themselves with such a practice. This is not to say that the Romans were unaware of the dangers inherent in the use of evidence gained by torture. Quintilian (*Institutio* 5.4.1) gives a list of arguments (familiar to us today) by which such evidence may be overthrown. But we must not suppose that torture was seen as something special. He goes on in his next section to show how to overthrow written documents.

The usefulness of torture lies in the way it provides for you the confession you want from the suspect's mouth. The vision the law-enforcement authorities had of crime would be confirmed by the enforced confession: torture validates the authorities' preconceived views about the nature of crime and the criminal. Recent research on criminal confessions suggests that the accused often attribute their crime to unconscious impulse, 'I don't know what made me do it'.[2] After such confessions society could rest secure that these outrages were perpetrated by men who were insane and bestial. 'In all those regions where the bestial madness of banditry, which cares not for its own safety, rages', opens one law (*Codex Theodosianus* 1.29.8).

A weak police force, discretionary laws and differential enforcement sounds like a recipe for disaster. Under such circumstances how was order maintained? We arrive at a silence in the sources. Let us try another line of approach.

South-west of ancient Cagrae lies the site of Emerye Kalesi. The most prominent remaining structure is a tower, built of well-squared masonry, with foundations of outbuildings to the north. An

---

[1] On torture see now Peters (1985).
[2] Cohen (1971), 27-61.

inscription above the doorway describes it as a *pyrgos* belonging to a family known from other inscriptions to have been resident in Cagrae.[1] *Pyrgos* seems to denote the centre of an estate, and as a technical term has figured prominently in recent discussions of the forms of seigneurial holdings of Achaemenid, Hellenistic and Roman Asia Minor.[2] The tower itself is square, with a small doorway, with many slots for bars. Outside the tower lie the remains of outbuildings. It is located in a fertile depression, with some remains of ancient field systems to the north. The physical ownership of much of the land, and control of tenant farms (as *pyrgos* seems to imply) must have kept many of the peasants of the in-fields close to the urban elites.

Another factor lies in the positioning of such towers. Emerye Kalesi, the tower at Söler, that at Avasun and that at Uzunkale, all lie on the edge of the cultivable land, in the interface between arable and pastoral territories. In such an area, the fruits of arable and pastoral production are fragile: they need protection from animal and human predators. The smallness of agrarian surpluses in this area must have exacerbated the problem. The smallness of peasant holdings may have led to a similar problem for the peasant, and the vulnerability of their flocks is a constant source of anxiety for transhumants:[3] all these features lead to a need for protection. Such protection was available in the estates of the wealthy. The towers we have considered would have been in an ideal position for such a purpose.

Yet protection in a rural society is competitive.[4] A 'protector' has to ensure that his protection is better than that of his rivals to obtain the greater following in the community, access to more resources and so increase his standing. Such a process turns protection into a protection racket:[5] the unacceptable face of patronage.

Protection rackets need strong-arm men, of whom, as we have seen, there was no shortage in the Taurus Mountains. The estate

[1] Described in Bean and Mitford (1970), 28-9.

[2] C.B. Welles, *Royal Correspondence in the Hellenistic Period* (1934) nos.18, 20 and 320ff; Robert (1963), 14f.; Broughton (1938) 628-9; Hunt (1947); Nowicka (1965); Briant (1973); Debord (1976-7); Kreissig (1977).

[3] On the insecurity of pastoral wealth see N.P. Khaznov (1984); Nelson (1973).

[4] Cf. Blok (1974).

[5] Cf. Scott (1977).

owners need not stoop to carry out their own strong-arm work (although there is a law forbidding the curial elite from indulging in banditry).[1] What is more revealing is the sequence of laws forbidding *curiales* to hide bandits on their estates.[2] As we have seen, such protection would be secure as the *curiales* were the agents of law enforcement. Bandits would have to court the patronage of *curiales* to survive for a reasonable period. The bandits who act in the peasants' interests are the heroes of popular legend, yet they are the failures who do not re-integrate themselves into society. Blok (1974) and Lewin (1979) have shown that successful bandits are dependent on the help of landlords and local administrative officials. Here the landlords were the administrative officials.

Tough men could be used to show the ineffectiveness of rivals' patronage by direct action, by and large consisting of robbery and rustling. Perhaps a similar system in late Roman Gaul lies behind Ausonius' letter to his friend:

> Or are you chasing thieves who wander throughout your area,
> who, finally fearing you, call you into partnership and share the
> booty? You, a gentle and idle chap, condone human bloodshed for
> money and call it all a mistake and impose a rate on rustled cattle
> and take the business from the courts. (Ausonius *Ep*. 14.22-7)

In such cases the laws against 'fences' would have little weight.

The situation was exacerbated by the principle of self-help. The *Lex Julia de Vi Publica* allowed people to carry arms to oppose bandits on their estates. Two laws of 243 AD[3] absolve murderers of brigands of guilt and a further law states that it is the right of all to resist banditry.[4] But, as we may now begin to suspect, the identity of the bandit was uncertain. The activity of murder is therefore open to several legal interpretations, one of which may make it legitimate. Presumably the local authorities (i.e. the law officers drawn from the curial classes) would have to decide who was helping himself in a

---

[1] *Digest* 48.19.27.2.

[2] *Cod. Theod.* 19.29.1; *Cod. Theod.* 9.29.2; *Cod. Theod.* 8.18.7; *Cod. Iust.* 9.39.1-2; *Cod. Iust.* 9.12.10.

[3] *Cod. Iust.* 9.16.2-3.

[4] *Cod. Iust.* 3.27.1.

legitimate cause and who was helping himself in an illegitimate cause. Presumably those who have property are more likely to be defending it than those who haven't: those who have a political stake in the community (which, in Roman times, meant the wealthy) were seen as more likely to act in a legitimate fashion. The system gives the propertied insider considerable leeway against the unpropertied outsider.

Consequently we hear of estate guards (*horophylakes*),[1] who are by profession strong-arm men. In view of the laws about harbouring bandits, who are the poachers and who the gamekeepers? A law of Leo in the fifth century AD suggests that such harbouring had by then become widespread: 'we wish to end the freedom of having *bucellarii* or Isaurians or armed slaves in fields and in the cities' (*Codex Justinianus* 9.12.10).

This may give us an insight into one of the more curious aspects of Cilician history. At the end of the revolt of 367 AD, the Isaurians

> by means of intermediaries asked for peace for themselves, at the instigation of the inhabitants of Germanicopolis, whose opinions (like those of standard-bearers in a unit) always hold sway among them. Consequently, after the Isaurians had handed over hostages as required, they attempted no warlike acts during a long period of peace and quiet. (Ammianus 27.9.7, trans. J.C. Rolfe)

The inhabitants of Germanicopolis, presumably the town-councillors, were able to negotiate with both the insurgents and the Romans. We must assume that their weight with the Romans was due to their status as local government officials and the local men of quality. What had the Germanicopolitani to do with the rebels? How could they instigate a peace? If my model is accepted, the disturbance arose from a breakdown of local order which was as much against the interests of the Germanicopolitani as of the Romans. Now that a Roman army was approaching, they were able to reimpose their authority. For the Romans, they were useful brokers[2] ensuring the avoidance of a troublesome war.

[1] M.A.M.A. 8.354; L. Robert, *Hellenica* 7, p.58.

[2] A useful analysis of this concept is that by Adams (1970). See also Boissevain (1974).

As brokers, they were able to provide the Romans with a peaceful Isauria by means of their reassertion of clientage networks, as well as provide the Isaurians with peace and no Roman invasion by means of their own status conferred by the Romans. As patrons of their countryside, yet clients of the Roman government, they performed a broker's role - ensuring to their patrons and clients access to resources in their respective areas of activity.

In the Roman relations with Cilicia, its administrators and people, we can see how patronage was a means by which the centre controlled the periphery.[1] This was a two-stage operation. The first step, which has been well-researched,[2] is the construction of patron-client networks between town-councillors and Rome, serviced by means of embassies, promising loyalty to Rome and receiving in return benefits for the cities. The second step was the patronage by the curial classes of their peasants, shepherds and strong-arm men in the countryside, granting 'protection' to peasants and bandits alike in return for the specialisms each was capable of. Is it possible to see such networks being 'serviced'? Possibly satirical hints in Ausonius are not enough. Laws against town-councillors playing the bandit point in the right direction; the law forbidding town-councillors to give their children to shepherds for rearing points to intriguing possibilities (*Codex Theodosianus* 9.31.1); the increased need for supervision of local by central government suggests that local government officers were playing a different game from that expected of them. Finally the abolition of the chief police officers in 408 as 'a race ruinous to the state' (*Codex Theodosianus* 12.14.1) perhaps hints at the transformation possible in such an office.

It was the enforcement of law and order by men of property who were themselves engaged in the competitive use of resources which must have tempted them to exercise their old power through new trappings. And as local agents of patronage their 'justice' supplemented the 'justice' of the bandits in the eyes of the peasants. As long as the system worked, everybody seemed to benefit: 'the ideology of patronage underwrote the status and authority of the elite' (Silverman 1977, 13). The apparent universalistic ascriptive criteria of the Roman state may then have been superseded locally by local

[1] Cf. the discussion of patronage in Morocco in Eisenstadt and Roniger (1984), 95-9.

[2] Cf. Millar (1977), ch.7; Bowersock (1969); Millar (1983).

paternalistic forces.[1] Within the laws which they enforced, social status was explicitly stated; patronage and 'influence' were inscribed within the interstices of the legal structure: that hidden 'supplement' needed to make sense of the edifice.

Bibliography

Adams, R.N. (1970), 'Brokers and career mobility systems in the structure of complex societies', *Southwestern Journal of Anthropology* 26, 315-27.

Bean, G.E. and Mitford, T.B. (1970), 'Journeys in Rough Cilicia 1964-1968', *Dentschriften der Österreichische Akademie der Wissenschaften in Wien* (Phil. Hist. Klasse 102 Band), 28-9.

Blok, A. (1974), *The Mafia of a Sicilian Village 1860-1960*. Oxford.

Boissevain, J. (1974), *Friends of Friends: Networks, Manipulators and Coalitions*. Oxford.

Bowden, T. (1978), *Beyond the Limits of the Law: a Comparative Study of the Police in Crisis Politics*. Harmondsworth.

Bowersock, G. (1969), *Greek Sophists in the Roman Empire*. Oxford.

Briant, P. (1973) ,'Remarques sur "laoi" et esclaves ruraux en Asie Mineure hellénistique', *Actes du Colloque de 1971 sur l'esclavage* (Centre Rech. Hist. nc. Vol. 140) 93-133. Besançon.

Broughton, T.R.S. (1938), 'Roman Asia Minor', in T. Frank (ed.), *An Economic Survey of Ancient Rome* vol. 4. Baltimore.

Cohen, S. (ed.) (1971), *Images of Deviance*. Harmondsworth.

Debord, M.P., (1976-7), 'Populations rurales de l'Anatolie Gréco-Romaine', *Atti Centro Studi e Documentazione sull' Italia Romana* 8, 43-69.

Dionisotti, A.C. (1982), 'From Ausonius' schooldays? A schoolbook and its relatives', *Journal of Roman Studies* 72, 83-125.

Eisenstadt, S.N. and Roniger, L. (1984), *Patrons, Clients and Friends*. Cambridge.

Gellner, E. and Waterbury, J. (eds.) (1977), *Patrons and Clients in Mediterranean Societies*. London.

---

[1] The opposition is that of Eisenstadt and Roniger (1984).

Hobsbawm E.J. (1985), *Bandits*. Harmondsworth.

Holl, K. (1908), 'Das Fortleben der Volksprachen in Kleinasien in nachchristlicher Zeit', *Hermes* XLIII, 240-54.

Hopkins, K. (1983), *Death and Renewal*. Cambridge.

Hopwood, K. (1983), 'Policing the hinterland: Rough Cilicia and Isauria', in S. Mitchell (ed.), *Armies and Frontiers in Roman and Byzantine Anatolia* (B.A.R. International Series 156), 173-87. Oxford.

Hopwood, K. (1984), 'Policing the Melas Valley', *Yayla* 5, 25-9.

Hunt, D.W.S. (1947), 'Feudal survivals in Ionia', *Journal of Hellenic Studies* 67, 68-76.

Khaznov, A.M. (1984), *Nomads and the Outside World*. Cambridge.

Kreissig, H. (1977), 'Landed property in the "Hellenistic" Orient', *Eirene* 15, 5-25.

Le Roy Ladurie, E. (1978), *Montaillou. Cathars and Catholics in a French Village 1294-1324*, trans. B. Bray. London.

Lea, J. and Young J. (1984), *What is to be done about Law and Order?* Harmondsworth.

Lewin, L. (1979), 'The oligrarchical limitations of social banditry in Brazil: the case of the "good" thief Antonio Silvino', *Past and Present* 82, 116-46.

MacMullen, R. (1963), 'The Roman concept robber-pretender', *Revue Internationale des Droits de l'Antiquité* (3) 10, 221-3.

MacMullen, R. (1966), 'Provincial languages in the Roman empire', *American Journal of Philology* 87, 1-17.

Millar, F.G.B. (1977), *The Emperor in the Roman World: 31 BC - AD 337*. London.

Millar, F.G.B. (1983), 'Empire and city, Augustus to Julian: obligations, excuses and status', *Journal of Roman Studies* 73, 76-96.

Mócsy, A. (1968), 'Latrones ardaniae', *Acta Antiqua Academiae Scientarum Hungaricae* 16, 351-4.

Nelson, C. (ed.) (1973), *The Desert and the Sown: Nomads in the Wider Society*. Berkeley.

Nowicka, M. (1965), 'Les maisons de tour dans le monde grec' *Bibliotheca Antiqua* 15.

Peters, E. (1985), *Torture*. Oxford.

Reinach, Th. (1908), *Bulletin de Correspondance Hellénique* 32, 499-513.

Robert, L. (1963), *Noms Indigènes dans l'Asie Mineure Greco-Romaine*. Paris.

Rougé, J. (1966), 'L'Histoire Auguste et l'Isaurie au IVème siecle', *Revue des Études Anciennnes* 68, 282-315.

Rudé, G. (1978), *Protest and Punishment*. Oxford.

Scott, J. (1977), 'Patronage or exploitation?' in Gellner and Waterbury (1977), 21-39.

Shaw, B.D. (1984), 'Bandits in the Roman empire', *Past and Present* 105, 3-52.

Silverman, S. (1977), 'Patronage as myth', in Gellner and Waterbury (1977), 7-20.

Syme, R. (1968), *Ammianus and the Historia Augusta*. Oxford.

Welles, C.B. (1934), *Royal Correspondance in the Hellenistic Period : a Study in Greek Epigraphy*. New Haven.

Wrightson, K. (1980), 'Two concepts of order: justices, constables and jurymen in seventeenth-century England', in J. Brewer and J. Styles (eds.), *An Ungovernable People: the English and their Law in the Seventeenth and Eighteenth Centuries*. London.

Chapter 9
Patronage in Roman Gaul and the problem of the Bagaudae[1]

John Drinkwater

According to Julius Caesar, dependence and patronage were established features of northern Gallic society at the time of the Roman conquest (58-50 BC). He describes how ordinary people, in order to protect themselves against powerful men in general, followed certain individuals and helped promote their political careers:

> for no leader allows his supporters to be oppressed or cheated, and
> if he fails to protect them, he loses his authority over them.
> (Caesar, *De Bello Gallico* 6.11.4, trans. Wiseman)

Only a little further on in his narrative, however, Caesar paints a somewhat gloomier picture of this relationship. The majority of Gauls, far from being able to choose freely as to whether they should follow great men, were compelled by poverty or fear to enter their service, and to be absolutely dependent upon them:

[1] This paper differs somewhat from that delivered at the Nottingham seminar, in which I dealt in more detail with the question of the reliability of our evidence for the Bagaudae (I hope to present this discussion elsewhere). I would like to thank members of the seminar for their help in revising my contribution for publication. I would also like to express my gratitude to Professor E.A. Thompson for having so patiently listened to my criticism of his views, and for subsequently having given me welcome advice and a number of very useful offprints.

Most of them, crushed by debt or heavy taxes or the oppression of more powerful men, pledge themselves to serve the nobles, who exercise over them the same rights as masters have over slaves.
(Caesar, *De Bello Gallico* 6.13.1-3)

The most important obligation performed by dependants for members of the Gallic nobility (Caesar's *equites* or 'knights') was to assist them in their military campaigns:

Whenever a war breaks out and their services are required ... all [knights] are involved in the campaign, each one attended by as many retainers and dependants (*ambactos clientisque*) as his birth and wealth make possible. The size of a knight's following is the only criterion of influence and power they recognise.
(Caesar, *De Bello Gallico* 6.15.1-2)

Elsewhere, indeed, Caesar refers to powerful and ambitious Gallic aristocrats using their wealth to increase the size of their armed retinues.[1]

Caesar's account of pre-conquest Gallic society has to be treated with care: he was no social anthropologist. Many of the details he gives are obscure (for example, in the third passage quoted above the exact significance of the words Caesar employs to distinguish between different degrees of dependence (Celtic *ambactus* and Latin *cliens*) is much debated).[2] Moreover, he may well have exaggerated certain features of Gallic social behaviour in order to comment on contemporary political developments in Rome.[3] However, in general terms his account of Gallic patronage rings true; and although the institution found its most visible expression in time of war, we may legitimately suppose that it was just as pervasive in time of peace, governing the lives not only of the fighting men, but also their families, and *their* dependants, down to the bottom of the social scale. In this respect, likely analogues of independent Gallic society are to be found in early-medieval Wales and Ireland; as Wightman, in an important survey of the subject, remarks:

[1] *De Bello Gallico* 1.18.4-5; 2.1.4.
[2] E.g. Rice Holmes (1911), 514-16; and, most recently, Daubigney (1983), 659-83.
[3] Drinkwater (1983), 176.

The evidence for all Celtic societies, including Gaulish society at
the time of the conquest, indicates a social hierarchy with strong
vertical ties of interdependency between the rich and the powerful
and the poor and weak. (Wightman 1978, 97)

The Roman conquest brought change. As Wightman also
suggests, the previously undefined relationship between lords and
dependants may, under the Roman system of taxation, have been
strictly formalised, with the latter becoming tenants (*coloni*) of the
former, rendering their dues in cash rather than kind.[1] Without doubt,
the supervision and protection of Gaul by the imperial army spelled
the death of the old military obligations.[2] However, even the military
tradition took some time to disappear: we may perhaps perceive its
continued operation during Germanicus' campaigns of retribution over
the Rhine, early in the first century AD;[3] and it must have played a
part in Julius Indus' formation of a Treveran cavalry-regiment to help
Rome during the rebellion of 21.[4] Possibly, too, it helped Vindex
raise the native militias against Nero in 68.[5] Thus Gallic patronage
was still a force to be reckoned with; and although its military aspect
eventually withered away, in civil life the close relationship between
those who owned the wealth of Gaul and those who created it
continued to be an important feature of Romano-Gallic life.

This was especially so in the countryside, where most of the
population lived. Always wary of radical change, Rome kept in being
the traditional Gallic nations (*civitates*). At her prompting each
civitas developed its own capital city, designed on Roman lines.
These *civitas*-capitals were to be the foci of activity of the Gallic
landowners, in order both that such might be easily supervised and
that they might learn the ways of the conquerors.[6] The Gallic
aristocrats complied, but do not seem to have forgotten their local
roots. This may be seen, for example, in inscriptions recording

1 Wightman (1978), 104.
2 Wightman (1978), 103.
3 Tacitus, *Annales* 1.56.1; cf. Drinkwater (1983), 26.
4 Tacitus, *Annales* 3.42.3; cf. Drinkwater (1978), 829 and nn.
5 Drinkwater (1983), 42.
6 Drinkwater (1983), 141; cf. Drinkwater (1985), 51.

aristocratic office-holding and munificence at tribal (*pagus*) level.[1] The most dramatic evidence is, however, archaeological. This does not, as one might expect, consist of large, palatial, country-houses, with coronas of subsidiary manors and farms: such an arrangement is uncommon in Gaul.[2] Rather, it is the existence of expensive and extensive complexes of religious and recreational facilities, of a type usually associated with the main urban centres, sited by minor townships or even deep in the countryside: the so-called *conciliabula*, which inscriptions indicate were built by local aristocrats.[3] Such lavish provision of urban-style amenities for the rural populace (significantly different from what occurred in other parts of the empire: see Hopwood above) is plausibly explained by the continuation of strong local ties, that would naturally find expression in mutual assistance: the rich provided buildings and entertainment, and were rewarded with popular adulation and support in the traditional manner.[4]

> In the late-Roman period, from the end of the third century, insecurity and fiscal pressures resulted in an intensification of the patron-client relationship between rich landowners and poor *coloni*. (Wightman 1978, 97)

Indeed, as conditions deteriorated great Gallic landowners attracted crowds of dependants. The Aquitanian, Paulinus of Pella, recounts how early in the fifth century he went about attended by 'deferential crowds and throngs of supporting clients' (*Eucharisticon* 437). In return the Gallic aristocrat would have been expected to protect his supporters from the demands of other notables and the imperial tax-collectors: in the first half of the fifth century the cleric Salvian of Marseilles deplored the state of affairs which forced the poor to seek relief from the rich in this way:

[1] Drinkwater (1983), 108f; cf. Drinkwater (1984), 360.
[2] Drinkwater (1983), 171-5.
[3] Drinkwater (1983), 179-81.
[4] Cf. Drinkwater (1985), 54.

They put themselves under the care and protection of the powerful,
make themselves the surrendered captives of the rich and so pass
under their jurisdiction.

(Salvian, *De Gubernatione Dei* 5.8.38, trans. Sandford)

The similarity with Caesar's account of pre-conquest society is
striking; it comes as no surprise that people again sought the safety
of hill-refuges and that the mid-fifth century Gallic warrior-nobleman
Ecdicius raised his own army against the Visigoths besieging
Clermont-Ferrand.[1]

It seems evident, therefore, that patronage and dependence persisted
as key factors in Gallic social relations throughout the period of
Roman rule, and beyond. The question that I wish to address myself
to here is whether we are therefore entitled to assume that their
operation was *continuous*, taking as a test-case a specific, extraordinary and fascinating development in Gallo-Roman social history:
the emergence of the Bagaudae.

The Bagaudae made their first appearance late in the third century.
According to Aurelius Victor and Eutropius, the emperor Diocletian,
following his victory over his western rival Carinus in 285, heard
that the Gallic countryside was being laid waste by 'a band of rustics'
under Aelianus and Amandus, and that these 'Bagaudae', as they were
called locally, were now attacking towns. He immediately appointed
Maximian as Caesar, and sent him to put down the troublemakers; by
the end of 286 the country was quiet.[2] This account is complemented
by a panegyric delivered before Maximian by the Gallic orator
Mamertinus in April, 289. Mamertinus does not mention the
Bagaudae by name, but scholars agree in seeing an allusion to them
in his embarrassed praise of Maximian's suppression of 'ignorant
farmers' who had donned military dress and, like the barbarian invader,
laid waste their own fields.[3]

The next direct mention of the Bagaudae is made in relation to
events over a century later. In 408, Zosimus relates (*Nova Historia* 6.

---

[1]   *CIL* 12.1524 (= *ILS* 1279), with Gilles (1985); Sidonius Apollinaris,
Epistulae 3.3.7. Cf. Wightman (1978), 115.

[2]   *De Caesaribus* 39.17-20; *Breviarium* 9.20.3. For this section in general see
Czúth (1965); and for a review of recent Bagaudic studies, Thompson (1982),
221-3. To the latter should be added Dockès (1980) and Drinkwater (1984).

[3]   *Panegyrici Latini* (ed. Galletier) 2(10).4.3-4.

2.5), Stilicho sent the Goth Sarus into southern Gaul against the usurper Constantine III. Sarus, however, was eventually forced to withdraw, and had to treat with Alpine Bagaudae to secure a safe passage to Italy. In addition scholars have generally accepted that we have three important indirect indications of continuing Bagaudic activity a decade or so later than the Sarus incident. The most significant of these is Rutilius Namatianus' *De Reditu Suo*, written to celebrate its author's return from Italy to his Gallic homeland in 416-7. The poem includes praise of his relative, Exuperantius, who was at the time 'teaching the regions of Aremorica to love the return of peace', and who had already restored liberty and the rule of law, and seen to it that (*sc.* respectable) people were 'not the servants of their own slaves' (1. 213-216). Namatianus' reference to trouble in Aremorica fits in well with Zosimus' account (*Nova Historia* 6.5.2-3) of a revolt there around 407, which led to the expulsion of Roman officials. It also seems to allow us to make sense of a short passage in a surviving fragment of an anonymous late Latin comedy, the *Querolus*, possibly dedicated to Namatianus himself, and therefore ascribable to the early fifth century. Here mention is made of life on the Loire, where men lived according to natural law, where there were no differences in status, where even the most important legal cases were held in the open, where peasants acted as advocates and private citizens as judges: where everything was allowed (ed. Ranstrand, p. 17). Taking all three passages together, it is not difficult to see why it has been supposed that between about 407 and 417 Aremorica was in the grip of Bagaudic revolution.[1]

If indirect reference to the Bagaudae is allowed for the early fifth century, it becomes possible to fill the long gap between 286 and 407/8 by accepting as Bagaudic the trouble in Gaul in 369, as recorded by Ammianus Marcellinus. According to him the emperor Valentinian I had to suppress 'a savage frenzy for brigandage' in the interior of Gaul, which had even led to the murder of a member of the imperial family.[2]

However, notwithstanding the efforts of Exuperantius, we find the Bagaudae at their most active in the middle years of the fifth century. Salvian, writing around 439/41 and, as we have seen, deploring the

---

[1] Thus Thompson (1952), 16.
[2] Ammianus 27.2.10 (not listed by Czúth, 1965).

helplessness of the weak and the poor in the face of the corruption and the rapacity of government officials and landowners, mentions the recent flight of certain of the oppressed to the Bagaudae, whom he depicts as poor outlaws, persecuted by the very authorities whose vices had brought them into being. Furthermore, he suggests that the Bagaudae were to be found throughout Gaul and Spain (*De Gubernatione Dei* 5. 21-27). As far as Gaul is concerned, Salvian's rather general remarks fit in well with particular notices in the *Gallic Chronicle of 452*, concerning a Bagaudic revolt, involving almost all the servile classes in 'Further Gaul' under the leadership of a certain Tibatto, just a few years before (in fact between 435 and Tibatto's capture in 437).[1] This in turn accommodates a remark in Sidonius Apollinaris (*Carmina* 7.246-8), concerning the military success of Litorius against 'the Aremoricans' in 437. Chronic Bagaudic unrest in Aremorica ties in well with events earlier in the century, and may also help explain a reference in Constantius' *Life* of bishop Germanus of Auxerre, written c.480, to the saint's aid being solicited by the Aremoricans in the mid- to late-440s. Their problem was that Aetius, the Roman commander-in-chief in the west, angered by their 'insolence', had charged Goar, king of the Alans, to bring them into line. Germanus agreed to intercede with Goar and the imperial government, and indeed a peace would have been settled, had not Tibatto once again inspired revolt among the 'fickle and undisciplined populace'.[2]

In the context of Tibatto's second rising is perhaps to be placed Sidonius Apollinaris' reference (*Carmina* 5.210-13) to the future emperor Majorian's defence of Tours; and in the context of Tibatto's ultimate defeat we may be able to put the poet Merobaudes' mention of the pacification of Aremorica by Aetius, described in terms of the abolition of brigandage, the restoration of agriculture and the acceptance of imperial law. Also emphasised is the ending of fraternisation with neighbouring barbarians.[3] Mention of Merobaudes takes us conveniently to Spain, where Salvian's information apparently fits in well with notices in his contemporary Hydatius'

[1] Ann. 452, 117.

[2] *Vita S. Germani* 28, 40. (The exact date of the incident is disputed.)

[3] *Panegyricus* 2.8-22. (The chronology of this undertaking is again controversial.)

continuation of Jerome's *Chronica*. According to Hydatius, Merobaudes' father-in-law, Asturius, and Merobaudes himself, as successive *duces utriusque militiae*, had, at a somewhat earlier date (c.441-3), to suppress Bagaudic activity in Tarraconensis. However, Hydatius also reveals that such trouble continued in the area even after their time, led by a certain Basilius, and that it was not until 454 that Frederick, brother of the Visigothic king Theoderic, acting under imperial Roman orders, put them down for good.[1]

The single most influential interpretation of the Bagaudae over the last three and a half decades has undoubtedly been that of E.A. Thompson.[2] His is essentially a modification of established Marxist thinking, which would see the Bagaudae as the product of growing social tension in the west, combatants in an ancient class war that eventually led to the disappearance of the slave-owning society of the classical period, as represented and protected by the imperial Roman government, and the appearance of medieval feudalism.[3] Thompson avoids the controversial issue of the relative importance of slavery in the west, but is at pains to bring out the revolutionary policies of the Bagaudae, in particular by laying great emphasis on the testimony of Rutilius Namatianus and the *Querolus*. Following the lead of Dmitrev, he also underlines the (perhaps even conscious) continuity of their movement by tracing its history back to the revolt of Maternus under Caracalla.[4] However, of late an alternative explanation has been gaining ground.

Like that which it seeks to displace, this interpretation is based on the acceptance of continuity, but not that of developing conflict between rich and poor. Rather its protagonists emphasise the long established tradition of *co-operation* between people of different wealth and status in Gaul, embodied in the institution of patronage: far from being mortal enemies, landlords and Bagaudae were bound together by mutual ties of dependence and obligation.[5] Such a concept

[1] Hydatius, 125, 128, 141, 142, 154.

[2] Thompson (1952), with Thompson (1956).

[3] See e.g. Dockès (1980); and de Ste. Croix (1981), 374-9.

[4] Thompson (1952), 12f. (and nn. 6, 10), 15, 18f.

[5] Wightman (1978), 103, cf. 111; Wightman (1985), 199f. (A complication here is that Wightman's thinking was shaped by the 1974 doctoral dissertation of R. Van Dam, on whom see below.) For 'barons' and 'dynasts' see Drinkwater (1978), 817 and n.1.

is not new. Its essentials were neatly expressed in Lady Brogan's comment that 'the incipient feudalism of the great estates is a theme running through the story of Gaul';[1] and its use as a tool in understanding the Bagaudae was perceived by MacMullen when, in a strong criticism of Thompson's hypothesis, he argued that the predominantly vertical social ties of ancient society would have prevented the polarisation of rich and poor 'as two compact armies facing each other', and proposed that greater emphasis should be laid on the dependence of the poor upon powerful patrons. He envisaged the rich as creating 'little realms', composed of people from all levels of society.[2] However, the implications of such thinking have only very recently been developed to their fullest by Van Dam (1985).

Like his predecessors Van Dam accepts 'the structural continuity of Gallic society', and envisages Roman Gaul throughout its history as being a land of 'small local tyrannies', each held together by 'the exercise of informal patronage' (1985, 14ff.). When imperial power was strong these local power nexus were lost to view, but when it flagged they reappeared, as people looked to their traditional leaders for direction and security. He sees this occurring in the troubles of the third century with the emergence of the 'Gallic' emperors and Carausius, and the Bagaudae. The last were not peasant revolutionaries, but the poor returning:

> to traditional ties of social dependence ... In this interpretation the Bagaudae become men rallying around local leaders out of a need for security. (Van Dam 1985, 27, 31)

These leaders were local Romanised aristocrats, condemned and crushed as outlaws, even barbarians, rather than as saviours of the Roman order, by harassed central administrations that knew and cared little about what they stood for. However, in Van Dam's opinion the modern historian should be prepared to regard at least some of them as failed imperial usurpers since, out of habit and education, they would have attempted to express their status through Roman titles and ceremonial (1985, 20-4).

Unlike Thompson, Van Dam does not attach any great importance to the revolt of Maternus, seeing in it just the illegitimate practice of

[1]   Brogan (1953), 129.
[2]   MacMullen (1966), 198f. cf. 233.

local power, which serves only to remind us of the protection that 'conventional' aristocrats could offer their dependants (1985, 19). Likewise, he discounts the impression of social revolution to be found in Rutilius Namatianus and the *Querolus* (1985, 41f., 46f.).

Such thinking is very attractive because it accords better with what we know about the workings of Gallic society than that of Thompson, and indeed it leads easily to the emergence of the Christian bishop as the local patron in late- and sub-Roman Gaul, one of the main themes of Van Dam's work. However, I would argue that the plausibility of his explanation of the Bagaudae is, in the event, no greater than that of its predecessor. For example, his dismissal of the Gallic emperors of the third century as 'local leaders with limited influence' is certainly mistaken, given the support afforded to them by the armies of Germany and Britain.[1] Likewise, since his model demands that local aristocratic leadership could only become effective in the absence of strong imperial authority, he has to deny the occurrence of serious trouble in Gaul under Valentinian I.[2] More important however, in my view, is the fact that he is unable convincingly to identify any Bagaudic leader as a usurping Gallic aristocrat or, conversely, any usurping Gallic aristocrat as a Bagaudic leader. As far as the former is concerned, his characterisation of Amandus and Aelianus as local landowners and of Tibatto as 'a local aristocrat' is entirely speculative.[3] With regard to the latter, the nearest he gets is his interpretation of Exuperantius: as a Pictonian landowner taking it upon himself to restore order locally following barbarian invasion (1985, 41f.). Yet Rutilius Namatianus clearly did not regard Exuperantius as exercising illegitimate power; most modern authorities indeed assume that he acted as he did as an official in the service of the Empire.[4]

[1] See Drinkwater (1987), ch. 4.

[2] Van Dam (1985), 33. Sirago (1969), 503f., would also see Julian's trouble with 'Alamannic' *laeti* as a Bagaudic disturbance.

[3] Van Dam (1985), 30f., 45. With regard to the former, the numismatic evidence (*RIC* v.2, p.595: three barbarous radiates of 'Amandus') is hardly to be trusted; and generally the archaeological evidence cannot support the weight that Van Dam puts on it. Cf. Thompson (1952), 18.

[4] Stroheker (1948), no. 141; *PLRE* ii, 448 (both, it must be conceded, acknowledged by Van Dam); also Dockès (1980), 221.

In fact I am profoundly sceptical of the thesis that any great Gallic landowner could have drifted from self-help into the kind of half-baked usurpation that Van Dam's ideas regarding 'the fuzziness of the distinction between legitimate and illegitimate authority at a local level' (1985, 19) suggest. The rules of accession were well-enough known in the later empire, as Gallic history of the fourth and fifth centuries clearly shows. Usurpers needed the proper imperial insignia, which had to be assembled and bestowed with great care and ceremony; and above all they needed to be able to depend on strong military backing. The careers of Magnentius, Silvanus, Julian, Eugenius, Jovinus and Avitus would have shown all Gallic aristocrats who aspired to the purple how the job should be done.[1]

A fundamental question here, however, is the very nature of the Gallic aristocracy, and this takes me to my main criticism of Van Dam's argument. In pressing for the continuity and power of the institution of patronage he has to press for the continuity of 'the essential ideology of local aristocracies and their relationships to the rest of the population' and so must ignore the severe disruption suffered by this society on at least four and possibly five occasions over the four hundred years of Roman rule: at the time of Caesar's conquest; towards the end of the first century; towards the end of the third century; perhaps in the middle of the fourth century; and certainly in the early part of the fifth century.[2] It seems unlikely that the Gallic aristocracy could have offered *continuous* local leadership because this aristocracy was at times subject to radical change, as old families disappeared, and were replaced by new. Certainly Ausonius cannot be regarded as a 'typical' great Gallic landowner of long standing;[3] and Paulinus of Pella, his grandson, died a refugee.

---

[1] See, for example, the contrived legitimacy of Julian's usurpation: Rosen (1978).

[2] Van Dam (1985), 14. For disruption and change within early Gallic society see Drinkwater (1978), and for the later period Drinkwater (1984), 366, with Drinkwater (forthcoming).

[3] So Van Dam (1985), 33. Ausonius is surely better seen as a *parvenu* whose career reflects the great opportunities for social advancement available to academics in fourth-century Gaul that resulted from the presence there of the imperial court; Wormald (1976), 220, rightly characterises the process as 'the rise of the gentry'.

What, therefore, was the relationship between the Bagaudae and Gallic patronage? This is not an easy question to answer; in the first instance, we should assess our sources rather more critically than has usually been the case: not all the incidents cited above should be treated as Bagaudic. (In particular, the *Querolus* passage is so obscure that it is unfitted to bear the weight of argument placed upon it.) Our most reliable sources appear to be Victor, Eutropius, Mamertinus, Ammianus Marcellinus, Rutilius Namatianus, the *Gallic Chronicle of 452*, Sidonius, Merobaudes and Constantius; and on the basis of what these offer I suggest that we should view periods of sustained social disorder in Gaul as resulting not from the *success* but from the *failure* of the established system of patronage - in peaceful times the mainstay of Gallic society - following severe dislocation caused by barbarian invasion and civil war. Subsequent reassertion of imperial authority, including the reimposition of taxation and punitive degradation of the people concerned to inferior or servile status, may itself have aggravated the unrest.

I have argued elsewhere that there is no evidence for the type of oppressed rural proletariat envisaged by Thompson in early imperial Gaul: the Bagaudae of the third century are to be explained only by reference to the very specific conditions obtaining in Gaul following the fall of the Gallic Empire in 274, namely the breakdown of an hitherto prosperous and well ordered society and hence the collapse of established authority and patronage.[1] A similar interpretation is possible for the events of the mid-fourth and early fifth centuries. Fifty years of peace in the west was ruined by the revolt of Magnentius (350-3); Julian restored order, but this was shattered by his death in the east, in 363. The gravity of the situation in Gaul is reflected in Valentinian I's decision, as senior emperor, to establish his court in northern Gaul in 365. The prestige, peace and wealth that the west began to enjoy from this date, as the location of a permanent imperial residence, came to an abrupt end in the early fifth century, first with the invasion of the Alans, Suevi and Vandals in 406/7, and then with the settlement of the Visigoths in Aquitania in 418. Many aristocrats fled.[2] It was not until the arrival of Aetius in 425 that the situation was taken in hand, but progress was slow and uncertain. To

[1]   Drinkwater (1984), 364-8.
[2]   Mathisen (1984).

borrow Shaw's concept, space had been created outside imperial control, and had been filled by those whom the government was pleased to call outlaws.[1] For many such people the restoration of imperial strength must have been a mixed blessing; indeed, one may surmise that it was the efforts of Aetius and his lieutenants to reimpose control that actually prompted the revolt of Tibatto.[2]

In conclusion it must be emphasised that there was no continuity of outlook or structure between the various Bagaudic disturbances. Indeed, it is probable that well within a hundred years after the word was first employed to describe those participating in the third-century *jacquerie* 'Bagaudae' had lost its exact meaning. The very nature of the crisis that had called forth the original Bagaudae, as traditional leadership collapsed and reappeared further down the social scale at the highest feasible level, must have brought some strange figures to the fore - lesser aristocrats and yeomen; even slaves, bandits and barbarians.[3] It is therefore likely that in succeeding years the term became a general label for anyone involved in illegal and violent activity in Gaul.[4] Thus it could be applied indiscriminately to mountain-brigands and renegade barbarians (as in Zosimus and Salvian), or not used at all in respect of people whose deeds genuinely resembled those of their third-century predecessors (as in Ammianus Marcellinus). Indeed, the renewal of its old force, when it came to be used again of 'authentic' Bagaudae in the fifth century, was possibly a fortuitous result of the unthinking or pejorative *re*-application of a common synonym for 'outlaw' to the quite different phenomenon of ordinary folk who, again deprived of Van Dam's 'conventional' leadership, were forced to make shift elsewhere.

---

[1] Shaw (1984), 50.

[2] Dockès (1980), 156, 177f., 220ff.

[3] Drinkwater (1984), 368.

[4] Cf. Jullian (1926), vol. viii, 176: '... le monde romain, par cela seul qu'on voulait le distribuer en cadres fixes et sous les vocables juridiques immuables, abonda en indisciplinés ... mais le régime impérial trouva quand même le moyen de leur donner un nom et de les grouper sous un rubrique, en imaginant ce mot des Bagaudes pour l'ensembler des déshérités de la campagne'.

Bibliography

Brogan, O. (1953), *Roman Gaul*. London.

Czúth, B. (1965), *Die Quellen der Geschichte der Bagauden* (Acta Universitatis de Attila Jozsef nominatae, minora opera ad philologiam classicam et archaeologiam pertinentia, vol. ix). Szeged.

Daubigney, A. (1983), 'Relations marchandes méditerranéennes et procès des rapports de dépendance (*magu-* et ambactes)', in *Modes de contacts et processus de transformation dans les sociétés anciennes* (Collection de l'École Française de Rome no. 67), 659-83. Pisa-Rome.

Dockès, P. (1980), 'Révoltes bagaudes et ensauvagement', in P. Dockès and J.M. Servet, *Sauvages et ensauvagés*, 143-262. Lyon.

Drinkwater, J.F. (1978), 'The rise and fall of the Gallic Iulii', *Latomus* 37, 817-50.

Drinkwater, J.F. (1983), *Roman Gaul: the Three Provinces 58 BC-AD 260*. London.

Drinkwater, J.F. (1984), 'Peasants and Bagaudae in Roman Gaul', *Classical Views* n.s. 3, 349-71.

Drinkwater, J.F. (1985), 'Urbanization in the Three Gauls: some observations', in F. Grew and B. Hobley (eds.), *Roman Urban Topography* (Council for British Archaeology Research Report no. 59), 49-55. London.

Drinkwater, J.F. (1987), *The Gallic Empire: Separatism and Continuity in the North-West Provinces of the Roman Empire, AD 260-274* (Historia Einzelschriften no. 52). Stuttgart.

Drinkwater, J.F. (forthcoming), 'Gallic attitudes to the Roman Empire in the fourth century', *Festschrift für Gerold Walser* (Historia Einzelschriften). Stuttgart.

Gilles, K-J. (1985), *Spätrömische Höhensiedlungen in Eifel und Hunsrück* (Trierer Zeitschrift Beiheft no. 7). Trier.

Holmes, T. Rice (1911), *Caesar's Conquest of Gaul*, 2nd ed. Oxford.

Jullian, C. (1926), *Histoire de la Gaule*, vol. viii. Paris.

MacMullen, R. (1966), *Enemies of the Roman Order*. Harvard.

Mathisen, R. (1984), 'Emigrants, exiles and survivors: aristocratic options in Visigothic Aquitaine', *Phoenix* 38, 159-70.

Rosen, K. (1978), 'Beobachtungen zur Erhebung Julians, 360-61 n. Chr.', in R. Klein (ed.), *Julian Apostata* (Wege zur Forschung no. 509), 408-47. Darmstadt.

Ste. Croix, G.E.M. de (1981), *The Class Struggle in the Ancient Greek World.* London.

Shaw, B.D. (1984), 'Bandits in the Roman Empire', *Past and Present* 105, 3-52.

Sirago, V.A. (1969), *Galla Placidia e la transformazione politica dell'Occidente.* Louvain.

Stroheker, K. (1948), *Der senatorische Adel im spätrömischen Gallien.* Tübingen.

Thompson, E.A. (1952), 'Peasant revolts in late Roman Gaul and Spain', *Past and Present* 2, 1952, 11-23, reprinted in M.I. Finley (ed.), *Studies in Ancient Society*, 304-20. London.

Thompson, E.A. (1956), 'The settlement of barbarians in southern Gaul', *Journal of Roman Studies* 46, 65-75, reprinted in Thompson (1982), 23-37.

Thompson, E.A. (1982), *Romans and Barbarians.* Wisconsin.

Van Dam, R. (1985), *Leadership and Community in Late Antique Gaul.* California.

Wightman, E.M. (1978), 'Peasants and potentates', *American Journal of Ancient History* 3, 97-128.

Wightman, E.M. (1985), *Gallia Belgica.* London.

Wormald, P. (1976), 'The decline of the western Empire and the survival of the aristocracy', *Journal of Roman Studies* 66, 217-26.

Chapter 10
The client-patron relationship: emblem and reality in Juvenal's first book

Duncan Cloud

In this paper I want to make three points: first, Juvenal's first book of *Satires* sets out a perfectly coherent account of the client-patron relationship. Secondly, the coherence of this account does not necessarily imply correspondence with the real-life institution. Thirdly, I would like to suggest in a highly tentative manner some criteria for distinguishing between social fact and elegant fantasy in Juvenal's *Satires*.

From the time that L. Friedlaender produced his commentaries on Martial and Juvenal and his monumental *Darstellungen aus der Sittengeschichte Roms* (which went into eight editions between 1861 and his death in 1909), two things appear to have been taken for granted by social historians of Rome: first, that, after allowances have been made for the hyperbole appropriate to an epigrammatist and satirist, the society Martial and Juvenal are describing is recognisably that of *their* Rome, *viz.* the Rome of c.80 to c.130 AD, and, secondly, that both poets are operating in much the same way. Such is the assumption made by Marache in 1961 as it was by Gérard in 1976. Of course, Gérard avoids Marache's mistake of regarding Juvenal as a social reformer dedicated to the moral improvement of the upper classes,[1] but he does regard Juvenal as guilty of no more than exaggeration in his depiction of Roman society and he does regard Martial and Juvenal as sources of much the same kind.

---

[1] 'Juvénal se consacre à la conversion des nobles, à leur amélioration morale', Marache (1961), 59.

The relation between Martial's *Epigrams* and social reality is more complex than this view of his work implies; there are occasions where the speaker in the *Epigrams* adopts a posture which is not so much an exaggeration of the situation of their author as a misdescription of it. For instance, the speaker in Martial's *Epigrams* is always complaining about his indigence, but we should be chary of identifying the speaker with Martial himself; Hardie (1983) points out the discrepancy between 'the mendicant facade' and the equestrian rank with estates to support it attested by the poems.[1] Nor is it difficult in this case to distinguish between Martial and his speaker: poets are traditionally poor,[2] but the Roman poet was usually a person of some status.[3] However, the point of an epigram does usually depend on some paradoxical relationship with reality. For example, the jokes about wine being cheaper and less valuable than drinking water in Ravenna (3.56,57) depend for their point on the fact, borne out by Strabo's account of the town, that there was no local source of fresh drinking water there.[4]

To take another example, when Martial contrasts the delicious, plump turtle-dove set before his patron Ponticus with the magpie, found dead in its cage, set before Martial himself (3.60.7-8),[5] it would be overliteral to assume that magpies, dead from natural causes, formed part of the regular diet offered to clients when dining with their patrons during the principate of Domitian, but it would be perfectly reasonable to assume that some patrons provided their clients with food of a lower standard than that eaten by themselves. Such behaviour is intrinsically plausible and attested by the younger Pliny (*Epistles* 2.6). Consequently, Martial as a source of

---

[1] Hardie (1983), 51, 54-6.

[2] Cairns (1979), 20. Tibullus is an excellent example of a well-off Roman poet of equestrian status whose speaker in the Elegies is a young man who makes a point of advertising his slender means (*paupertas*) in his first, programmatic, poem (1. 1.5).

[3] White (1982), 52.

[4] Strabo (5.1.7) speaks of Ravenna as being situated in the midst of marshes and streams, into which the sea flows at high tides. In the circumstances it would be surprising if there were any local drinking water other than that collected in cisterns (cf. Mart. 3.56).

[5] aureus inmodicus turtur te clunibus implet, /ponitur in cavea mortua pica mihi.

information is to be preferred to Juvenal, not because he aims, any more than Juvenal, to provide Mayhewesque reportage on lower-middle-class Rome in the late first century, but because his favoured form of entertainment is to exaggerate to the point of absurdity rather than rearrange existing elements in the social situation into a novel pattern.[1]

The relationship of Juvenal's poetry with reality is more complex; Feinberg (1963) speaks in general of the satirist's technique as a 'playfully critical distortion of the familiar' and in Juvenal's case the familiar includes literature, its stock themes and standard responses.[2] Above all, Juvenal is not giving us slices of autobiography. Juvenal may himself have been a client, if the Juvenal of Martial 12. 18.2 is the subsequent composer of satires and if the picture of Juvenal haunting, toga-clad, the thresholds of the mighty in lines 4 and 5 depicts the satirist's life-style c. 101 and is not there to afford a conventional contrast between a life of dependence in Rome and Martial's new life as independent landowner in Spain.[3] But it would be very foolish to go further and identify the intemperate and declamatory fantasist who inveighs against the current state of client-patron relationships from the pages of Book 1 with the artful and sophisticated composer and organiser of that book.[4]

Silverman (1977) suggests that we look at patronage in two related but distinct ways: as the way in which people think of behaviour defined as patronage in their society and the way in which an outsider might look at the structure of relationships and networks and the exchange of services involved. Even from the standpoint of the literary analysis of Juvenal's first book this distinction is a helpful one, since the speaker contrasts patronage as it is conceived as

---

[1] See Saller (1983) for a convincing defence of this way of using Martial.

[2] I owe the reference to Feinberg (1963), and to Fredericks (1979).

[3] The Juvenal of this epigram is certainly engaged in the early morning *salutatio* of patrons by clients; Juvenal is wearing his toga (line 5), *de rigueur* on these occasions, and in lines 13-16 Martial contrasts his current practice in Spain of sleeping beyond the third hour with his former rising before dawn, one of the prime disadvantages of being a client, since the patron expected his attendance from first thing in the morning. Presumably Martial is continuing the contrast with Juvenal.

[4] For a demonstration of the art with which Book 1 (Satires 1-5) is constructed, see Braund and Cloud (1982).

operating by the client with the sordid reality of the relationship as it
exists within the world of the satires. Since Juvenal is a poet and his
speaker a second-century irascible declaimer not a late twentieth-
century sociologist, the techniques used are not those of Silverman
but they nevertheless exist. For example, it has been shown by Saller
(1982) that the word 'client' (*cliens*) is not much used by clients of
themselves or indeed by patrons of their dependents when either party
wishes to advertise the relationship, since the word draws attention to
its asymmetricality. Instead, they use the word *amicus* (friend) and its
cognates. Juvenal, however, uses *amicus* in a consistently derogatory
or ironic manner throughout the book. Mostly, the offensiveness or
irony is that of his speaker; examples are numerous and indeed the
word occurs as often in Book 1 as in all the other four books of
satires put together.[1] One case will suffice; Umbricius, whose tirade
occupies most of *Satire* 3, remarks of the client:

> Who nowadays is held dear (*diligitur*) except the accomplice and he
> whose seething heart boils with secrets ever to be concealed? The
> man who has shared an honourable secret (*secreti.... honesti*) with
> you considers he owes you nothing and will grant you nothing in
> the future; that man will be dear (*carus*) to Verres[2] who at any time
> he chooses can bring a prosecution against Verres. Do not regard
> all the gold-laden sand that wooded Tagus rolls down to the sea as
> a prize great enough to lose your sleep for it and take bribes that
> later have to be resigned, sorrowfully (*tristis*), and be ever feared
> by your mighty friend (*a magno semper timearis amico*).
>
> (*Satire* 3.49-57)

Affection might be expected to characterise the relationship between
the two 'friends', but the only 'affection' Verres feels is for the
subordinate who has been his associate in plundering his province and
can 'turn him in' (the apt adaptation of Peter Green 1967) whenever

[1] See LaFleur (1979), *passim*; particularly acute are L.'s comments on the
use of *amicus* of Umbricius in *Satire* 3. The word is so discredited by its other
contexts in Book 1 that, when the speaker in 3. 1 characterises Umbricius as
his old friend (*vetus amicus*), we should be put on our guard and warned not
necessarily to accept him on his own terms as a hard-up honest Roman too
decent to make his way in Trajanic Rome. Winkler's 'priggish and self-
righteous "redneck"' (1983, 223), though not quite right, is nearer the mark.

[2] Verres typifies the corrupt provincial governor.

he wants. Thus the feeling that should characterise friendship is devalued by its criminal context and the guilty conscience of the subordinate, seething and bubbling away (*fervens / aestuat ... animus*); it is specifically dissociated from what is honourable; when Umbricius turns from irony to the real feelings experienced by the parties to the relationship, it is not surprising that one feels sorrow and the other continual fear. When the word 'friend' finally occurs - in highly emphatic position, since it not only ends the line but the paragraph - it is totally discredited by its associations with guilty consciences, crime and feelings of distress and terror.

The gulf between the mythology or ideology of patronage and its reality within the book is exposed mainly by the way in which that reality is described. When the services performed by the client are traditional, the speaker suggests that the tradition has become travesty; the *salutatio* or early morning call upon patron by his clients preliminary to escorting the patron to the forum has been turned into an undignified competition for dole-money (the *sportula*) engaged in not simply by the humble citizen-client but by senior magistrates and rich ex-slaves as well.[1] Or the services described are such that either a decent Roman could not perform them convincingly or could not perform them at all; as examples of the first type Umbricius instances forms of flattery like throwing up one's hands in incredulous admiration at the euphony of one's patron's belches or the accuracy of his pissing.[2] As examples of services that the decent Roman could not perform, Umbricius lists praising the patron's books, using one's knowledge of astronomy to predict his father's death, acting as go-between betwixt patron and mistress and, possibly, poisoning or putting spells on an opponent.[3]

---

[1]   1. 95-126: for praetors and tribunes cf. 101, the consul (*summus honor*) cf. 117, the old republican nobility (*Troiugenae*) cf. 100; for the rich Syrian freedman cf. 102-11.

[2]   ....iactare manus, laudare paratus / si bene ructavit, si rectum minxit amicus (3. 106-7). The relationship is diminished not merely by what the successful client is expected to do but by the structure of the line which juxtaposes *amicus* and *minxit* (has pissed) while placing *amicus* illogically but emphatically *after* the verb, thus highlighting the degrading depths to which this 'friendship' has sunk.

[3]   3. 41-6. The investigation of frogs' guts mentioned at line 44 could refer to poisoning or maleficent magic - cf. Duff (1898) and Green (1967) a*d loc* . - as well as extispicy.

If we turn now to the other side of the relationship, namely the benefits (*beneficia*) that the patron was expected to bestow upon the client, these are in Book 1 in effect restricted to two, the money-dole of 25 asses distributed to each client at the morning *salutatio* and the occasional but regular dinner provided. The bestowal of gifts in cash or kind mentioned by Pliny the Younger, Martial and Persius as being a significant form of *beneficium* are only twice mentioned in the book - at 5.32, where the speaker says that the patron will never send even a ladleful (*cyathum*) of decent wine to an *amicus* with indigestion, and at 5.107-13, where the bestowal of gifts is regarded as characteristic of good patrons in the Neronian and Augustan ages but, by implication, not to be expected of a contemporary patron.[1] One might suppose (if Juvenal were writing contemporary social history) that the practice of bestowing goods on clients had ceased by the time Juvenal came to write Book 1,[2] but the evidence cited in n.18 shows that it still continued.

There is another way in which the satirist of Book 1 presents a historically false picture of the client: he is a very poor man. He does *not* possess the equestrian census (3.155); he requires the *sportula* of 25 asses to pay for toga, bread and fire (1.119-20); denied a free dinner from their patron, clients are styled wretched in having to pay for their own cabbage and firing (1.133). In fact, there is sufficient evidence to show that Rome was no different from many other societies in excluding the very poor from the client-patron relationship; although the relationship is asymmetrical, the client has to be able to contribute *something* and under the empire the very poor citizen has not even a vote to deliver.[3]

[1] For gifts of wine to clients in Persius, cf. *Sat.* 3. 92-3; for Martial gifts in kind from a patron occupy more epigrams than the dole. I note roof-tiles to replace others blown off in a winter storm (7. 36), mules (8. 61.7), a loan of 5000 sesterces requested but refused (10. 14), togas, cloaks, plate and pieces of gold (12. 36) and gifts increasingly minute (8. 71). Togas are obsessional with the epigrammatist (8. 28; 9. 49; 10. 73).

[2] The publication of Book 1 is to be dated to 'around 112' (Courtney (1980), 2) but could be even later.

[3] The clinching reference is provided by Tacitus (*Hist.* 1. 4) who places clients among the 'pars populi integra et magnis domibus adnexa' - the section of the people that was sound and attached to great houses - a class which he places between the leaders of the equestrian order on the one hand and the *sordida plebs* - the filthy plebs - on the other.

The 'reality' of the world of Book 1, though internally coherent, is thus in two ways not the reality of the world in which Juvenal lived. As it happens, in *Satire* 9, where Juvenal's techniques of distortion are different, the bisexual gigolo client, Naevolus, is not on the bread line (11) and receives gifts from his patron (28-31, 41); of course he rails at the stinginess of his patron, but the gifts which he thinks that as a client (71) he should have received - capital yielding interest of 20,000 sesterces, some moderately good silver vessels, two Moesian slaves, an engraver and a portrait painter (140-6) - are hardly the fantasies of a poor man. When he chooses to do so, Juvenal can depict a client who is conventional in status and is the recipient of gifts, though strikingly unconventional in the services he performs for his patron and his patron's wife!

This brings us to the point where, in reading Juvenal, we must add a third to Silverman's two ways of looking at patronage; one of the satirist's traditional roles is that of critic of society. The aim of the satirist may be entertainment rather than conversion, but whatever his aim, readers of satire from Lucilius onwards will expect him to attack the wickedness of the times. The furious moralist of Book 1 amply satisfies these expectations. His point is that purely materialistic considerations have replaced the traditional humane values of the past and he chooses the client-patron relationship, and particularly the *sportula*, to exemplify the inversion of moral standards. Of course, he makes the point directly - the Romans now worship money (1.112-3) and what is fundamentally wrong with the patron Virro is that because he is rich and his client Trebius is poor he feels no need to treat him like a fellow-citizen or humble friend (5.111-13). But he also makes it indirectly and the *sportula*, which provides the set-piece for *Satire* 1 (95-126) places before our eyes an institution which, instead of serving as a medium for the exchange of a variety of services, exhibits patrons bent on giving as little and clients grabbing as much as they can. The speaker draws attention to four features: (1) the patron is suspicious of interlopers; (2) Roman magistrates as well as the poor queue up for their 25 asses; (3) rich ex-slaves (*liberti*) push past magistrates and poor client alike - because they are better off, they deserve to be paid first; (4) some people bring their wives along so as to double their dole-money or even bring an empty sedan-chair which they pretend contains a sick or pregnant wife. Indeed, a hundred *lecticae* (litters for rich matrons) are at the patron's gate. The first and last of these features illustrate the *avaritia* of both patron and

client; the other two suggest something more striking - an inversion
of traditional Roman values: the dole - a substitute for free food - was
intended for the humbler client, not for praetors or tribunes or rich
liberti; *liberti* as citizens without all the rights of citizens should not
have jumped the queue but should have waited till the others had
received the *sportula*.

In terms of social comment the use made of the frightful dinner in
Satire 5 is less original: as in Martial 3.60, the patron's food is
expensive and delicious, the client's cheap and nasty. Yet there are
differences between Martial and Juvenal; Juvenal's Virro is not merely
stingy. He is also a sadist who knows that Trebius will suffer any
indignity for the honour of dining with him (156-72). Juvenal's
speaker, moreover, draws a different conclusion from Martial:
Martial's plea is that patron and client should eat the same food,
whereas the speaker thinks that Trebius should prefer the life of a
beggar to that of a client on Virro's terms.

I have already noted two forms of distortion which occur in Book
1 and which can be corrected from Pliny and Martial (and indeed from
Satire 9), namely the suggestion that patrons had given up bestowing
gifts in cash or kind upon their clients and the suggestion that the
typical client was poor enough to need 25 asses to purchase the basic
necessities of life. However, the distortion of reality in Book 1 takes
a more precise form; there is something fundamentally wrong with
Juvenal's account of the *sportula*. What is wrong with it was
observed long ago by one H.M. Stephenson (1887), known, if at all,
to the world of classical scholarship as a tireless late-nineteenth-
century producer of school editions of Livy. But as it was impossible
to accept Stephenson's bizarre conclusion - that Juvenal was a skilful
late-Latin poet pretending to an early-second-century date, but let
down from time to time by ignorance of social history - his dossier
of unhistorical items in Juvenal has been undeservedly neglected. To
read what he wrote is enlightening:

> The first [difficulty] I will notice is the custom of the *sportula* as
> represented by Juvenal, which in two or three important particulars
> is quite unknown to Martial, who beyond a doubt was an eye-
> witness of what he described. Juvenal represents it as distributed in
> the morning (Martial 10. 70, 13-14 at the tenth hour).

Stephenson finds the discrepancy very puzzling:

> Suppose two writers describing Cambridge University life should one of them represent the time for boating practice as regularly beginning at 9.0 A.M. and the other at 2.0 P.M., it would surely raise doubts as to the accuracy of one of them.

He further points out that Martial's account makes sense in a way that Juvenal's does not: the *sportula* is a substitute for the evening meal with the patron and should therefore be distributed in the late afternoon; moreover, patrons, especially those as stingy as the general run are made out to be by both poets, would surely only pay out the 25 asses when the client has completed his services for the day. Stephenson points to two other improbabilities in Juvenal's account of the *sportula* in Juvenal's first satire; what we know of Roman social practice allied with the silence of our other sources makes it most unlikely that women collected the *sportula* in their own right or indeed attended *salutationes*. Secondly, while the rich and noble did attend the *salutationes* of imperial favourites and others richer than themselves, there is no evidence that they queued up for their dole-money as well. Stephenson's immediate conclusion that Juvenal's *sportula* is not a picture of contemporary practice seems to me unassailable. Attempts to reconcile the Martial evidence with Juvenal's in the first *Satire* smack of desperation rather than plausibility. Friedlaender (1895) *ad loc.* suggested that the time of day for the distribution of the *sportula* changed under Trajan from late afternoon to early morning, but this is unlikely because (1) Martial's tenth book happens to be the latest of his works, dated by Friedlaender to 98, early in Trajan's reign, and the dramatic time of Book 1 is mainly Domitianic - the most recent event mentioned in it is the trial of Marius Priscus (1. 49-50) which took place in 100; (2) the other objections to the morning *sportula* stand; there is some slight support in Pliny for the late afternoon *sportula* well into Trajan's reign.[1] Gérard suggests that the time at which the *sportula* was distributed varied from one great household to another,[2] but this

---

[1] *Ep.* 2.14.4, a passage which associates the distribution of *sportulae* with the dining-room and therefore with a meal-time.

[2] (1976), 180-1.

move would not save Juvenal's credit, since Juvenal represents *all* clients as receiving the dole in the morning (cf. esp. 1. 127-34).

In short, it is a pointless exercise to try and reconcile Juvenal with Martial and the reality of social practice in Trajanic Rome; Juvenal has fused two customs - the early morning *salutatio* attended by the great man's friends as well as his clients and the late afternoon *sportula* at which the clients received their dole or tip. His motive is obvious: his speaker is castigating the shift from traditional to money-based values and his description of the rich and distinguished queueing up for the *sportula* with the rich elbowing past the merely distinguished makes his point in a way which a boring adherence to the social facts would never have done and which an audience, trained on the mixture of fact and fantasy presented by the declamations, would have been the first to appreciate.

If we accept that the *salutio-sportula* of *Satire* 1 is a fantasy-product or literary equivalent of Canaletto's capriccio technique, then we are entitled to cast a sceptical look upon the strange *sportula* which figures briefly in *Satire* 3. 249-53. An almost literal translation would run:

> Do you not see with what a mass of smoke the *sportula* is
> celebrated / thronged (*celebretur*)? A hundred banqueters, each
> followed by his kitchen. Corbulo [a Neronian general of huge size,
> cf. Tacitus *Annales* 13.8] could scarcely sustain so many huge
> vessels, so many objects piled upon his head as the wretched little
> slave carries with head upright, fanning the flame as he runs
> along.

On all the other five occasions on which the word *sportula* occurs in Juvenal, it refers to the dole handed out by the patron, probably in the form of cash.[1] One would therefore expect a reference to the dole here too. On the other hand, the speaker's description conjures up a communal picnic, enjoyable for the guests but not for the slave or the speaker for whom the crowd, smoke and vessels merely provide further impediments to his passage along the street. It used to be maintained until Friedlaender (1895) *ad loc.* was convinced by Wissowa of the error of his ways that the clients had converted their dole-money into food and were now cooking their lunches in the

---

[1]   1.95, 118, 128; 10.46 cash distributions; 13.33 cash or food distribution.

street, since their small apartments possessed no kitchens. But as Wissowa pointed out to his friend, 25 asses would not buy the sort of meal which would require the vast array of pots carried by the slave and in any case at this stage of the day the client would be still in attendance on his patron. This also rules out Gérard's suggestion[1] that the patron is providing his clients with a special distribution of food for a supper meal. Nowadays it is the fashion to suppose that the speaker is referring to a club (*collegium*) picnic[2] but while there is evidence of the word *sportula* used of food or cash distributed by a *collegium* to its members, there is none, as far as I know, that suggests that the word is used of a meal to which the members bring their own portable stoves.

The fact that the inscriptions mentioning the *sportula* in this sense often also mention the distribution of hot water (*calda*) suggests that means of heating up food were provided on the club's premises.[3] Surely these rather desperate moves suggest once again that we should not be trying to cash this *sportula* with any specific social institution. The passage comes half-way through Book 1 which begins in *Satire* 1 with the Juvenalian *sportula* as the paradigm case of the perversion of the traditional client-patron relationship and ends in *Satire* 5 with the evening meal as a further paradigm case of that perversion. This unfocussed scene, with its emphasis on the discomfort of the slave and of Umbricius, looks forward with its reference to banqueters / diners (*convivae*) to *Satire* 5 and backwards with its reference to *sportula* to *Satire* 1.[4] Just as the sportula represented the devaluation of the client-patron relationship, so will dining; the function of the passage is chiefly structural, but in the process Juvenal takes elements from other social phenomena, the carrying away of food from the *thermopolia* (hot food takeaways), street cooking and the club dinner, to convey a further impression of crowds and obstacles.

---

[1] (1976), 184-91.

[2] Thus Duff (1898), Ferguson (1979) and Courtney (1980) *ad loc*.

[3] See the material collected by Traenkle (1978).

[4] *Conviva* turns up three times in *Sat.* 5 (25, 74 and 161), always in contexts which suggest the devaluation of the word; note also that *culina* occurs only here, at 5. 162 and 14. 14, although meals are a frequent topic in Juvenal's Satires. For *sportula* cf. n.1, p.215.*Ventilat* occurs in Juvenal only here and in *Sat.* 1 (28).

This investigation should suggest that historians should use Juvenal with the greatest caution. First of all, never trust Juvenal when he is the only witness to a custom or institution and never trust Juvenal - or any poet - when he is exploiting a commonplace. For example, poets are always poor and so when in 7.82-7 the poet Statius is saved from starvation by selling his *Agave* to the actor-dancer Paris we have every reason to be sceptical.

Secondly, historians should study the rules of the satirical game; Roman satirists regularly move from one topic to another not too far removed from it and, in *Satire* 3, Juvenal switches from the impossibility for a traditionally honest Roman of making a living as a client to the lot of the urban poor. Umbricius, with still enough capital to retire to Cumae, is in a different league from the allegedly leek-eating cobbler's associate who gets mugged at the end of the poem. The transition is so artfully managed that we associate, and are meant to associate, the misery of the mugged diner-out and the poet reduced to beggary when his attic flat is destroyed by fire with the situation of Umbricius, the honest, old-fashioned, client; we *feel* that *all* clients must be very poor indeed.

Thirdly, for poetry as a whole, the point or points that the poet is trying to make may be dictated by the rules of the *genre* or by his own fancy or more probably in ancient Rome by a mixture of the two, but will rarely be an unmediated report of some personal experience: any appearance of naturalism is delusory. Juvenal, even less than Martial, is not a second-century Mayhew, as our dissection of the vividly recounted but purely fantastic early-morning *sportula* has shown. And, to return to my beginning, satire based on the schools of declamation is a most unreliable source for social history. The declamatory element makes it a treacherous source even for attitudes. The speaker in Juvenal's first book is an enraged declaimer prepared to invent institutions to give substance to his indignation. Unless we have supporting evidence from elsewhere, we cannot tell whether what we read are the comic exaggerations of a more rhetorical Alf Garnett or sheer fantasy. For attitudes as well as for facts the historian would be well advised to make wary use of Martial but give a very wide berth indeed to Juvenal.

Bibliography

Braund, S.H. and Cloud, J.D. (1982), 'Juvenal's Libellus - a farrago?',
Greece and Rome 29, 77-85.
Cairns, F. (1979), *Tibullus, a Hellenistic Poet at Rome*. Cambridge.
Courtney, E. (1980), *A Commentary on the Satires of Juvenal*.
London.
Duff, J.D. (1898), *D. Iunii Iuvenalis Saturae* XIV. Cambridge.
Feinberg, L. (1963), *The Satirist: His Temperament, Motivation and
Influence*. Ames, Iowa.
Ferguson, J. (1979), *Juvenal: The Satires*. Basingstoke.
Fredericks, S.C. (1979), 'Irony of overstatement in the Satires of
Juvenal', *Illinois Classical Studies* 4, 178-91.
Friedlaender, L. (1895), *D. Junii Juvenalis Saturarum Libri* V.
Leipzig.
Friedlaender, L. (1922), *Darstellungen aus der Sittengeschichte
Roms*, (10th ed.). Leipzig.
Gérard, J. (1976), *Juvénal et la réalité contemporaine*. Paris.
Green, P. (1967), *Juvenal: the Sixteen Satires* (an English
translation). Harmondsworth.
Hardie, A. (1983), *Statius and the Silvae: Poets, Patrons and
Epideixis in the Greco-Roman World*. Liverpool.
LaFleur, R.A. (1979), 'Amicitia and the unity of Juvenal's first
book', *Illinois Classical Studies* 4, 158-77.
Marache, R. (1961), 'La revendication sociale chez Martial et
Juvénal', *Rivisita di Cultura Classica e Medioevale* 3, 30-67.
Saller, R.P. (1982), *Personal Patronage under the Early Empire*.
Cambridge.
Saller, R.P. (1983), 'Martial on patronage and literature', *Classical
Quarterly* 33, 246-57.
Silverman, S.F. (1977), 'Patronage as myth', in E. Gellner and J.
Waterbury (eds.), *Patrons and Clients in Mediterranean Societies*,
7-19. London.
Stephenson, H.M. (1887), 'Difficulties in Juvenal', *Classical Review*
1, 243.
Traenkle, H. (1978), 'Zum zwei umstrittene Stellen in der dritten
Satire des Iuvenal', *Zeitschrift für Papyrologie und Epigraphik* 28,
169-72.
White, P. (1982), 'Positions for poets in Early Imperial Rome', in
B.K. Gold (ed.), *Literary and Artistic Patronage in Ancient Rome*,
50-66. Austin, Texas.

Winkler, M.M. (1983), *The Persona in Three Satires of Juvenal* (Altertumswissenschaftliche Texte und Studien, 10). Hildesheim.

Chapter 11
Patronage: relation and system

Terry Johnson and Christopher Dandeker

In this paper we develop a perspective which in certain respects is the reverse of that adopted by the other authors in this volume, most of whom are concerned with the usefulness of the concept of patronage for the analysis of Roman society at particular historical moments - early republic, late republic, empire, etc. Our foremost concern is with patronage as a tool of comparative analysis; that is, its capacity to reveal structural similarities between such diverse historical societies as the Roman republic and eighteenth-century England.

The literature on patronage as a tool of comparative analysis can be divided into two broad approaches. The first concludes that patronage is a phenomenon limited to certain historical societies: particularly those characterized by the break-up of kinship and tradition, or those in the early throes of modernisation or industrialisation. Patronage is of significance, it is argued,

> only in societies where political integration and social mediation
> are limited by the weakness of market forces and the
> ineffectiveness of central government. (Bourne 1986, 8)

Patronage, according to this approach, has no place in a 'properly run', modern bureaucratic state. The implication of such a view is that patron-client relations are associated essentially with a transitional phase in state development and the wider processes of modernisation. That is to say, patronage emerges to facilitate economic and political relationships where the ties of kinship are no longer effective and the integrative and distributional functions of market and state do not yet operate. We should, then, look for patron-client relationships only in the transition from tradition to modernity.

The alternative approach is represented by Marc Bloch who regarded patronage as a universal phenomenon; universal across time, across culture, across class:

> To seek a protector or to find satisfaction in being one - these things are common to all ages. (Bloch 1961, 147)

This approach accedes to the undoubted fact that the public and the private bureaucracies of both east and west in the modern world are infested with 'powerful friends' and 'obligated clients'. Patronage ties cement the institutions of modernity, it is argued, just as they did when the 'old corruption' defaced both metropolitan and provincial life in eighteenth-century England or when clients legitimately sought advancement through their patrons in republican Rome.

As is usually the case when such alternative conceptions are proposed there also exists a literature of compromise, which argues that while patronage is 'never absent', being a universal phenomenon, it is historically 'subject to fluctuations in importance and intensity' (Bourne 1986, 8). However, again as is usually the case with such compromise, insofar as the literature is silent about the conditions determining such fluctuations, the concept tends to lose analytic purchase as a tool of comparison.

The origins of this divide, between those who see patronage as a universal phenomenon and those who identify it as an historically specific structure can be found, we will argue, in a common failure to distinguish between two levels of the analysis of patronage. Such a distinction not only explains the contradictory approaches identified above, but also helps to disentangle a number of confusions which have arisen in the literature of Rome, including the papers which make up this volume.

The distinction to which we draw attention is that between patronage, defined as a *particular kind of relationship* and patronage as a *system of relationships*. Patronage, it is suggested, can be understood as either a *social relationship* or a *social system*. In the first and more common case, patronage is defined as an elementary or cell structure of social life with discrete, yet universal, characteristics. In the second, patronage is identified as a system of such relations, constituting a social mechanism which functions strategically in the reproduction of the major social institutions of power. Such a distinction would allow us to argue that any seeming decline of patronage in the course of 'modernisation' would not necessarily lead to the disappearance of patron-client relations, but could lead to a shift in their strategic significance. Our position can be identified with the literature of 'compromise' but is distinctive in allowing us to specify the most important conditions of variation. It is not, however, a position which commits us to the evolutionary assumptions inherent in the modernisation thesis, a problem we will return to in the conclusion below.

Patronage as a social relation

There is general agreement among the contributors to this volume that the essential and irreducible characteristic of patronage is that it is a *personal* relationship - akin to friendship - but existing between unequals (see, for instance, Saller, Garnsey and Woolf, Drummond and Wallace-Hadrill). These 'relational' definitions often include a number of other crucial elements, such as the existence of a process of reciprocal exchange (Saller, Millett, etc.) or the claim that the patron-client relation is entered into on a voluntary basis (Garnsey and Woolf, Drummond). Such agreement reflects the widespread tendency, not just among ancient historians, to launch the analysis of patronage from the base of such a relational definition. For example, Scott has argued that patronage is a

> ... largely instrumental friendship in which an individual of higher
> socio-economic status (the patron) uses his own influence and
> resources to provide protection or benefits, or both, for a person of
> lower status (the client) who for his part reciprocates by offering
> social support and assistance including personal services to the
> patron. (Scott 1977)

The essence of patronage, defined in such a fashion, Bourne concludes, is 'inequality, reciprocity and intimacy' (5); a durable, two-way relationship of 'lop-sided' or 'vertical' friendship (Perkin 1969, 49).

Further, the added stress on voluntarism along with reciprocal exchange - unequal in varying degrees - distinguishes patronage quite

222 Johnson and Dandeker

clearly from master-slave or lord-serf relationships. Also the patron-client relationship is personal, intimate and diffuse (or 'many-stranded'); all factors which clearly contrast it with characteristically impersonal and highly specific relationships existing between, say, the industrial-capitalist entrepreneur and the 'formally free' worker of modern capitalist society. However, at the same time the 'intimacy' of the patron-client relationship is not one of blood or kinship, because the latter ties of reciprocity are not the product of voluntary action. It also follows that while the moral bond of 'loyalty' or *fides*, between patron and client may well be expressed through a terminology of kinship, it cannot be conceived merely as an extension of kin solidarity.

Conceptualised in this way, as a dyadic social relation, patronage is revealed as a ubiquitous and elementary form of social life, found in the most diverse social settings; from the internal power struggles of modern bureaucracies, and the hierarchical relations of organised crime, to those personalised relations which have periodically been constructed between landowners and peasants throughout history.

At this level of analysis any attempt to pose the question, 'Under what social conditions does patronage arise?' is bound to generate answers which are both abstract and vacuous. For example, the claimed universality of patronage is sometimes explained as resulting from a 'human' tendency to look to those in more favoured circumstances for protection and advancement. The relational concept of patronage has the effect of tearing the cell-relationship of patron-client out of its historical and social conditions of existence, depriving the analyst of any possibility of answering the most important questions. For example, under what conditions does patronage constitute a *system* of relations, such that complex chains of asymmetrical 'friendship' relations constitute *the* primary form of resource allocation in the reproduction of society as a whole? More simply, in what kind of society does the answer to the question, 'Who are your friends?' become of decisive importance? To tackle such questions a second and complementary level of analysis, what we call the system level, must be developed.

Patronage as a social system

As we have suggested, a patronage *system* can be understood initially not as a type of relationship but as a complex and hierarchically organised series of chains of such relationships. Such a system is not exhaustively defined by reference to the essential characteristics of the patron-client relationship because it has emergent properties which cannot be conceptualised in terms of one-to-one asymmetrical reciprocation. A patronage system cannot be described by aggregating individual patron-client relationships. Once we recognise that a complex network of such relations can function as the prime mechanism in the allocation of scarce resources and the dominant means of legitimising the social order, then we can also understand that there have existed societies in which such a system has played a strategic role in the maintenance and reproduction of power relations. At this level of analysis, there is a displacement of the crucial theoretical and empirical questions. We are no longer solely concerned with those questions which consume much of the attention of our fellow authors - e.g. Do patron-client relations exist? Are they reciprocal on a one-to-one basis? Rather, we need to discover whether or not they play a dominant (not exclusive) role in the organisation of the economy, polity and society.

Among the emergent properties of patronage as a system to which we will pay particular attention are, first, the dominance of vertical over horizontal relations of solidarity and, second, the systematic effects of voluntarism in inhibiting the emergence of stable, inherited forms of power holding.

Briefly, the vertical relations of solidarity connecting patron to client in a hierarchical structure have the effect of inhibiting the social significance of class or status forms of horizontal solidarity, as well as undermining the potential legitimacy of egalitarian forms of ideology. This does not mean that communal, status or class action is unknown, but that patron-client ties and loyalties reduce the potentiality and centrality of such forms of integration. Similarly, the institutionalisation of personalised ties which are, in principle, the product of individual choices, has the generalised effect of undermining the emergence of stable, hereditary structures of power holding. The incorporation of voluntarism into a system of resource allocation introduces a destabilising factor: patronage tends to operate as a competitive and pluralistic system in which patrons are dependent on maintaining a high level of client support in a situation where clients are neither owned nor entirely controlled. That is to say, client choice is a significant dynamic in the system and clients constitute a major resource within it.

Patronage in antiquity: relation and system

It is our argument, then, that the analytic utility of the concept of patronage, as a tool of comparison, has been impaired by a failure to distinguish between these two levels. This failure is particularly marked in the literature on Roman patronage, where seminal contributions such as that of Saller (1982), while clarifying issues at the relational level, have also generated theoretical and empirical penalties associated with such a one-dimensional view. We can best justify such claims by considering the ways in which our co-authors, in their analysis of Roman society, have been affected by the commitment to a relational concept. In focussing our critique on the papers in this volume we are in no sense suggesting that ancient historians are unique in concentrating their attention on the relational aspect of patronage. It is a commitment which could be identified equally in the sociological and social anthropological literature. Indeed, in the contributions of Saller, Drummond and Wallace-Hadrill, for example, we find attempts to move beyond a purely relational account. We confine our remarks to the papers in this volume because such a decision forces us, as sociologists, to make a specific contribution to the issues current in classical studies while more properly representing our role as commentators in the seminars which were the basis of this book. The comparative value of what we have to say will be illustrated by reference to eighteenth-century England.

The various papers we will be considering largely share Saller's view (1982, 1) that patronage is an asymmetrical friendship relation, involving: (1) a reciprocal exchange of goods and services, (2) a personal relationship of some duration, (3) two parties of unequal status offering different kinds of goods and services in exchange. The definition of the elementary patron-client relation is extended by several other authors to include (4) the principle of voluntarism (Garnsey and Woolf, 154; Drummond, 101).

a) *Relations versus systems of reciprocation*

The general acceptance of Saller's definition (with modifications) has led directly to the construction of a series of 'empirical' problems and issues which currently exercise ancient historians concerned with patronage. Take first the issue of reciprocation: by defining the patron-client relation as involving the reciprocal exchange of goods and services, Saller effectively captures a number of red herrings in the net of his concept. The first 'empirical' issue which has been subsequently identified is illustrated by the question: is it, in fact, the case that patron-client relations in Rome were reciprocal? It has been argued, for example, that it is often impossible to identify such reciprocal exchange relations between patron and client. The potential irrelevance of any such empirical quest becomes apparent once we move from a relational to a system level of analysis. At the system level the empirical issue is not the existence of one-to-one exchanges over the short-term but the existence and operation of a complex network of vertical and cross-cutting ties which have wider integrative and social control functions than those identified through the discrete reciprocations of single patrons and clients

It is many years since Malinowski revealed the integrative functions of serial rather than directly reciprocal exchanges among the Trobriand islanders and there is no reason to reject the possibility that Roman patronage was also characterised by a more complex system of personalised exchange (Malinowski 1922). In particular, the notion that patrons would require or even expect immediate reciprocation of a benefit bestowed is almost certainly misconceived. For example the operation of patronage in eighteenth-century England suggests that it was in the patron's interest to maintain client indebtedness, so ensuring a high measure of personalised, local control (Johnson 1982). In seeking to determine whether reciprocation operated as a strategic mechanism of resource allocation then the reciprocation between individual pairs of patron and client is less important than the extent to which networks of reciprocal exchanges can be identified. Wallace-Hadrill, who comes closest to the system concept through his notion of a patronage network, argues for example that

> ...what justifies talk of the network as a whole as a patronage
> network is that it involves exchanges between those closer to the
> centre of power and those more distant from it. (above, p.77)

Despite its tautological context, the implication of this claim is that patronage is not only a structure of power but a system for the reproduction of power relations on a personalised basis. Wallace-Hadrill also identifies a major condition of patronage as a system when he claims:

> The secret of the game is the manipulation of scarce resources: where all need resources that are in short supply, it is easier for the patrons to secure control of the routes of access, so rendering access impossible except through a patron. (above, p.73)

Leaving aside for the moment the complicating factor that the clients themselves are a resource of the system, Wallace-Hadrill provides us with one of the criteria for determining whether a patronage system exists; that is to say, is access to resources so governed? While it is unlikely that access to resources is ever determined by a single set of relationships, except in very simple kinship societies - that is, there are always competing institutions operating - what we need to be convinced of in order to conclude that what we are looking at is a patronage system, is that access to resources is predominantly mediated by such personalised relationships.

Equally, it should be remembered that patronage systems may well vary considerably in the social distance and intimacy existing between patron and client and the patterns of reciprocal exchange which operated between them and such intermediaries who might exist. As Bourne pointed out for Victorian England (1986, 7), it was 'not uncommon for patron and client to be entirely unknown to one another'. Gibbon and Higgins (1974) have shown in another context that the maintenance of intimacy might lie in the mediating role of brokers rather than in any direct encounter between patron and clients. In the context of the distribution of naval patronage in the England of the late eighteenth century, personal, kin or political connections with naval patrons were normally decisive in determining whether one would be able to make the first step into the occupation of naval officer. However, relatively distant connections could ensure success. One good reference and the hard work of brokers or third parties could make all the difference (Dandeker 1978).

Such brokerage may itself vary between the extreme of commercialised agency, where the market is more dominant, or kinship, where consanguinity operates as an effective principle of allocation. Garnsey and Woolf (p.158) make this point in relation to the Roman provinces.

> Access to work and even the market might be in the gift of a powerful man and a peasant might make overtures to a kinsman to gain access to *his* patron or might represent his village to a rich man whose client he already was.

Thus a patronage system may remain personalised and based on reciprocal exchange, but these processes are neither bounded by, nor describable in terms of, the patron-client dyad.

Once we view personalised, reciprocal exchange in terms of a systemic rather than a relational principle, we are also able to move away from the static assumptions which are built into the idea of one-to-one reciprocation. The very notion that a patronal benefit requires a client response in the short-term implies an inherently self-regulating process in which the principle of reciprocal exchange maintains not only a given structure of power but - because it is personalised - particular groups or persons as the powerful. At the system level we can more easily conceptualise what appears to be closer to the reality of Roman patronage: that is, networks of interconnection and cross-cutting ties, the outcome of which was continually shifting alliances of powerful patrons competing for resources including the resource inherent in client loyalty.

It is equally the case that in eighteenth-century England the significance of patronage lay not in the quantity of reciprocal exchanges between individual patrons and clients. Rather, patronage was a strategic mechanism for the reproduction of a structure of power in which fractions of the great landed families dominated the political life of the kingdom. They controlled the electoral system, and manned the benches in both Houses of Parliament. In addition they provided the majority of the clergy of the Church of England, the officers corps of the Army and Navy and senior positions in the diplomatic service. They commanded the militia, and with the clergy monopolised the magistracy and governed the countryside (Perkin 1969, 38-44, 65-8). In the hands of this landed oligarchy lay the power of patronage which at 'all levels ... was the instrument by which property influenced recruitment to the positions in society which were not determined by property alone' (Perkin, p.45).

Notwithstanding the hegemonic power of the landed class, *fluidity* was a key feature of eighteenth-century England, as with any social structure rooted in patronage. First, the great landed families did not constitute a unified elite but were divided into factions competing for power resources, including clients. Secondly, membership of the most privileged status groups could be gained through the circulation of wealth; patrons did not comprise a closed society. Thirdly, the landed class led a society characterised by a complex social hierarchy with multiple sources of patronage. As Perkin has argued, between the landed class and the largely propertyless labouring classes

> stretched the long diverse but unbroken chains of the middle ranks.
> Between the extremes the whole interim was filled by parallel
> business and professional hierarchies of an infinity of graduated
> statuses. (Perkin, p.23)

b)   *Competition and choice - the pluralist system*

Wiseman has documented the degree to which competition was a dominant feature of relationships within the Roman elite (Wiseman 1985), while Braund comments on the fact that members of the elite 'could even compete for particular clients' (above, p.148). Drummond also argues of early Rome that:

> As a consequence of ... aristocratic rivalry, there may well have
> been competition for the adhesion of dependents, a situation
> further complicated by ... the fact that changes in the balance of
> power within the ranks of the aristocrary meant a varying and
> fluctuating ability to provide the protection and assistance required.
> (above, p.106)

Where client loyalty is voluntarily given, patronage remains a highly fluid structure, adapted to change, driven by the twin motors of patron competition and client choice. It is this adaptive capacity which is identified by Wallace-Hadrill (p.74) as a major factor explaining the potentiality of Roman culture and institutions to absorb an expanding empire. It is also a feature of the *system*; a capacity and a consequence which cannot be adequately addressed from the conceptual starting point of the relational concept alone. The systemic consequences of the interplay between patron competition and client choice effectively create both instability - the inherent tendencies for the system to move toward other forms such as kinship or bureaucracy - and adaptability; the capacity of patronage institutions to carry out new imperial functions. For once a patron-client hierarchy freezes into relatively permanent social strata reflecting the established power of a given family or group, particularly where it is institutionalised through hereditary succession, then patronage is already in process of decay, giving way to personalised bureaucratic control or tyranny.

While stressing the capacity for change it is important not to lose sight of the integrative functions of patronage as a system. As we suggested above, patronage is characterised by the dominance of vertical over horizontal relations of solidarity. As Drummond points out in relation to early Rome, patronage

> as a voluntary personal bond between full citizens can be seen as fulfilling an integrating role, reconciling the realities of power and its unequal distribution with the need to preserve the sense of common citizen identity ... (above, p.109)

This point is reinforced by Garnsey and Woolf:

> it has frequently been observed that the power of patronage is in opposition to that of horizontal associations in society, and that the vertical bondings that it creates undermine the solidarity of individual status groups, especially those of the clients.
>
> (above, p.157)

The question which arises from such systemic considerations is not that relating to the possibility of asymmetrical friendship and its existence in Rome. Rather the problem is the degree to which clients are 'reconciled' to inequality by virtue of ties of friendship and loyalty and the extent to which status and class solidarities fail to emerge, or play a less significant role in social action.

Similarly the patronage system of eighteenth-century England involved the predominance of vertical over horizontal principles of group formation. As Perkin argues, class was a latent phenomenon (Perkin 1969, 261). Notwithstanding the existence of status groups, stratified in terms of property and social honour (e.g. gentle and common), those individuals found at each level had more in common with their social superiors and inferiors with the same functional interests and activities than with others of the same broad social level. Those in the middle and lower reaches of the social structure, in seeking social advancement and security for themselves and their families, looked upwards to patrons for assistance rather than outwards to those at a similar social level in order to pursue collective class-bound interests against those of a higher and privileged social level. Not even the collective outbursts of violence such as the food riots have been found to be homogeneous in terms of status or class (Rudé 1964).

A further issue which has emerged as a result of the commitment to a relational concept is that of multiple patrons. This is a central issue in Saller. A number of papers in this volume provide evidence of clients admitting to or even boasting of relations with several patrons (Braund, p.148). The incidence of multiple patrons does suggest that the ethic of personal loyalty was often strained to its limits. It is clear, at least, that Saller's relational concept is deficient in coping with this problem, particularly as he does not include in his definition the principle of voluntarism, emphasised by Drummond and Garnsey and Woolf. However, once we admit to the principle of choice then it is clear that a system of patronage will be characterised by fluidity, the movement of clients from one patron to another, and by competition between patrons for clients. Loyalty and choice are in tension in the system in such a way as to suggest strongly that multiple patrons could exist. Once again, the instability of the system is highlighted in those societies where the exercise of client choice is associated with an increasing dominance of the market in the system, heralding the arrival on the scene of the entrepreneurial patron. Alternatively, the long-term primacy of the ethic of personal loyalty may well stabilise the system into some form of *hereditary* structure. In both cases patronage as a system is threatened. The fact that clients seek and sometimes obtain the protection of two patrons may well strain loyalty as an individual practice, but it does not necessarily undermine 'the personal ideal' or *fides* as the centrepiece of a system of legitimation nor the personal character of such multiple ties.

It is clear from the papers in this volume that multiple patrons existed in Rome at particular times and places, and we would argue that this is in no sense indicative of a weakening of patronage as a system. In fact, if we accept that Roman society was characterised by the tolerance of such ambiguity, then this may well help to explain the failure of scholars to identify a clear or stable set of meanings associated with Roman usage of such terms as patrons, *clientes*, *amici*, etc. For not only can one conclude, as does Saller, that any technical definition of such terms is essentially a modern construction imposed on what was a constantly changing set of meanings - a process of change and adaptation to emergent shifts in power and status - but that patronage as a system is characterised by ambiguity. As Drummond points out of the early period:

> ... the reciprocal obligations involved, and the bond itself, were never prescribed by legislation and hence were potentially flexible according to the status and the needs of the parties concerned. It follows that the relationship was not sustained by legal sanction.
>
> (above, p.101)

Crucial to the maintenance of a patronage system are those legitimating meanings and beliefs cohering round such concepts as 'loyalty' or *fides* which may themselves be rooted in fictive kinship or the ethics of friendship. Such meanings function as the cement of the system. Nevertheless, the operation of the principle of choice, however extensive or restricted this might be (e.g. choice may operate effectively only in the upper reaches of the patronage hierarchy) the web of relations which make up the system is constantly and necessarily subject to 'failures' or discrepancies between the ideal and the reality. If such discrepancies become regular in occurrence, then the terms of discourse themselves may be subject to shifts of meaning and ambiguity. Where choice is sustained yet *fides* is entrenched, then ambiguity becomes an inherent feature of the system. Tolerance of such ambiguity, of the discrepancy between the ideas and the reality is reflected in individual relations and becomes enshrined in the language itself. Paradoxically, without its 'failures' the system would degenerate. In short, tolerance of ambiguity is an adaptive feature of the system.

c) *Dependence and exploitation*

A further set of issues which can be identified as arising from an unbalanced commitment to the relational level of analysis are those which cohere around questions of dependence and exploitation. Are clients dependent upon patrons in much the same way as slaves upon masters or serfs upon lords? Are clients exploited by patrons? There are seemingly contradictory answers to such questions to be found in the contributions of Drummond on the one hand, and Millett on the other. Drummond's argument, while not excluding the possibility of exploitation, is that the patron-client relationship being, in principle, voluntaristic was one in which 'the normal expectation was of the observance of customary obligations and mutual rights on both sides' (p.102). Millett, however, in exploring the 'fit' between Athenian democracy and patronage concludes that patronage would have been inimical to such democratic institutions because of its inherent elitism. The patron-client relationship is, he argues,

> conducted along lines largely determined by the party of superior status. It is this that opens up the way for the exploitation that is so common in patron-client relations. (above, p.16)

The inadequacy of both these claims and the seeming contradictions arising from them, can again be viewed as the product of a failure to consider the system level.

For example, whilst we agree that choice is an important factor in assessing the significance of dependence or exploitation, we cannot accept the adequacy of the implicit argument, that patrons cannot systematically exploit clients if clients have, in principle, the capacity to withdraw from the relationship. We reject this insofar as it is an argument which operates only at the relational level. The resultant problem becomes clear if we remember that the classic case of 'exploitation' was identified by Marx as arising out of the contradiction between the system and relational levels. Marx begins his analysis of capitalism by pointing out that labour is 'formally free'; that is to say in relational terms, labour is always able to withdraw from the contract. The central focus, of Capital, and Marx's creative contribution, was to explain how this 'freedom' could co-exist with 'exploitation'; the existence of exploitation being a systemic consequence arising out of the exclusive possession of the means of livelihood (*not* the dependency of the labourer), manifest in the private ownership of capital. Whatever the validity of Marx's substantive thesis, the *form* of the argument - the move from the relational to the system level - is, we would argue, crucial to an adequate analysis. To return to patronage, voluntarism inhibits exploitation not only because of the capacity of clients to withdraw from the relationship, but because that capacity exists in the system in which neither land nor labour can be exclusively possessed. While land is owned it is also an element in the process of reciprocation which arises out of the needs of both patron and client. Where a patronage *system* exists, it functions as the primary means of allocating such strategic resources. From the patron's viewpoint clients are also one such strategic resource, but patron competition and client choice ensure that this resource cannot be guaranteed.

In the patronage system, vertical ties of reciprocation not only undermine horizontal forms of solidarity but also weaken exclusivist forms of property relations. The means of livelihood are part of the reciprocal exchange process and, therefore, cannot be exclusively possessed. Equally, in such a system labour cannot be transformed into abstracted 'labour power' because the relationship is, above all, personal. This is not to argue that the poor in Rome were integrated into a patronage system, nor does it follow that neither dependence nor exploitation existed. Rather, it is suggested that insofar as patronage existed as a system it did not *systematically reproduce* exploitative relationships and that where such relations existed or gained ground, patronage was absent or in the process of decay.

To return to Millett's argument then, we would suggest that neither democracy nor client dependency provides an adequate explanation for the inhibition of patronage networks in Athens. Rather, as Millett himself suggests, the relative economic independence of the poorer citizens of Athens was buttressed by alternative institutions: namely, the existence and effective operation of institutions of public support. That is to say, in Athens the potentiality for the development of private and personalised ties of patronage was inhibited by the existence of both an 'ethic' of 'euergetism' (public benefaction) (Clapham 1982) and the institutions of public allocation. Wallace-Hadrill (p.69) also refers to such an alternative arising out of the rapid population increase in Rome in the late republic and the consequent crises resulting from the failure of the market to ensure food supplies. These conditions led, he argues, to the emergence of the embryonic 'universal patron', the Gracchi, distributing land and corn to the poor. Such popular leaders as the Gracchi and Clodius, reacting to the reality and threat of violence, acted as patrons of the 'mob', so reducing dependence on competing individual patrons. We will come back to the question of the 'universal patron' in discussing the state, here merely agreeing with Wallace-Hadrill that mass patronage of this kind had the effect of undermining the competitive pluralism of the patronage system while introducing into the system the alternative principle of public allocation. It is interesting to note here that we normally associate the emergence of an effective ethic of public allocation with the rise of the modern state and notions of welfare, and that this process in England at the end of the eighteenth century was associated with rapid urbanisation and land dispossession. The questions remain, however, whether the Roman state was transformed through this process and to what extent institutions of public allocation became increasingly central to the distribution of resources.

d) *State, empire and community*

Mention of the state brings us to the final set of issues we wish to identify as contentious in the accompanying papers, and the seminars out of which they have developed. These issues relate to the use of various collective concepts such as state, empire, community and once again bear upon our distinction between relational and systemic analysis.

The first problem area concerns conceptions of the state and the relationship of the state to patronage, and it is raised in its most acute form by Garnsey and Woolf who conceive of patronage as:

> ... an alternative way of doing things because it is voluntary, an option which an actor may (but need not) take up, because he thinks it offers some advantage over the 'official system', over the 'normal' status quo. It is a gap filler, doing what the open and established order cannot do or does less efficiently. (p.154)

It is clear that these authors fall into the category of those analysts who, starting from a dyadic relational concept, do not conceive of the possibility that patronage may itself be the dominant and generalised form of institutionalised resource allocation which, we would argue, was probably the case in Rome for a considerable period. Secondly, they see the state - the established order - as the 'normal' structure of power relations; distinct and separate from patronage.

While we would agree that alternative and competing systems of resource allocation may co-exist, we wish to leave open the possibility which Garnsey and Woolf effectively reject altogether, that patronage, as the dominant system can constitute the form that the state takes; that the formation of the Roman state, including its imperial extension, was effected through the creation and adaptation of patronage institutions.

The difficulty entailed in conceptualising the relationship between the state and patronage is best brought out by Drummond, who while making the point that whereas in the archaic period, patronage lay outside 'the formal power structures of the Roman state' (p.109); that it was never, 'so far as is known employed as a mechanism for the determination or allocation of public authority, rights or obligations..' He nevertheless insists that patronage 'is itself a product of the distribution of power in Roman society ...'

> And for the aristocracy collectively these arguments embedded their power in the social fabric, made its exercise more acceptable and offered a means of controlling those subject to it and of countering the claims of those outside it; as an instrument of social and political control, therefore, its importance was considerable.
>
> (above, p.110)

Drummond's ambivalence is rooted in the claim that the client bond is a product of the 'distribution of power'. Should we insist on the equally acceptable counter-claim that patronage is the main mechanism of such distribution then together we either end up in the grip of an unhelpful tautology - the client bond is the consequence of patronage - or we are forced back into the untenable claim that there exist formal power structures of the Roman state which are both separate from and conditioning of patronage. But what is this power structure distinct from patronage relations? What are its resources unmediated by a patronage network? What are the agencies of its operation from which the patronage principle is absent? Whether we conceive of the state as those 'agencies' or an 'apparatus' mediating the common affairs of a political community, or, as sometimes defined, as a set of functions (e.g. social integration, goal attainment) or follow Weber in identifying such functions with the monopolisation of means (i.e. of the means of violence, taxation and administration) we are forced to the conclusion that in Roman society such agencies are patronage structures; that the operation of such functions and the utilisation of such means are impossible even to describe except in terms of patronage.

In short, for much of its history Rome was a society in which public agencies and official functions were mediated by the private personal ties of patronage. State offices - senator, provincial governor or the emperor - were enmeshed in patronage relationships to a degree that it becomes entirely misconceived to maintain a distinction between the 'formal power structures' of the state and the private bonds of patronage. As Braund argues in relation to Cicero's correspondence with the governor of Asia,

> public and private are scarcely distinguishable as the complex of patronage is deepened and extended. (above, p.142)

'Public office,' he writes, 'tended to generate patronage' (p.122), so focussing the resources of the patronage system. Nevertheless, Braund continues to conceive of the state as something other than patronage: the state and patronage constituted distinct entities. Braund's commitment to this distinction is highlighted by his theme of the dysfunctions of patronage, suggesting that 'personal patronage could undermine the functioning of the imperial state' (p.145). The contradiction which exists in Braund arises, we believe, out of a tendency implicit in a number of the papers in this volume to assume that the state, 'the official system', 'the formal power structures', must, almost by definition, be constituted by something other than patronage. We get the impression that there always exists a legal, rational core to any state, however infected it might be by *fides* or personal loyalty.

The difficulty which exists in separating out the patronage system from the state is equally the case when we consider the more developed state apparatus of eighteenth-century England. Contrary to the view of nineteenth-century Whig critics, the state in the eighteenth century could not be regarded as a formal bureaucratic organisation within which informal patronage networks operated as corrosive elements of favouritism and corruption. In systemic terms the state was an integral element of the patronage system, despite the fact that there existed competing criteria of placement and promotion in the most developed branches of the state - the armed services. As Dandeker has shown in relation to the navy (1978) bureaucratic criteria of 'seniority', 'seatime', and 'technical merit' were all mobilised in promotion decisions, yet all these operated within the constraints of patronage obligation. Seniority was accepted by the Lords of the Admiralty as vocationally relevant, yet they also accepted that their duty was to look after the interests of family, followers and friends, and would have responded with moral repugnance to any attempts to prioritise merit, so disrupting the conventional balance between the generalised exercise of patronage and the local use of merit in the determination of career progress. Such centralised state agencies were, then, integral to the patronage system, but were a part of that system in which there existed areas of discretion for decisions operating on the basis of criteria other than that of 'connection'. It was the widening of these areas of discretion, fed by the new codes of ethics and morality expressed by an emergent urban middle class, which in the nineteenth century saw the gradual shift to the dominance of bureaucratic forms.

If it is possible to conclude that Rome of the late republic was characterized by the dominance of a patronage system which not only mediated the major lines of resource allocation (Wallace-Hadrill, p.78) but was the structural form through which state activities were mobilized then it is also possible to identify those trends, associated with imperial expansion, which were to modify the system.

Perhaps the most significant effect of this process was the degree to which the hierarchical chains of patronage increasingly focussed in the emperor, who by virtue of his position was able to control access to more and more of the resources of the system. The potential of such a process is succinctly outlined by Wallace-Hadrill:

> It would appear axiomatic that if one patron achieves monopoly control of resources, he destroys the system and becomes the state itself. (above, p.78f.)

While not suggesting that the emperor ever gained such a monopoly, it was the case that the role of emperor did reduce the competitive pluralism of the system, so narrowing the apex of the patron-client hierarchy. To follow Braund, under the principate:

> the emperor and his household had taken over, effortlessly, much of the role of the republican elite in exercising personal patronage outside Rome. (above, p.151)

Again it would be a mistake to suggest that the emperor acted as the sole patron of the provincial elite or that brokerage was not becoming a more significant feature of the system, particularly as the rate and

scope of expansion outran the organisational capacity of the emperor's household to achieve such a monopoly.

Rather, the process of expansion, involving the successive inclusion of new peoples into the political community of Rome, necessitated the increasing reliance on adaptive forms of patronage, and in particular its various collective forms such as 'universal patronage' and the 'collective client'. The very notion of the collective client - that is the patronage of a community, town or region - raises the issue of whether we can even conceive of such relationships as patronage in the relational sense at all. Certainly, as Rich argues, these relationships were common under the empire:

> ... thus we find the patron-client terminology being freely used of the relationships between individual members of the Roman elite and municipalities and foreign communities. (above, p.127)

It is clear that the existence of the collective client is difficult to subsume under a relational definition which requires above all that the patron-client bonds be personal; a problem which is not resolved by Wallace-Hadrill's observation that such relationships were always 'mediated through individuals' (p.75) so retaining the character of patronage. This is not an acceptable resolution insofar as all human institutions are mediated by individuals, but that does not allow us to conclude that bureaucracy is thereby a form of patronage. Rather it is important to recognise that the emergence and growing significance of the collective client was an adaptive form which weakened patronage as a system. First, its growing significance was linked to the concentration of resources under the empire: as the resource base was extended so was the increased basis for mass clientage. At the same time such resource concentration provided the structural basis for the exercise of universal patronage, identified by Wallace-Hadrill, as we have seen, as first emerging in Rome with the universal patronage of the 'mob' (p.79) and very much extended by the control of resources exercised by the emperor. Perhaps the most important effect of such trends was that the patron-client bonds necessarily became less diffuse and all-encompassing; that such ties were much more specific regarding the reciprocal expectations of the parties involved, being in some cases reduced to the exchange of benefaction and honour alone. Such trends suggest that we are here observing a systemic shift toward increased impersonality in the forms of patronage, and that these adaptive forms exhibit a potential for the development of 'personalised' bureaucratic institutions.

In short, under the empire a variety of adaptations were occurring which weakened patronage as a system. The phenomenon of the universal patron, weakened competitive pluralism and client choice, and the increasing significance of the collective client, created institutions of reciprocation and control which were more specific in their functions and less personalized in their full institutional operation.

Finally, we are forced to depart from the conclusions drawn by Rich who argues that the utilization of adaptive patronage ties in structuring imperial relations - ensuring that *fides* was central to inter-state relations - suggest that the political system of the Roman empire was itself a patronage system. While both Rich and Braund are correct in suggesting that a society whose institutions were saturated by the meanings and language of patronage could not in extending its relations on an inter-state basis construct such relations on entirely new principles, the dynamics of the emergent system are not those of patronage. For as Rich indicates, not only did the Romans themselves avoid patron-client terminology in referring to relationships with peoples over whom Rome extended its hegemony, but they did so because '... it was only felt to be appropriate in a world where there could be a multiplicity of patrons' (p.127). That is, they identified the significance in patronage of the dynamic of client choice and patron competition as crucial to the system. If Rome were patron, 'there could be no other' (p.127), at least, Rich argues, from the second century BC. In effect, while the construction of Rome's empire was dependent on the existing institutions of patronage, the very process of expansion led to a reliance on adaptive forms of patronage which themselves had the effect of undermining the system. This is not to argue that the patron-client bond disappeared but that the dynamics of the system in which patronage played the strategic role in the maintenance and reproduction of power relations were weakening.

Conclusion

At the outset of this paper we argued that discussions of patronage had drawn on two contrasting perspectives - the universalist and the historical. Our own view takes as its point of departure the 'compromise literature' which has sought to recognise the universal, elementary structures of patronage, yet also poses the historical problem of patronage as a system: of the conditions under which patronage can become significant as the strategic mechanism of a social order.

In the discussion we have argued that when patronage operates as a social system, it is characterised by an essential fluidity, ambiguity and flexibility. Central to a patronage system is the tenuous process through which the power structure is reproduced: essential to the system is rivalry between patrons for clients and the ability to change patrons or to have multiple allegiances to them. At the same time the system is characterised by the relative ease with which patrons can be joined by new members, or lose existing ones.

To this tenuous process of power holding must be added the feature of ambiguity. In the context of eighteenth-century England, Perkin has argued, patronage can be conceptualised as lying half-way between systems of medieval homage on the one hand, and, on the other, the relations of contract, characteristic of modern capitalism. Patronage shares with the former the commitment to deference and thus the predominance of vertical over horizontal relations of social solidarity. It shares with the latter the idea of voluntarism in respect of the social basis of participation in these relations.

With regard to flexibility, a number of writers in this volume have shown how patronage could serve as an adaptive mechanism in the expansion of Roman imperial administration. This is an illustration of a more general point made by those who have considered patronage from the perspective of modernisation theory: that patronage can operate as a system when kin ties are no longer effective mechanisms of economic and political integration, and where the rational legal state and market economy are insufficiently developed to carry out such functions.

However, this view of patronage as an intermediate social system falling between tradition and modernity need not be associated with an unqualified support of modernization theory. Two related grounds can be adduced in support of this contention. First, as we argued earlier, it is misleading to suggest that patronage relations have no place in modern bureaucratic societies. Such an argument would be to conflate the distinction between relation and system, and to view the decline of patronage as a strategic mechanism of social order in terms of a simple process of attenuation. However, patronage relations in modern societies are not anomalies or instances of cultural lag. Rather, they are inevitable features of modern bureaucracies. Yet this does not detract from the fact that such organisational structures are quite distinct from the patrimonial administrations characteristic of pre-capitalist societies.

This argument links with a second, broader, problem concerning modernisation theory. It tends to be associated with a teleological view of history which is construed as a developmental process, each stage providing successive conditions for the unfolding of modernity. However, typological and historical analyses are quite different exercises; the classification of different types of social structure need not be linked with unwarranted evolutionary assumptions about processes of transition. For instance, it should not be supposed that the decline of a patronage system necessarily involves a rise of modernity. Equally possible is a 'return' to the prevalence of kin solidarity, or the construction of a tyranny with a monopolistic patron heading a personalised bureaucracy. The potentiality for change of patronage as a system involves the possibility of quite different outcomes depending on the peculiarities of the historical context in which its dissolution takes place.

Bibliography

Bloch, M. (1961), *Feudal Society*, translated by L.A. Manyon. London.

Bourne, J. (1986), *Patronage in Nineteenth Century England*. London.

Clapham, C. (ed.) (1982), *Private Patronage and Public Power: Political Clientelism and the Modern State*. London.

Dandeker, C. (1978), 'Patronage and bureaucratic control: the case of the naval officer in English society', *British Journal of Sociology* 29, No. 3, 300-20.

Gellner, E. (1977), 'Patrons and clients' in E. Gellner and J. Waterbury (eds.), *Patrons and Clients in Mediterranean Societies*. London.

Gibbon, P. and Higgins, M.D. (1974), 'Patronage, tradition and modernization; the case of the Irish gombeenman', *Economic and Social Review* 16, No. 1 Oct-Nov, 27-43.

Johnson, T. (1982), 'The state and the professions: the peculiarities of the British', in A. Giddens and G. Mackenzie (eds.), *Social Class and the Division of Labour*, 186-208. Cambridge.

Malinowski, B. (1922), *Argonauts of the Western Pacific*. London.

Perkin, H. (1969), *Origins of Modern English Society, 1780-1880*. London.

Rudé, G. (1964), *The Crowd in History: a Study of Popular Disturbances in France and England 1730-1848*. New York.

Saller, R.P. (1982), *Personal Patronage under the Early Empire*. Cambridge.

Scott, J. (1977), 'Patronage or exploitation?', in Gellner and Waterbury (eds.) 21-39.

Weber, M. (ed.) (1977), *Economy and Society*, Vol. 1. Berkeley.

Wiseman, T.P. (1985), 'Competition and co-operation', in Wiseman (ed.), *Roman Political Life 90 BC to AD 69*, 13-19. Exeter.

Appendix

Dionysius of Halicarnassus, *Antiquitates Romanae* 2.9-11

9. (1) When he had divided the lesser men from their betters, Romulus then prescribed and regulated the duties of each. The patricians were to act as priests, magistrates and judges, conducting the affairs of the community in partnership with himself and concentrating on business in the city. The plebeians were to be released from these concerns because they had no experience of them and their poverty deprived them of the necessary leisure; rather, they were to engage in agriculture, the rearing of livestock and gainful occupations. The purpose of this arrangement was to avoid the dissension that arises in other cities through the abuse inflicted on the weak by their superiors. (2) He also entrusted the plebeians to the care of the patricians, allowing each of the common people to have a protector of his own choice. In this he improved on an old Greek custom which the Thessalians long continued to observe, as initially did the Athenians. For they treated their dependants arrogantly, imposing on them duties that did not befit free men, whipping them for any failure to carry out their orders and generally maltreating them like bought slaves; the Athenians called their dependants 'thetes' because of their status as hired labourers, whilst the Thessalians used the term 'penestai', a name that was itself a degrading reminder of their circumstances. (3) In contrast, Romulus not only selected a genial term to enhance the relationship by calling the protection of the poor and humble 'patronage', but he also assigned each party obligations that were beneficial, organising the ties between them on a humane basis and one appropriate to citizens of the same community.

10 (1) The customary practices of patronage which Romulus then defined and which long remained in force among the Romans were as follows. The patricians had to expound the law to their clients, who were ignorant of it; whether their clients were present or absent they had to look after their interests, omitting nothing that fathers do for their sons, in respect both of money and of pecuniary contracts; where clients were wronged in contractual matters, the patron had to bring a suit on behalf of the injured party and he had to defend any suit brought against the client. In short, one could say that it was the patron's duty to ensure for his client that tranquillity in personal and public affairs of which he had a particular need. (2) For their part, clients had to assist their patrons with dowries for their daughters' marriages, if the father lacked means, and to pay a ransom to an enemy if any of them or their children were taken captive; if the patron lost a private suit or incurred a public penalty which involved a monetary fine, the clients had to meet it from their own resources as a favour, not a loan; on a par with kinsmen they had also to contribute to their patron's disbursements in magistracies, offices and all other public expenditures. (3) As a common obligation on both parties it was impious and unlawful for either to prosecute the other, give evidence or vote against them or range themselves with their enemies. Should anyone be convicted of any such act, he was liable under the law of betrayal which Romulus enacted and it was for anyone who wished to kill the guilty party as a sacrifice to subterranean Zeus. (It was a Roman custom to dispose of those whom they wanted to kill with impunity by devoting their persons to one of the gods, particularly the subterranean divinities.) These then were the arrangements Romulus instituted at that time.

(4) In consequence, the bonds of clients and patrons persisted for many generations, identical to the ties of kinsmen, and still held good between their descendants. It was a source of great credit to men of distinguished family to have as many clients as possible, both by preserving the patronage ties which they had inherited from their forebears and by acquiring others through their own merit. And it is remarkable how intensely both parties competed with each other in their demonstrations of goodwill, each anxious not to be outdone in generosity by the other: clients resolved to perform every service they could for their patrons, whilst patrons were anxious to inconvenience their clients as little as possible and accepted no gifts of money - a testimony to the self-discipline of their conduct with respect to any kind of pleasure and to their use of virtue, not fortune as the measure of happiness.

11 (1) The patronage of the patricians was not restricted to the city and the common people, but each of Rome's colonies, the cities that became her friends and allies and those subjugated in war had Romans

of their own choosing as their protectors and patrons. Indeed, the senate often referred the disputes which came from these cities or peoples to their patrons and regarded their decision as binding.

(2) Hence the practices instituted by Romulus initiated so firm a concord among the Roman people that for six hundred and thirty years there was no internal bloodshed or murder despite the numerous major political conflicts which developed between the people and their rulers and which are to be expected in all cities, both large and small. (3) Instead, by mutual persuasion and education, by mutual give and take they succeeded in resolving their grievances in a manner consistent with their common citizen status. But from the time that Gaius Gracchus used the power of the tribunate to destroy the harmony of the state, there has been no respite in their efforts to murder or exile each other and to commit any and every abuse purely to secure their own victory.

General Index

Index of Authors

LIST OF CONTRIBUTORS

David Braund is Lecturer in Classics at the University of Exeter.

Duncan Cloud is Senior Lecturer and Head of Department of Classics at the University of Leicester.

Christopher Dandeker is Lecturer in Sociology at the University of Leicester.

John Drinkwater is Lecturer in Ancient History at the University of Sheffield.

Andrew Drummond is Lecturer in Classics at the University of Nottingham (formerly at the University of Sheffield).

Peter Garnsey is University Lecturer in Ancient History and Fellow of Jesus College, Cambridge.

Keith Hopwood is Lecturer in Classics at St David's University College, Lampeter.

Terry Johnson is Professor of Sociology at the University of Leicester.

Paul Millett is University Lecturer in Ancient History and Fellow of Downing College, Cambridge.

John Rich is Lecturer in Classics at the University of Nottingham.

Richard Saller is Associate Professor of Ancient History at the University of Chicago.

Andrew Wallace-Hadrill is Professor of Classics at the University of Reading (formerly Lecturer in Ancient History at the University of Leicester).

Greg Woolf is a postgraduate student at Trinity College, Cambridge.